Your Pro Tools® Studio

Robert Correll

Course Technology PTR
A part of Cengage Learning

COURSE TECHNOLOGY
CENGAGE Learning™

Australia • Brazil • Japan • Korea • Mexico • Singapore • Spain • United Kingdom • United States

COURSE TECHNOLOGY
CENGAGE Learning™

Your Pro Tools® Studio
Robert Correll

Publisher and General Manager, Course Technology PTR: Stacy L. Hiquet

Associate Director of Marketing: Sarah Panella

Manager of Editorial Services: Heather Talbot

Marketing Manager: Mark Hughes

Executive Editor: Mark Garvey

Project Editor: Dan Foster, Scribe Tribe

Technical Reviewer: Brian Jackson

PTR Editorial Services Coordinator: Erin Johnson

Copy Editor: Kevin Kent

Interior Layout Tech: ICC Macmillan Inc.

Cover Designer: Mike Tanamachi

Indexer: Larry Sweazy

Proofreader: Carolyn Keating

For product information and technology assistance, contact us at **Cengage Learning Customer & Sales Support, 1-800-354-9706**

For permission to use material from this text or product, submit all requests online at **cengage.com/permissions**
Further permissions questions can be emailed to **permissionrequest@cengage.com**

Digidesign, Avid, Pro Tools, M-Audio, and Mbox are registered trademarks of Digidesign and/or Avid Technology, Inc.

Microsoft, Windows, and Internet Explorer are either registered trademarks or trademarks of Microsoft Corporation in the United States and/or other countries.

Apple, Mac, and Macintosh are registered trademarks of Apple, Inc.

iLok is a trademark of PACE Anti-Piracy, Inc.

Library of Congress Control Number: 2008902377

ISBN-13: 978-1-59863-530-0

ISBN-10: 1-59863-530-1

Course Technology
25 Thomson Place
Boston, MA 02210
USA

Cengage Learning is a leading provider of customized learning solutions with office locations around the globe, including Singapore, the United Kingdom, Australia, Mexico, Brazil, and Japan. Locate your local office at: **international.cengage.com/region**

Cengage Learning products are represented in Canada by Nelson Education, Ltd.

For your lifelong learning solutions, visit **courseptr.com**

Visit our corporate website at **cengage.com**

Printed in the United States of America
1 2 3 4 5 6 7 11 10 09 08

To Anne, who bought me my first guitar for my birthday and who continues to encourage and inspire me to make music. For my kids: Benjamin, Jacob, Grace, and Samuel.

Acknowledgments

I have many people to thank. This book was a team effort from start to finish.

Thanks to David Fugate, my agent and the founder of LaunchBooks Literary Agency.

Many thanks to all the great people at Course Technology PTR, a part of Cengage Learning. Thanks to Mark Garvey, for believing in me and pairing me up with this concept, and to Dan Foster, for working closely with me and shepherding the book through the process.

Special thanks go to Brian Jackson, who reviewed the book for technical accuracy. Brian, I enjoyed e-mailing back and forth and getting to know you.

Thank you to many people at Digidesign. Special thanks to Claudia Cook for ensuring that I received such wonderful support from Digi. Many thanks also to Jason Lakis and Alex Steinhart.

Thank you to M-Audio. Special thanks to Dina Butler for your excellent support. Also, thanks go out to Vanessa Mering, Eric Krug, and Kevin Walt.

Thank you Anne, Ben, Jake, Grace, and Sam for believing in who I am and loving me for that, and for supporting and encouraging me. Special thanks to Don and Mary Anne for your support.

About the Author

Robert Correll is creative, passionate, artistic, and dedicated. He loves composing, arranging, performing, engineering, recording, mixing, producing, and mastering his own original music. Robert plays the guitar, bass, and dabbles with his MIDI keyboard. He is a Pro Tools fanatic who just can't get enough of it.

Professionally, Robert Correll is a freelance music producer, audio engineer, artist, and author. He was trained in audio engineering and music production at the Recording Workshop of Chillicothe, Ohio, and graduated with honors. His recent books include *Your Pro Tools Studio* (Cengage Learning, 2008) and *Photo Restoration and Retouching Using Corel Paint Shop Pro Photo* (Cengage Learning, 2007). He has written software workshop articles for *Music Tech* magazine (UK) and has created several 8-hour multimedia tutorials for the Virtual Training Company.

Robert is proficient or expert in many audio technologies and applications, including Digidesign Pro Tools, Sony ACID Pro, Sony Vegas+DVD, Propellerhead Reason, Cakewalk SONAR, Native Instruments applications, IK Multimedia Amplitube, Steinberg WaveLab, Image Line Software FL Studio (formerly Fruity Loops), Ableton Live, Waves, and other plug-ins. His audio hardware expertise ranges from analog consoles and virtually every computer DAW to electric and acoustic guitar, USB/Firewire/PCI audio interfaces, MIDI controllers, outboard music production hardware (EQ, compression, etc.), and more. Robert is also an expert in numerous computer technologies and applications.

Robert has been an author for close to a decade and has been a consultant/independent contractor in the marketing and design industry. Robert graduated with a Bachelor of Science degree in History from the United States Air Force Academy in 1988 and served in the United States Air Force as an intelligence officer.

You can reach Robert by sending an e-mail to protools@robertcorrell.com. His Web address is www.robertcorrell.com, and he is active on MySpace at www.myspace.com/robertcorrell and www.myspace.com/robertcorrellmusic. Robert encourages you to contact him.

Contents

Chapter 3
Setting Up Your Studio

Chapter 4
Preparing to Install

Chapter 5
Installing Pro Tools LE   93

Chapter 6
Installing Pro Tools M-Powered   117

Chapter 7
Configuring Pro Tools   153

Chapter 8
Using Pro Tools   179

Chapter 9
Recording Audio   211

Chapter 10
Editing Audio   241

Chapter 11
Using MIDI   269

Chapter 12
Plug-Ins and Mixing   297

Introduction

Making music is a challenge. Setting up a recording studio—no matter how small—takes hard work and thought. Learning how to use an advanced computer application like Pro Tools is tough. Deciding what to buy is daunting. Even when you figure out where all the menus and buttons are and what they theoretically do, you've got to put that into practice by using Pro Tools to record, edit, mix, and produce music. Whether you're making music as hobby, part-time gig, or profession, your goal should be to create a professional-sounding product that appeals to people.

Using Pro Tools is not the same as launching a text editor and learning how to write a letter. Music and audio production require a distinct and specialized set of skills and knowledge that most people don't have. Learning how to put together and run your Pro Tools studio will set you apart from the crowd.

Your Pro Tools Studio is a thorough, practical guide that walks you through the steps of starting your own small home or project studio and using Pro Tools as your centerpiece digital audio workstation. You'll learn about the different Pro Tools LE and M-Powered systems, which one is best for you, and how to install and get it running smoothly. You'll learn how to set up your studio for recording and mixing. You'll learn how to use Pro Tools to produce a professional audio product.

Your Pro Tools Studio approaches this daunting task by breaking it into manageable chunks that are easy to digest. Each chapter is focused and gives you perspective on what you're learning as you learn it. *Your Pro Tools Studio* is for the beginning to intermediate user.

What You'll Find in This Book

Your Pro Tools Studio is packed with an incredibly wide range of practical information. Everything is written to help you set up and run your own Pro Tools studio. You'll find, among many other things, topics like these in this book:

- Selection Criteria
- Pro Tools LE Systems

- Representative Pro Tools M-Powered Systems

- Pro Tools Options and Extras

- Setting Up Your Studio

- Installation Workflow

- Computer Maintenance

- iLok

- Installing an Mbox 2

- Installing an M-Audio FireWire 410

- Updating Pro Tools

- The Setup Menu

- Preferences

- The Edit Window

- The Mix Window

- Engineering Primer

- Microphones

- Recording in Pro Tools

- Basic Editing

- Elastic Audio

- Automation

- What Is MIDI?

- MIDI-Pro Tools Basics

- Plug-Ins

- Mixing

Whom This Book Is For

Your Pro Tools Studio is for anyone who wants to set up and use Pro Tools in their home or project studio. My focus is on teaching beginner to intermediate users the basics of audio production and engineering in general while introducing them to Pro Tools in particular.

Your interest in Pro Tools might fall along many lines. Most likely, you are in one of these categories:

- **Musician**—From beginner to professional, you want to start using Pro Tools to record yourself or your band.

- **Audio Engineer (Sound Guy)**—New to audio engineering and interested in starting up your own home or project studio and running Pro Tools. Even if you've got some audio experience under your belt, if you are new to Pro Tools this book will help you along your path.

- **Amateur**—Interested in music but aren't going to spend tens of thousands of dollars and every waking hour of the day. You still want to create something that sounds good.

- **Enthusiast**—More devoted than a hobbyist, but you want to invest your time and money wisely. Looking to improve your sound.

- **Professional**—Looking to get started down the path of making music professionally and want a solution to get you in the door. You want to make professional-caliber music but not at professional-studio prices.

We decided to present this information in a small and very affordable package. To give you some perspective, the *Pro Tools 7.4 Reference Guide* is 981 pages in length. Given the size of this book and the breadth of information I cover, I have not attempted to write about every possible feature in Pro Tools or describe every hardware configuration in detail. I have also not attempted to elaborate on all aspects of audio engineering or production. To do so would be a fool's errand.

On the contrary, I think it is exceptionally valuable to have just this type of book to learn from. I have used my professional experience, insights, and authoring skills to reduce the thousands of pages of manuals, reference guides, specifications, charts, and other engineering and music books to something much more manageable. This makes it easier for you to learn and get started—without feeling like the entire world has been dumped on your shoulders.

Having said that, there's still a tremendous amount of information in this book. That's a result of my personal commitment to you. By buying this book, you've hired me to help you get up and running. I take that seriously.

How This Book Is Organized

Your Pro Tools Studio is organized into twelve chapters. The first half of the book covers information on how to choose which version of Pro Tools to buy, setting up your studio, and getting Pro Tools up and running. The latter half of the book dives into the various aspects of working with Pro Tools.

- **Chapter 1, "A Pro Tools Buying Guide"**—This chapter's goal is to help you find the right Pro Tools LE system for you. It begins with a description of Pro Tools LE and M-Powered, introduces different selection criteria to consider, and concludes with extensive information that compares and contrasts each current Pro Tools LE rig.

- **Chapter 2, "Buying Guide: Part Deux"**—Chapter 2 continues the buying guide and describes different Pro Tools M-Powered options and hardware types, reviews legacy Pro Tools LE systems, and finishes with information on buying used systems.

- **Chapter 3, "Setting Up Your Studio"**—The task of setting up a studio to use Pro Tools can be daunting but is not insurmountable. This chapter describes many of the challenges you will face and offers guidance on how to succeed. You'll learn how to set up your studio and furnish it like pro, taking factors into account such as size, shape, acoustic treatment, furniture, studio accessories, and even lava lamps.

- **Chapter 4, "Preparing to Install"**—Successfully installing Pro Tools requires preparation. This is a critical step in ensuring your computer and workspace are ready for this demanding application. You'll review a general installation workflow, learn how to prepare your computer, and set up an iLok account if necessary.

- **Chapter 5, "Installing Pro Tools LE"**—This chapter contains a complete step-by-step installation of a Digidesign Mbox 2 system and Pro Tools LE. You'll learn how to unpack, install hardware and software, and update the software.

- **Chapter 6, "Installing Pro Tools M-Powered"**—Pro Tools M-Powered installation is sufficiently different from Pro Tools LE that it warrants its own chapter. In this chapter, you'll follow along with each step as the author installs an M-Audio FireWire 410 and Pro Tools M-Powered. You'll learn how to install, test, and update the system.

- **Chapter 7, "Configuring Pro Tools"**—To make the most out of Pro Tools, you must be able to set it up and configure it. This chapter explains every important audio engine setting, how to optimize Pro Tools for the task at hand, and reviews the extensive program preferences.

- **Chapter 8, "Using Pro Tools"**—The Pro Tools interface has many different aspects to it and can be very intimidating for a new user. This chapter shows you the Edit and Mix windows, introduces other interface elements, and explains how they all fit together to enable you to make music. Along the way you'll learn interface tips and tricks that will help you work more efficiently in Pro Tools.

- **Chapter 9, "Recording Audio"**—Recording audio well requires a fundamental understanding of the general principles of sound, microphones, and recording techniques. Among the many topics in this chapter, you'll learn what sound is, how we measure it, the difference between recording at different bit depths and sample rates, stereo versus mono, microphone types, patterns, and placement techniques, and how to bring all this knowledge to record in Pro Tools.

- **Chapter 10, "Editing Audio"**—Editing audio is one of the most important tasks in Pro Tools. You can save a mediocre performance by making sure each beat lands when it should. You'll learn how to work in the Edit window, make audio selections, separate and nudge regions, create fades and crossfades, use the Beat Mapper, work with Elastic Audio, and automate in this chapter.

- **Chapter 11, "Using MIDI"**—MIDI is an amazingly powerful and flexible method of making music, and in this chapter you'll learn what MIDI is, how to use MIDI and Instrument tracks, how to connect and record with an external MIDI instrument, and how to edit MIDI data manually.

- **Chapter 12, "Plug-Ins and Mixing"**—In the last chapter you'll learn about a number of different types of plug-ins (EQ, compression, reverb, etc.) and how to use them in Pro Tools. You'll also learn the fundamental principles of mixing multiple tracks together to form a cohesive whole.

1   A Pro Tools Buying Guide

S o you want to record something, mix it, make it sound great, bounce it, convert it to an MP3, and put it on MySpace. Maybe you want to build your own home studio and record yourself or bring in bands to work with. Fantastic! Perhaps you've already got a digital audio workstation (DAW) and are making the move to Pro Tools. Any way you slice it, you've got some big decisions to make.

Figuring out what to buy is an important task. One of my primary goals for this book, and certainly in these first few chapters, is to help you decide what direction to take. And choosing a direction is a good analogy for this decision. Many roads can lead you to the same place. Which road, in terms of time, money, purpose, and personality, is the best for you?

Because this is *Your Pro Tools Studio*, you're clearly leaning in the Pro Tools direction. That's cool. You aren't going to go wrong there. Although you find many preferences among audio engineers and artists, Pro Tools is right up there at the top of the list. However, deciding what Pro Tools system to buy and set up takes some sound thinking and an understanding of what Pro Tools is. Do you want an Mbox, Mbox 2, Mbox 2 Micro, 001, 003 Rack, 003 Factory, HD, or M-Powered? Do you need 2, 4, 8, or 16 inputs? Do you need S/PDIF, ADAT, preamps, 96 kHz or more?

Some of this chapter is going to read like an audio gear catalog, because that's the best way to distill the enormous amount of data describing these systems into manageable chunks to help you make a decision. I've poured over the spec sheets, gone through the product documentation, looked at the websites, sat and thought about what is most important to tell you, and physically handled much of the gear itself. This is my passion, and I want to help you on your way.

Introducing Pro Tools

What is Pro Tools? Why do I want it? How do I get it? What can it do for me? How is it different from any other DAW on the market? Each one of these questions is important. I want to start by looking at Pro Tools in the context of professional audio in general and then move to more specific information on Pro Tools itself.

Professional audio goes far beyond making music. Ranging from music production to radio, television, movies, software, video games, and live sound events such as concerts and weekly worship services, you are constantly exposed to professionally produced audio. One version of Pro Tools or another is often behind the scenes, helping the artists, engineers, and producers turn their creative vision into reality.

Pro Tools Usage   Throughout this book I use the general term *Pro Tools* to refer to the entire family of Pro Tools LE and M-Powered systems unless I want to purposefully delve into a specific product. In those cases, I'll be more exact in my terminology. I also specifically use the term *Pro Tools HD* when I want to refer to that more advanced (and costly) system.

Professional Tools

Creating professional audio requires professional tools. Prior to the advent of digital audio, music and audio production was done on large analog consoles and performed live or recorded to tape. That process seems somewhat crude by today's standards, yes, but it was neither cheap nor low quality. At that time gear did not have anything to do with a computer, and the price tag was far beyond what most people could afford. It took very wealthy people using the best and most expensive gear and the best artists available to create the classic albums from the Beatles, Rolling Stones, Pink Floyd, and many more.

Going to the Moon   It's amazing what you can do with analog gear, an understanding of physics, sound engineering, and quality manufacturing. Remember that's the technology with which we went to the moon.

Today, most audio products are created using computers, and the cost of entry into the world of professional audio has never been lower. You can create fantastic music that while it is being recorded to a hard disk drive is being converted from an analog signal to a digital data stream that can later be edited and mixed entirely using the computer. Enter Pro Tools. Pro Tools is a powerful combination of hardware and software designed to work seamlessly together to record, edit, mix, master, and produce professional digital audio products.

Notice I said "hardware and software." That is one of Pro Tools' greatest strengths. Some people complain that you can't just hook up any old thing to your computer and run Pro Tools. Yes. Exactly. That's the point. The Pro Tools software is tightly integrated with the hardware and they are guaranteed to work together (you should, however, check compatibility guidelines when upgrading your operating system and other key components). You're buying a hardware/software *system* when you buy into Pro Tools.

I'll get more into describing the specific Pro Tools hardware later in the chapter, but you have several hardware and software options to choose from that are designed to meet many different needs and budgets. Digidesign has two primary lines of Pro Tools products, one aimed at the traditional studio system (called Pro Tools HD) and one for the home and small professional studio (called Pro Tools LE). Pro Tools M-Powered is very similar to Pro Tools LE, but is designed to run with M-Audio hardware interfaces.

Flexibility   You have more hardware flexibility when choosing an M-Audio interface (which runs Pro Tools M-Powered), but at some cost in compatibility. Some of the higher-end products, such as the DV Toolkit 2, are optimized for LE and not M-Powered compatible.

The Pro Tools software that runs the hardware is very consistent. The software runs equally well on Windows and Macintosh computer systems, desktops and laptops. In fact, the software's portability makes it a necessity that it work well on laptops. Except for the details of how it interacts with the specific hardware, the software running Pro Tools HD, LE, and M-Powered is all remarkably similar. That's an absolutely fantastic benefit. Just think about it. You can get into Pro Tools with a very modestly priced LE or M-Powered system, learn the ropes, record, mix, and master (pun intended) the software at home and at your own pace. After you know your way around and are comfortable with it, there's nothing to stop you from going into any studio in the world that runs any version of Pro Tools, from HD on down, and working with the software. I'm not going to say you'll be able to do everything in any version across the board after learning on Pro Tools M-Powered, but the training to get you started is invaluable.

For over 20 years, Digidesign has been developing and perfecting its Pro Tools software package and building specific hardware components designed to work with the software. It's a marriage made in California. In one form or another, it is the industry standard for creating professional audio. I love the Pro Tools software. I love the design, the interface, and the concept. After you set it up, it steps out of the way and lets you make music (with the advent of Instrument racks, MIDI is getting better too).

Why Pro Tools?

It's been said many times and in many places that Pro Tools is the industry standard. A good reason for this exists. It works, and it works very well. Pro Tools is powerful, very capable, has had a long and productive life cycle, is stable (both from a software/hardware point of view and from the business side of things), reliable, widespread, and well-supported.

Pro Tools hardware and software are designed and created to work together. That's a huge deal. I can't stress the importance of that fact enough. If you buy any version of Pro Tools, you're guaranteed to have the hardware and software work together. That eliminates many serious headaches. If you go the M-Powered route, you're no less certain of the fact that your hardware and software will work together. It's guaranteed.

Guaranteed?   Yes, the hardware and software work together—no ifs, ands, or buts about that. Aside from the occasional bug or known issue, the main problems you might have with Pro Tools revolve around your computer and possibly other audio hardware. Make sure your computer is compatible, powerful, reliable, and not full of spyware and viruses, and be very careful to read beforehand how software upgrades (especially Pro Tools software) can affect the stability of your system.

Pro Tools software runs natively on both Windows and Macintosh platforms. This is a really big draw. That means you don't have to go out and buy a new computer just to get into the Pro Tools arena if you've got the "wrong platform."

Whether the arena is in music, television, movies, video games, radio, live sound, pre-production, or post-production, Pro Tools is there, behind the scenes, helping engineers and producers create audio. Digidesign has won a Grammy Award for Outstanding Technical Achievement, and the Academy of Motion Picture Arts and Sciences awarded the company an Oscar statuette for Scientific and Technical Achievement in 2003. The reason? It won for the "design, development, and implementation of the Pro Tools digital audio workstation."

Other DAWs

Although this is a book about Pro Tools and how to set up your Pro Tools studio, I want to be up-front about other digital audio workstations and their relationship to your studio in this section. I've used many other DAWs, and I like several of them. I think it's wise to branch out and have some experience in multiple DAWs as your career grows, and to possibly have more than one DAW in your studio to be able to open certain file types natively. You can also run many of these DAWs using the Digidesign Pro Tools LE or M-Audio hardware.

Still, hands-down, I would go with Pro Tools as the main DAW in my studio. For all the reasons I've mentioned previously, it's a winning combination. I love making music with it, editing in it, and mixing with it. However, I would encourage you to research other DAWs on your own and see if they are worth integrating into your Pro Tools studio. Knowledge, experience, and competition are good things.

Selection Criteria

I don't think you can go wrong with any of the Digidesign products. They're all very well designed and manufactured. They're top of the line. The issue is getting the right system for you and your budget.

I remember when I was first introduced to Pro Tools. I came to a pretty quick understanding of the basics of how to operate the software because it looked the same from system to system. What I did not initially understand, but have come to learn, is that a wide variety of Pro Tools systems use different hardware. Each hardware package is optimized for a certain set of needs and purposes. Therefore, when you are making the decision to buy one version of Pro Tools over an other, your decision will be based on the hardware, not the software. The software is basically the same, and you use it basically the same way from system to system. It differs only inasmuch as it needs to be able to interface with a given hardware unit.

Because Digidesign has gone to great lengths to create a wide range of Pro Tools products that cater to different needs, it's important for you to be able to identify your needs and prioritize them. A sound assessment of your needs helps ensure you get the right system, which helps you to be productive and happy. It also ensures that you don't waste money on features you don't need, or fail to purchase those you do.

Inputs

An important feature you can look at to determine which Pro Tools package is right for you is related to inputs. I've expanded this into two questions:

- **Number:** Does the system have enough inputs for me?

- **Type:** Are they the right type?

Number is pretty straightforward. How many inputs do you need? If you are buying Pro Tools only to mix and master, you're not going to need many inputs. You might need none, in which case, Pro Tools Micro or Mini is a good fit. If you want to record yourself singing, playing keyboards or the guitar, a few inputs are all you need. If you're setting up a studio for your band and need eight inputs for the drums, four for vocals, and four more for instruments, you're going to need a lot of inputs. Really think this one through. It's far easier to buy the right system now than it is to go back later to try to fix things.

Type is very important. If you are running microphones with XLR cables, you should look for systems with XLR inputs. This is an issue with the Pro Tools Mini. It has two inputs with preamps, but only one of them is XLR. That can catch you if you're not careful. Nothing is wrong with the Mini; it just is what it is. If you need something else, keep looking. If you run 1/4-inch balanced/unbalanced inputs out of a small mixer with preamps, you need 1/4-inch line inputs.

Preamplifiers

Related to the issue of inputs is how many preamplifiers (preamps) you get with each system. Pay close attention to this. The number of inputs is not always the same as the number of preamps. For example, the Mbox 2 Pro has eight inputs but only two pre-amps. The preamps are on the XLR/line/DI inputs (inputs 1–2) only. The rest of the inputs are auxiliary line inputs and S/PDIF. The M-Audio Delta 66 has four inputs and no preamps. If you purchase the Delta 66 because it fits your other needs and forget the preamps, you'll be very disappointed. Factor the number of preamps into what Pro Tools system you buy and make sure it has enough, or make plans that involve using external preamps.

Outputs and Headphones

The number of outputs a system has is an indication of how flexible your studio and engineering can be. To connect studio monitors, you need at least two line outs. Many times these are referred to as "Monitor Outputs," and there will be a physical volume control on the unit. Everything from the Mbox 2 Mini on up has at least two monitor outs (one left and one right). If you need to run more signals to external gear (you can run two channels of output through S/PDIF on the Mbox 2), you should consider the Mbox 2 Pro or a 003. Aside from digital I/O, these units start with four or more outputs, which come in mighty handy if you want to run true outboard gear. Some examples of possible outboard gear are an external reverb unit, more than one set of studio monitors, a sound enhancer, a mixer, a boutique mastering limiter, a headphone amp, or a vintage compressor.

By the same token, the number of headphone outs determines how easy it is to "grab a set of cans" and monitor a tracking session or set up a cue mix through a headphone amplifier. All the Digidesign hardware has at least one stereo headphone output, and some have more than one. The M-Audio products are more variable. For example, the

Delta 66 has four 1/4-inch mono outputs and no dedicated headphone connection. In that case, you would have to route two outputs (the left and right channels of your main mix) to a mixer or headphone amp to be able to listen in using headphones. Don't be surprised. Make sure the system you choose has what you need.

Digital I/O

Digital I/O is a powerful method of routing signals in your studio. It has been around for some time now, although it is less common than traditional analog connections. Pro Tools LE and M-Powered systems carry two versions of digital I/O: S/PDIF and ADAT Optical.

Technically Speaking   USB and FireWire could also be considered digital I/O, but are never referred to as such. In professional audio, USB and FireWire are referred to as the interface, or host, connection between external audio hardware and the computer and are not called digital I/O. Using this paradigm, digital I/O connects two audio devices together, as opposed to an audio device and a computer.

Sony/Philips Digital Interconnect Format (S/PDIF) is a common type of digital I/O found on a lot of gear, and two channels are normally carried on a 75 ohm coaxial cable with RCA connectors. S/PDIF in allows you to record signals from external gear such as preamplifiers, keyboards, or synths that have S/PDIF out. Digidesign and M-Audio hardware almost always carries two channels of S/PDIF I/O on each line, so the S/PDIF in has a left and right component, as does the out. Often, the S/PDIF out mirrors the main monitor outputs. S/PDIF can also be carried over optical lines.

Alesis Digital Audio Tape (ADAT) Optical is a great way to dramatically increase the number of inputs in a system. ADAT is a digital protocol created by Alesis to record eight channels of audio to a digital audio tape. Even though ADATs have been surpassed by hard disk drives as the digital storage medium of choice, the data transmission protocol has stuck. You need an external multichannel preamp that has ADAT Optical out, of course, to take advantage of this fact. PreSonus, Mackie, and MOTU (among others) all make high-quality, eight-channel ADAT Optical preamps.

Lightpipe?   ADAT Optical is also known as ADAT Lightpipe. For consistency with the Digidesign documentation, I've chosen to use ADAT Optical terminology. ADAT Optical uses the same optical cabling as S/PDIF Optical, although it carries eight channels instead of S/PDIF's two. S/PDIF carried over fiber-optic cables is referred to simply as S/PDIF (TOSLINK).

Sampling Rate

All of the Pro Tools LE and M-Powered products can produce professional audio. Have no doubts about that. They do, however, differ in the maximum sample rate at which they can convert analog signals to digital and back.

All of the Digidesign products are capable of recording and playing back at least 24-bit/ 48 kHz. You won't find anything higher than a 24-bit depth, but you can get a higher sampling rate. Of the current line of Digidesign products, here is a summary of the bit depths and sample rates offered:

- **Mbox 2 Micro:** 24-bit/48 kHz (output only)

- **Mbox 2 Mini:** 24-bit/48 kHz

- **Mbox 2:** 24-bit/48 kHz

- **Mbox 2 Pro:** 24-bit/96 kHz

- **003 Factory:** 24-bit/96 kHz (ADAT Optical, 48 kHz)

- **003 Rack:** 24-bit/96 kHz (ADAT Optical, 48 kHz)

M-Audio M-Powered-compatible hardware tends to be more variable in bit depth and sample rate capabilities than Pro Tools LE. M-Audio bit depths and sample rates, summarized by interface line, are as follows:

- **PCI:** Ranges from 24-bit/96 kHz to 24-bit/192 kHz

- **USB:** Ranges from 16-bit/48 kHz to 24-bit/96 kHz

- **FireWire:** Mostly 24-bit/96 kHz

- **ProjectMix I/O:** 24-bit/96 kHz

You can see from the preceding lists that if you must work in the 96 kHz range, you have to choose the Mbox 2 Pro, a 003 from Pro Tools LE, or a specific M-Audio product that supports that capability.

Additional Factors

These factors might not be included in your main needs analysis and therefore won't affect the system you buy, but you should be aware of what the different capabilities or options are and what they mean to you.

The total number of simultaneous inputs determines how many inputs you can record at once. The Mbox 2 line (excepting the Micro) goes from two simultaneous inputs for the Mini to six for the Pro. Six simultaneous inputs sounds great, but you should realize they aren't all XLR microphone inputs with preamps. The Pro allows you to record two mic/line/DIs from inputs 1–2 (these are the channels with preamps), two additional aux line inputs or phono inputs on channels 3–4, and two channels of S/PDIF at the same time. The question ends up being this: "How many inputs of what type do you need to be able to record at the same time with built-in or additional preamps?"

Current Pro Tools LE systems offer two types of interface: USB 1.1 and FireWire 400. I am somewhat disappointed that these interfaces are not the latest and highest speeds (USB 2.0 and FireWire 800), but they do work and are capable of supporting the current hardware. FireWire is used in the higher-end interfaces because it can transmit a lot more data more efficiently. Current M-Audio products also include PCI cards that are installed in your computer. These have breakout cables or breakout boxes with a cable going back to the PCI card.

Pro Tools LE Systems

In this section I describe each Pro Tools LE system and look at representative M-Powered hardware. To compile these descriptions, in addition to calling on my experience using Pro Tools HD and LE systems, I spent time on the Digidesign website (www .digidesign.com) collecting information and looking at high-resolution photos, specifications, and documents; discussed various matters with our technical editor; and examined every piece of hardware in person. The purpose of this section is to highlight the main points so you have a head start and can use the information here to either make your decision or investigate further.

Consider your needs as you read through this section. The whole point is finding the right system for you. They're all great at what they do, but only you can define what it is you do.

The Mbox 2 Family

The Mbox 2 family, which has evolved from the original Mbox, represents the main line of Pro Tools LE systems. These are the most affordable and easily accessible Pro Tools systems. They are also all very portable.

This section moves through the Mbox 2 family from smallest to largest.

Mbox 2 Micro

I'm convinced this little pup is Digidesign's way of allowing you to run Pro Tools LE without a "proper" audio interface, or as close to it as you'll ever get. In other words, this is like having a hardware security dongle attached to your computer that authorizes you to use Pro Tools. I love it!

Given its price and limited hardware functionality, the Micro generally appeals to users who already have Pro Tools LE in their studio and want an ultra-portable copy for editing or mixing on the go. Figure 1.1 illustrates the Micro in its miniature glory.

Figure 1.1   The Mbox 2 Micro.

Table 1.1 summarizes the Micro's key features.

Table 1.1 Mbox 2 Micro Feature Summary

Feature	Details
Simultaneous Inputs	N/A
Analog Inputs	N/A
Preamps	N/A
Phantom Power	N/A
Analog Outputs	N/A
Headphone Outputs	1/8-inch stereo with volume control
Digital I/O	N/A
MIDI	N/A
Monitoring Latency	Low-latency software
Audio Interface	USB 1.1
Power	Bus powered
Bit Depth (max)	24-bit
Sample Rate (max)	48 kHz

Why the Mbox 2 Micro might be just the thing for you:

- It's cool.

- You get Pro Tools on the go.

- It's a mixer's delight.

Why it might not be:

- For mixing only—no recording inputs.

- Not to be a downer, but I wonder about the digital-to-analog (D/A) conversion quality from such a small package.

Mbox 2 Mini

The Mbox 2 Mini (Figure 1.2) is the smallest Pro Tools package you can get with inputs for recording. It's a tiny little guy, but it doesn't skimp on performance. You can record two simultaneous inputs, but be aware that you have only one balanced XLR connection with phantom power. The XLR input (Input 1) can also serve as a 1/4-inch line/DI connection. Input 2 is another unbalanced 1/4-inch line/DI. That means you can record, for example, a keyboard or electronic drum kit with 1/4-inch stereo line outputs with no problem. You can also put a mic on a guitar amplifier cabinet using the XLR on Input 1 and go direct using the DI on Input 2 at the same time. Use your imagination; these inputs can go a long way.

Figure 1.2 The Mbox 2 Mini.

However, you can't mic up a piano using a stereo XY technique, use two microphones in a spaced pair, or mic up a full drum kit with eight inputs with the Mini. If your needs are in that direction, you need a Pro Tools system with more XLR or digital inputs. You should also note that you have no peak light on this unit. You have to monitor levels by ear to discern clipping and look at the meters in Pro Tools to see how much headroom you have. That's not the end of the world, because you should be using your ears a lot anyway.

Another strong feature of the Mini is zero-latency monitoring, which is built right in. Mute the armed track(s) in Pro Tools and use the Mix control on the front panel to listen to a mix of what you are recording before it goes to the computer.

Table 1.2 summarizes the Mini's key features.

Table 1.2 Mbox 2 Mini Feature Summary

Feature	Details
Simultaneous Inputs	2 analog
Analog Inputs	1 balanced XLR input
	2 unbalanced 1/4-inch (TS) line/DI inputs
Preamps	2 channels
Phantom Power	Yes (on XLR input)
Analog Outputs	2 unbalanced 1/4-inch (TS) outputs
Headphone Outputs	1 1/4-inch stereo headphone output with volume control
Digital I/O	N/A
MIDI	N/A
Monitoring Latency	Zero-latency hardware
	Low-latency software
Audio Interface	USB 1.1
Power	Bus powered
Bit Depth (max)	24-bit
Sample Rate (max)	48 kHz

One final word about the Mini: I would call this a "cool" feature, but every Pro Tools LE system has it except for the Micro—monitor outputs. Dedicated monitor outputs connected to reasonably capable active studio monitors are critical to professional mixing, and Digidesign has included this from essentially the ground up. Don't forget they are there. You can also connect the monitor outputs to a mixer and use that as a switching bank to listen to one of several audio sources. Go out there and be imaginative!

Why the Mbox 2 Mini might be just the thing for you:

- Very small footprint and portability.

- You don't need many inputs.

Why it might not be:

- One microphone input

- No MIDI

Mbox 2

The Mbox 2, as seen in Figure 1.3, is the bread and butter of Pro Tools LE. It's the mainline system, which is still very portable and more powerful and "feature rich" than either the Micro or Mini. It's got a little bit of everything. For starters, you've got

Figure 1.3 The Mbox 2.

two analog inputs that can simultaneously record microphones (XLR) or line/DI signals. That means you can easily track a drum kit in stereo using your favorite stereo miking technique (I'm very partial to MS for many stereo applications). You can also record two guitar amplifier cabinets, or use two different mics on the same cab to blend together.

The Mbox 2 also has digital I/O in the form of two channels of S/PDIF (RCA). Hook up an extra preamp that has S/PDIF out, and you've got two more inputs, which means you can record four simultaneous inputs. The possibilities abound with two more inputs. Using just three, you can get a good drum kit sound. Set one mic up in the kick and use two more for overheads. You can also track two stereo keyboards, four vocalists, or use the two extra channels of input as talkback mics.

Things are really getting exciting, and I haven't even mentioned MIDI yet. The Mbox 2 has MIDI I/O, which for many artists, engineers, and producers is a must. Set up your external MIDI controllers, drum pads, and keyboards, and go to town. You've got 16 channels to work with, which is a great start.

The Mbox 2 is definitely a step up from the Mini. Aside from the inputs, it has clipping indicator lights (labeled Peak) on the front panel as well as separate volume controls for headphones and monitors.

Table 1.3 summarizes the Mbox 2's key features.

Why the Mbox 2 might be just the thing for you:

- Two analog inputs (mic/line/DI)

- Digital I/O (S/PDIF)

- MIDI I/O

Why it might not be:

- Need more inputs

- Need more outputs

- Only goes up to 48 kHz

- USB interface (you may prefer FireWire)

Mbox 2 Pro

The Mbox 2 Pro (Figure 1.4) is the pinnacle of the Mbox line. It includes all the features of the previous models, and more. Why? People wanted something to bridge the gap between the functionality of the older Mbox (which evolved into the Mbox 2) and the

Table 1.3 Mbox 2 Feature Summary

Feature	Details
Simultaneous Inputs	4 (2 analog, 2 digital)
Analog Inputs	2 balanced XLR inputs
	2 balanced 1/4-inch line (TRS) inputs
	2 unbalanced 1/4-inch DI (TS) inputs
Preamps	2 channels
Phantom Power	Yes (on XLR inputs)
Analog Outputs	2 unbalanced 1/4-inch
Headphone Outputs	1 1/4-inch stereo headphone output with volume control
Digital I/O	2 channels S/PDIF (RCA)
MIDI	1-in/1-out (16 channels)
Monitoring Latency	Zero-latency hardware
	Low-latency software
Audio Interface	USB 1.1
Power	Bus powered
Bit Depth (max)	24-bit
Sample Rate (max)	48 kHz
Word Clock	N/A

002 (which is now the 003). Digidesign heard this call and took several features of the 002 and made them available in the Mbox 2 Pro.

The features that set the Pro apart are things like BNC Word Clock, a FireWire interface, more inputs than any other Mbox 2 interface, and also a relatively large number of outputs for a box of this nature. All these things elevate the Pro to a level beyond a high-quality casual recording interface.

BNC What?   Word Clock is a signal that synchronizes gear that is simultaneously using digital I/O by providing a timing reference. In other words, if you have three devices in your studio (such as a Pro Tools LE interface, an external effects unit, and a preamp with S/PDIF out) and they are all running S/PDIF at a 48 kHz sample rate, the only way to keep them on (or near) the same sample is to provide a central timing reference.

Bayonet Neill-Concelman (BNC) is simply the name of the cable connector.

You can connect an external Word Clock source (such as Apogee's BIG BEN) to units with BNC Word Clock I/O and benefit from improved timing. Many consider using a high-quality external clock source to be a valid technique for improving the quality of your audio.

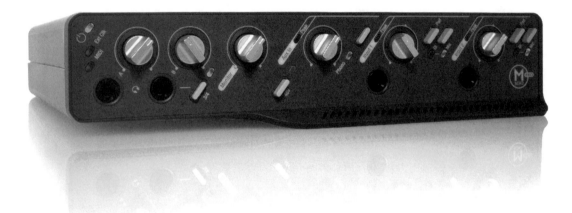

Figure 1.4   The Mbox 2 Pro.

Table 1.4 summarizes the Mbox 2 Pro's key features.

Why the Mbox 2 Pro might be just the thing for you:

- Good number of inputs
- Digital I/O
- FireWire
- MIDI
- BNC Word Clock

Why it might not be:

- More inputs than you need
- Still not enough inputs

- Need more outputs

- Need a control surface

Table 1.4 Mbox 2 Pro Feature Summary

Feature	Details
Simultaneous Inputs	6 (4 analog, 2 digital)
Analog Inputs	2 combo jack (balanced XLR, 1/4-inch line/DI) inputs
	2 unbalanced 1/4-inch (TS) DI inputs
	2 balanced 1/4-inch (TRS) line inputs
Preamps	2 channels
Phantom Power	Yes (on XLR inputs)
Analog Outputs	4 balanced 1/4-inch (TRS) line outputs
	1 unbalanced 1/4-inch stereo (TRS, 2 channels) line output
	2 balanced 1/4-inch (TRS) monitor outputs with dedicated volume control
Headphone Outputs	2 1/4-inch stereo headphone outputs with independent volume controls
Digital I/O	2 channels S/PDIF (RCA)
MIDI	1-in/1-out (16 channels)
Monitoring Latency	Low-latency software
Audio Interface	FireWire 400
Power	Bus powered or A/C power adapter
Bit Depth (max)	24-bit
Sample Rate (max)	96 kHz
Word Clock	BNC Word Clock I/O

Mbox 2 Factory Option

The Mbox 2 and Mbox 2 Pro come with a Factory option, which provides you with a number of additional plug-ins. I've used all of the plug-ins, and they are all powerful and fun. If you are on a tight budget, however, you can safely pass these by. Although cool, they don't add anything that you can't already do in one way or another in

Pro Tools using the existing bundle of plug-ins (with the possible exception of the Maxim, but you still have the stock compressor/limiter). Here's what is included:

- **Moogerfooger Analog Delay:** An analog delay that emulates the legendary Bob Moog's analog stomp box effects

- **JOEMEEK SC2 Photo Optical Compressor:** A photo optical compressor that warms and "fattens" without muddying. Photo optical compressors (of course this is a plug-in and not the real thing) use photoelectric cells to indirectly measure the intensity of the audio signal rather than the voltage of the incoming signal itself

- **JOEMEEK VC5 Meequalizer:** Another equalizer, but a good one

- **Cosmonaut Voice:** A sound effect that makes the track sound like it is being transmitted over the radio or an old telephone, complete with noise and beeps

- **Digidesign Maxim:** Limiter and loudness maximizer

- **iLok USB Smart Key:** Hardware security key that holds software authorizations

The plug-ins in the Factory option (iLok not included) are also available as the Producer Factory Bundle, should you want to go back and pick it up later, or purchase it for a Micro, Mini, 003 Rack, or M-Powered system.

The 003 Family

The Digi 003 family is the more capable, higher-end, and more expensive Pro Tools LE option. You're going to get a lot more power, features, and capabilities. The 003 line is a direct evolution from the 002, so don't expect anything dramatically different from the 002. If after looking at the 003 line you still need something more powerful or with more inputs, you should seriously look at getting Pro Tools HD or another solution entirely.

003 Factory

The 003 Factory (Figure 1.5) is the "mac daddy" of Pro Tools LE. It's ideal for tracking larger groups and mixing with a control surface. The total package here is significantly cool, but the 003 Factory's unique power comes with the control surface. Mixing is more natural and intuitive using faders as opposed to a mouse. Not only that, but it's easier to hit the Solo, Mute, and Arm buttons to quickly perform those functions. On top of that, you get real transport controls: Play, Record, Stop, Loop, Quick Punch, and so on. I can't say enough positive things about the 003 Factory, although it's the most

Figure 1.5 The Digi 003 Factory.

expensive Pro Tools LE variant. With all this power and a control surface to boot, it's a bargain. Did I say it was portable, too? It is.

Table 1.5 summarizes the 003 Factory's key features.

Why the Digi 003 Factory might be just the thing for you:

- Integrated control surface
- Significant number of inputs
- Significant number of outputs
- ADAT Optical I/O

Why it might not be:

- Don't need the control surface
- Too powerful

Table 1.5 Digi 003 Factory Feature Summary

Feature	Details
Simultaneous Inputs	18 (8 analog, 10 digital)
Analog Inputs	4 balanced XLR inputs
	4 balanced 1/4-inch (TRS) line/DI inputs
	2 balanced 1/4-inch (TRS) aux inputs
Preamps	4 channels
Phantom Power	Yes (on XLR inputs)
Analog Outputs	8 balanced 1/4-inch (TRS) line outputs
	2 balanced 1/4-inch (TRS) main monitor outputs
	2 balanced 1/4-inch (TRS) alternate monitor outputs
Headphone Outputs	2 1/4-inch stereo headphone outputs
Digital I/O	2 channels S/PDIF (RCA)
	2 channels digital optical (ADAT [8 channels] or S/PDIF [2 channels])
MIDI	1-in/2-out (16/32 channels)
Monitoring Latency	Low-latency software
Audio Interface	FireWire 400
Power	A/C power adapter
Bit Depth (max)	24-bit
Sample Rate (max)	96 kHz
Word Clock	BNC Word Clock I/O

003 Rack

The 003 Rack (see Figure 1.6) is the 003 without the control surface. The 003 is perfect for the LE user who needs a large number of inputs and outputs, but doesn't need or want the control surface. The price is significantly less than the 003 Factory because of the lack of a control surface, making the 003 Rack a real bargain.

Table 1.6 summarizes the 003 Rack's key features.

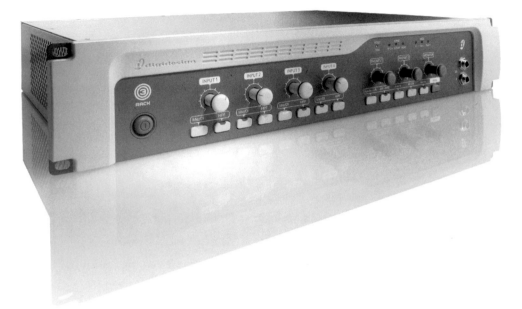

Figure 1.6 The Digi 003 Rack.

Why the Digi 003 Rack might be just the thing for you:

- Significant number of inputs
- Significant number of outputs
- ADAT Optical I/O

Why it might not be:

- Need control surface
- Too powerful

Premium Factory Option

The Digi 003 line comes with a Premium Factory option, and as its name indicates, it is a step up from the Factory option available for the Mbox 2 line. These plug-ins are already included in the 003 Factory product. You have the option of getting them only for the 003 Rack, which turns it into the 003 Rack Factory.

Table 1.6 Digi 003 Rack Feature Summary

Feature	Details
Simultaneous Inputs	18 (8 analog, 10 digital)
Analog Inputs	4 balanced XLR inputs
	4 balanced 1/4-inch (TRS) line/DI inputs
	2 balanced 1/4-inch (TRS) aux inputs
Preamps	4 channels
Phantom Power	Yes (on XLR inputs)
Analog Outputs	8 balanced 1/4-inch (TRS) line outputs
	2 balanced 1/4-inch (TRS) main monitor outputs
	2 balanced 1/4-inch (TRS) alternate monitor outputs
Headphone Outputs	2 1/4-inch stereo headphone outputs
Digital I/O	2 channels S/PDIF (RCA)
	2 channels digital optical (ADAT [8 channels] or S/PDIF [2 channels])
MIDI	1-in/2-out (16/32 channels)
Monitoring Latency	Low-latency software
Audio Interface	FireWire 400
Power	A/C power adapter
Bit Depth (max)	24-bit
Sample Rate (max)	96 kHz
Word Clock	BNC Word Clock I/O

Here's a summary of what you get in the Premium Factory package. This includes the plug-ins (and iLok) that come with the standard Factory option, plus the following:

- **Digidesign Bomb Factory BF-3A Classic Compressor:** A compressor modeled after the classic Universal Audio LA-3A Audio Leveler

- **Digidesign D-Fi bundle (Lo-Fi, Sci-Fi, Recti-Fi, Vari-Fi):** Cool sound effects and processing

- **Digidesign Moogerfooger Ring Modulator**: Modulation, low-frequency oscillation, and general moogulation effects from a company that knows a thing or two about sound synthesis

- **Digidesign SansAmp PSA-1**: Tube amp simulation

- **Digidesign Tel-Ray Variable Delay**: Delay and echo effects

- **Digidesign Voce Spin**: Rotating speaker effects

- **Digidesign Voce Chorus/Vibrato**: Chorus and vibrato effects

As was the case with the standard Factory option, you won't find anything here you can't live without. I've used many or all of these effects, and they are certainly cool, but can be saved for later if you have to keep your budget in line. The plug-ins in the Premium Factory option (iLok not included) are also available as the Producer Factory Pro Bundle should you want to go back and pick it up later or purchase it for a different LE or M-Powered system.

2 Buying Guide: Part Deux

This is Part Deux of the Pro Tools Buying Guide, also known as "Return of the Buying Guide," "More of the Buying Guide," or "The Buying Guide Strikes Back (Episode V)." It continues the tale of Pro Tools where the previous chapter left off, starting with an exploration of representative Pro Tools M-Powered systems by M-Audio. After that, the chapter covers some options and extras. It finishes up with information on legacy systems and buying used gear. So, without further ado . . .

Representative Pro Tools M-Powered Systems

After the acquisition of M-Audio in 2004 by Avid, the parent company of Digidesign, select members of M-Audio's line of gear were integrated into the world of Pro Tools through Pro Tools M-Powered software, which was spun off from Pro Tools LE. Suitable gear is clearly designated as "compatible with Pro Tools M-Powered."

You will find a number of differences between the worlds of Pro Tools LE and M-Powered. First, and most obvious, is the fact that you have many more hardware options to choose from within the M-Audio line of products. They range from PCI cards to USB and FireWire interfaces. I highlight four M-Audio products in this section to give you an idea of their capabilities. With the exception of the PCI card, they are roughly comparable with the Mbox 2 and 003 lines.

Delta 66

The M-Audio Delta 66 is a PCI card that mounts inside your computer. I've had the Delta 44 and Delta 66 (the 66 is the 44 with S/PDIF I/O) and have found them to be very good interfaces, provided you know what you're getting into. Unlike many of the other interfaces here, they have no preamps. Therefore, you've got to have a standalone preamp, channel strip, or other product such as a small format mixer (like I have) with preamps. Figure 2.1 illustrates the Delta 66. I got it because I wanted to try an interface that was internal and be able to set up different front and back ends.

Figure 2.1 The M-Audio Delta 66.

The Delta 66 has a breakout box that connects to the card by a proprietary cable. The box, which is the size of a few decks of cards, is very basic. It has four inputs and four outputs, but no stereo headphone connection, knobs, lights, or anything else.

Table 2.1 summarizes the Delta 66's key features.

MobilePre USB

The MobilePre USB (Figure 2.2) is comparable to the Mbox 2 Mini and Mbox 2. This is the interface I started my audio career with, so it has a special place in my heart. It's a nifty USB-powered interface that, although packing some power, is more suited to mobile recording and situations where you're not competing with higher-quality

Table 2.1 Delta 66 Feature Summary

Feature	Details
Simultaneous Inputs	6 (4 analog, 2 digital)
Analog Inputs	4 balanced 1/4-inch (TRS) line/DI inputs
Preamps	N/A
Phantom Power	N/A
Analog Outputs	4 balanced 1/4-inch (TRS) line outputs
Headphone Outputs	N/A
Digital I/O	2 channels S/PDIF (RCA, on PCI card)
MIDI	N/A
Monitoring Latency	Zero-latency hardware
	Low-latency software
Audio Interface	PCI Card
Power	PCI Bus
Bit Depth (max)	24-bit
Sample Rate (max)	96 kHz
Word Clock	N/A

interfaces. I used it for voiceover work initially (I was narrating computer tutorials) and then moved on to recording my own music on guitar.

It's got the basics covered. Two simultaneous inputs (XLR and line) with preamps, USB, stereo headphone out with volume control, and zero-latency hardware monitoring. Its major limitations are its bit depth, lack of MIDI connectivity, and consumer-level output signal (–10 dB).

Table 2.2 summarizes the MobilePre's key features.

FireWire 410

The FireWire 410 (see Figure 2.3) is a powerful unit that is comparable to the Mbox 2 Pro. As the name suggests, it's FireWire, and it has four inputs and ten outputs. The number of outputs is tremendous compared to similar products, and it has S/PDIF (RCA or Optical) and MIDI. I have enjoyed using these outputs to send signal to my mixer and mix "outside the box" for a change.

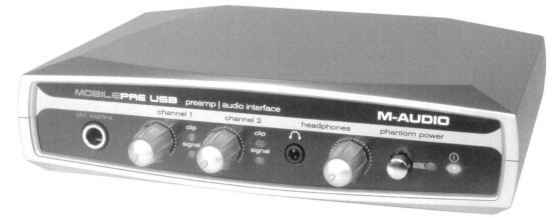

Figure 2.2   The M-Audio MobilePre USB.

Table 2.2   MobilePre USB Feature Summary

Feature	Details
Simultaneous Inputs	2 analog
Analog Inputs	2 balanced XLR inputs
	2 balanced 1/4-inch (TRS) line/DI inputs
Preamps	2 channels
Phantom Power	Yes (on XLR inputs)
Analog Outputs	2 unbalanced 1/4-inch [TS] line outputs
	1 1/8-inch stereo line output
Headphone Outputs	1 1/8-inch stereo headphone output
Digital I/O	N/A
MIDI	N/A
Monitoring Latency	Zero-latency hardware
	Low-latency software
Audio Interface	USB 1.1
Power	USB Bus
Bit Depth (max)	16-bit
Sample Rate (max)	48 kHz
Word Clock	N/A

One FireWire 410 limitation is that its outputs are –10 dB, which might not be powerful enough to drive external gear that expects a +4 dB professional signal. This is not a fatal exception, however, and surely represents one reason the unit is very modestly priced. Being forewarned is forearmed, as they say. You can compensate for a weaker output in the external gear (if possible, turn the gain up to get a hotter level) if you need to.

Figure 2.3   The M-Audio FireWire 410.

Table 2.3 summarizes the FireWire 410's key features.

Table 2.3 FireWire 410 Feature Summary

Feature	Details
Simultaneous Inputs	4 (2 analog, 2 digital)
Analog Inputs	2 combo jack (balanced XLR, unbalanced 1/4-inch [TS] line/DI) inputs (1–2)
	2 unbalanced 1/4-inch (TS) line inputs (on back, 1–2)
Preamps	2 channels
Phantom Power	Yes (on XLR inputs)
Analog Outputs	8 unbalanced 1/4-inch (TS) line outputs (1–8)
Headphone Outputs	2 1/4-inch stereo headphone outputs
Digital I/O	2 channels S/PDIF (RCA or optical)
MIDI	1-in/1-out (16 channels)
Monitoring Latency	Zero-latency hardware
	Low-latency software
Audio Interface	FireWire 400

Table 2.3   Continued

Feature	Details
Power	FireWire bus or A/C power adapter
Bit Depth (max)	24-bit
Sample Rate (max)	96 kHz
Word Clock	N/A

ProjectMix I/O

The ProjectMix I/O (Figure 2.4) is comparable to the Digi 003 Factory and is a high-quality, flexible, professional interface and control surface in one. It has a large number of inputs, FireWire interface, S/PDIF or ADAT Optical digital I/O, BNC Word Clock, and of course, motorized faders.

Figure 2.4   The M-Audio ProjectMix I/O.

Table 2.4 summarizes the ProjectMix I/O's key features.

Table 2.4 ProjectMix I/O Feature Summary

Feature	Details
Simultaneous Inputs	18 (8 analog, 10 digital)
Analog Inputs	8 balanced XLR inputs
	8 balanced 1/4-inch (TRS) line/DI inputs
Preamps	8 channels
Phantom Power	Yes (on XLR inputs)
Analog Outputs	4 balanced 1/4-inch (TRS) line outputs
Headphone Outputs	2 1/4-inch stereo headphone outputs
Digital I/O	2 channels S/PDIF (RCA)
	2 channels digital optical (ADAT [8 channels] or S/PDIF [2 channels])
MIDI	1-in/1-out (16 channels)
Monitoring Latency	Zero-latency hardware
	Low-latency software
Audio Interface	FireWire 400
Power	A/C power adapter
Bit Depth (max)	24-bit
Sample Rate (max)	96 kHz
Word Clock	BNC Word Clock I/O

Pro Tools Options and Extras

Several additional packages are available for Pro Tools LE and M-Powered users, ranging from additional software capabilities to control surfaces and keyboards. I won't go into depth here, but I want to mention each one in turn and briefly describe what it does. None of these extras is essential to get you up and running, so take your time to decide if any are right for you.

- **DV Toolkit 2:** Offers many specialized video post-production features, increases the total track count in Pro Tools LE to 48 mono or stereo tracks (up to 96 kHz if your interface supports it), includes an MP3 option (which is a necessity in today's world), import/export file format translation, and more. I would strongly consider this or the Music Production Toolkit as part of an initial studio setup.

M-Powered Compatibility The DV Toolkit 2 is not compatible with Pro Tools M-Powered systems.

- **Music Production Toolkit:** Has some of the same features as the DV Toolkit (track boost, MP3 option) and many other features oriented toward-music production (Digidesign Hybrid high-definition synthesizer, TL Space Native Edition convolution reverb, Smack! LE compressor, and so on) rather than post-production. I would strongly consider this or the DV Toolkit 2 as part of an initial studio setup. The Music Production Toolkit is compatible with Pro Tools LE and M-Powered systems.

- **Producer Factory Bundle:** The same plug-ins (without the iLok) that come with the Mbox 2 and Mbox 2 Pro Factory. For Pro Tools LE and Pro Tools M-Powered systems.

- **Producer Factory Pro Bundle:** The same plug-ins (without the iLok) as the 003 Premium Factory. For Pro Tools LE and Pro Tools M-Powered systems.

- **C|24:** This is the pinnacle of the Pro Tools LE or M-Powered world (although it can also be used with Pro Tools HD), providing a complete hands-on control solution. You hardly need to touch your mouse with this bad boy sitting in your studio. It has the works: preamps, 24-bankable channel strips, 5.1 analog monitoring, I/O galore, transport controls, plug-in controls, meters, and more. Awesome.

- **Command|8:** This is a control surface that looks and acts somewhat like the 003 Factory. However, it does not have the preamps or the I/O capabilities of the 003 (it's a control surface without the features of an audio interface), and it's USB (not FireWire). Compatible with any LE or M-Powered system, this is like having a big mouse sitting on your desktop that enables you to control the mixing and editing functions in Pro Tools.

- **Pro Tools Custom Keyboard:** A very good idea if you are going to spend a lot of time working in Pro Tools, especially editing. It gives you keyboard shortcuts on the keys themselves. This can make you work faster and help you shine in front of your clients. I've used this and wholeheartedly endorse it. It's modestly priced, and different models are available for Windows and Macintosh computers.

Legacy Systems

Although many of you will buy your Pro Tools LE system new from the factory, there are older "legacy" Digidesign products that can still be considered capable. They range from the fairly recently discontinued Mbox and 002 family to the much older (and for all intents and purposes, obsolete) 001. With this information, you'll be able to evaluate whether or not one of these older systems meets your needs, should you run across one. Even if you never buy a legacy system, you will have an understanding of what it is capable of should you see one in someone else's studio.

Mbox

The Mbox was Digidesign's first portable, easy to connect, and relatively inexpensive system. This is the product that put Pro Tools LE on thousands of computers outside of the traditional studio system, and many within it. Figure 2.5 illustrates the original Mbox.

Figure 2.5 The original Mbox.

It is still a very capable system, despite being replaced by the Mbox 2. It comes in only one version, which relies on USB for its connectivity. It has two analog TRS inserts, which is very cool (those have been removed in the Mbox 2). The inserts allow you to easily hook up outboard gear and use the hardware inserts in Pro Tools. Table 2.5 summarizes the Mbox's key features.

Table 2.5 Mbox Feature Summary

Feature	Details
Simultaneous Inputs	2 analog
Analog Inputs	2 combo jack (balanced XLR, 1/4-inch line/DI) inputs
	2 balanced 1/4-inch (TRS) line inputs (inserts)
Preamps	2 channels
Phantom Power	Yes (on XLR inputs)
Analog Outputs	2 balanced/unbalanced 1/4-inch (TRS/TS) line outputs
Headphone Outputs	1 1/4-inch stereo headphone output
	1 1/8-inch stereo headphone output
Digital I/O	2 channels S/PDIF (RCA)
MIDI	N/A
Monitoring Latency	Zero-latency hardware
	Low-latency software
Audio Interface	USB 1.1
Power	Bus powered or A/C power adapter
Bit Depth (max)	24-bit
Sample Rate (max)	48 kHz
Word Clock	N/A

The Digi 002 Family

As the numerical designations indicate, the Digi 002 family evolved from the 001 and is the direct predecessor of the 003. Like the 003, the 002 family is for serious recording. It gives you a lot of input/output options, the ability to track 18 inputs at the same time at a high sample rate, and FireWire connectivity to the mothership (your computer).

Advantage: 003   There is a consensus in the community that the preamps and digital converters on the 003 are noticeably better than the 002.

The 002 line is still sought after and a very capable package. Internally, there is no tremendous difference between the 002 and 003 systems. The Factory package comes with the 002 control surface, and the 002 Rack has everything the 002 Factory has except the control surface.

002 Factory

The 002 Factory (Figure 2.6) is the flagship of the 002 line. It has a ton of capability and a nifty integrated control surface. You can even use the control surface as a standalone 8-channel digital mixer if you like. Some of the main differences between the 002 and 003 can be found in the control surface. If you look closely, you can see that the 002 has no automation controls; no built-in jog/shuttle wheel; no Save, Undo, or Enter functions; no MIDI mode switches; and so on.

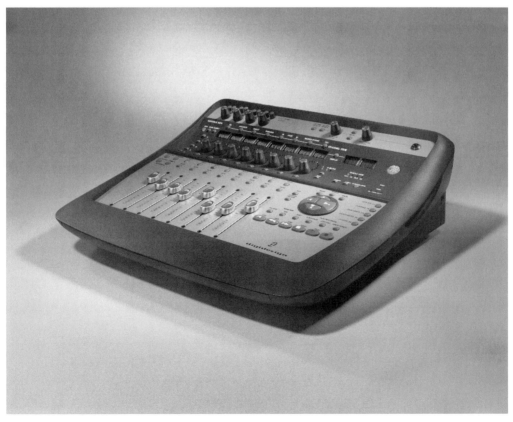

Figure 2.6 The Digi 002 Factory.

Table 2.6 summarizes the 002 Factory's key features.

Table 2.6 Digi 002 Factory Feature Summary

Feature	Details
Simultaneous Inputs	18 (8 analog, 10 digital)
Analog Inputs	4 balanced XLR inputs (1–4)
	4 balanced 1/4-inch (TRS) line/DI inputs (1–4)
	4 unbalanced 1/4-inch (TRS) aux inputs (5–8)
	2 alt inputs (RCA)
Preamps	4 channels
Phantom Power	Yes (on XLR inputs)
Analog Outputs	6 balanced 1/4-inch (TRS) line outputs (3–8)
	2 balanced 1/4-inch (TRS) main monitor outputs (1–2)
	2 fixed line outputs (RCA)
Headphone Outputs	1 1/4-inch stereo headphone outputs
Digital I/O	2 channels S/PDIF (RCA)
	2 channels digital optical (ADAT [8 channels] or S/PDIF [2 channels])
MIDI	1-in/2-out (16/32 channels)
Monitoring Latency	Low-latency software
Audio Interface	FireWire 400
Power	A/C power adapter
Bit Depth (max)	24-bit
Sample Rate (max)	96 kHz
Word Clock	BNC Word Clock I/O

002 Rack

The 002 Rack is shown in Figure 2.7, and it is functionally similar to the 003 Rack. This option is great if you need the power of the 002 but not the control surface. The 002 Rack mounts in a rack, which takes it off the table top and blends it in with the rest of your rack-mounted studio gear. It's very similar to the 003 Rack, but the 003 has a few more switching options on the front panel as well as a second headphone jack with volume control.

Figure 2.7   The Digi 002 Rack.

Table 2.7 summarizes the 002 Rack's key features.

Table 2.7 Digi 002 Rack Feature Summary

Feature	Details
Simultaneous Inputs	18 (8 analog, 10 digital)
Analog Inputs	4 balanced XLR inputs (1–4)
	4 balanced 1/4-inch (TRS) line/DI inputs (1–4)
	4 unbalanced 1/4-inch (TRS) aux inputs (5–8)
	2 alt inputs (RCA)
Preamps	4 channels
Phantom Power	Yes (on XLR inputs)
Analog Outputs	6 balanced 1/4-inch (TRS) line outputs (3–8)
	2 balanced 1/4-inch (TRS) main monitor outputs (1–2)
	2 fixed line outputs (RCA)
Headphone Outputs	1 1/4-inch stereo headphone outputs
Digital I/O	2 channels S/PDIF (RCA)
	2 channels digital optical (ADAT [8 channels] or S/PDIF [2 channels])

Table 2.7   Continued

Feature	Details
MIDI	1-in/2-out (16/32 channels)
Monitoring Latency	Low-latency software
Audio Interface	FireWire 400
Power	A/C power adapter
Bit Depth (max)	24-bit
Sample Rate (max)	96 kHz
Word Clock	BNC Word Clock I/O

The Digi 001

Pro Tools LE started with the Digi 001, which was and is a very capable system, although for all intents and purposes it is now obsolete. Digidesign has stopped supporting the 001 and the latest version of Pro Tools that the 001 can run is 6.4. Despite this, you can still get used 001 systems easily.

The 001 is comparable to the 002 and 003; it has a large number of inputs and outputs, and has digital I/O and MIDI. The main differences are the fact that the 001 relies on an internal PCI card rather than FireWire to communicate with the computer, and the 001 is not compatible with recent versions of the Pro Tools LE software. Table 2.8 summarizes the 001's key features.

Buying Used Systems

My advice to you from the outset is to buy a system fresh from the factory. You can trust that it's real, it works, and you can send it back or exchange it if something doesn't work or you don't like it. Further, you'll have all the packaging and documentation that comes with an original product. The documentation is more important that you may realize. Changing ownership is so critical, in fact, that Digidesign has a Web page and documentation for the specific purpose of transferring ownership. Visit Digidesign's web site (www.digidesign.com) and search for "Transfer of Ownership" to take you to the correct page.

However, if you want something that is no longer sold new or a legacy product, you have no other choice than to purchase it used. I also understand the desire to get

Table 2.8 Digi 001 Rack Feature Summary

Feature	Details
Simultaneous Inputs	18 (8 analog, 10 digital)
Analog Inputs	2 combo jack (balanced XLR, 1/4-inch line/DI) inputs (1–2)
	6 balanced 1/4-inch (TRS) line/DI inputs (3–8)
Preamps	2 channels
Phantom Power	Yes (on XLR inputs)
Analog Outputs	6 unbalanced 1/4-inch (TRS) line outputs (3–8)
	2 balanced 1/4-inch (TRS) main monitor outputs (1–2)
Headphone Outputs	1 1/4-inch stereo headphone output
Digital I/O	2 channels S/PDIF (RCA)
	2 channels digital optical on PCI card (ADAT [8 channels] or S/PDIF [2 channels])
MIDI	1-in/1-out (16 channels)
Monitoring Latency	Low-latency software
Audio Interface	PCI card
Power	PCI bus
Bit Depth (max)	24-bit
Sample Rate (max)	96 kHz
Word Clock	N/A

something less expensive than new retail. If you're on a strict budget and want to get started, buying a used system might be just the ticket.

Be Careful!   Protect yourself, your identity, and your money. Buying used gear online, even through a reputable establishment, is dangerous. Yes, dangerous. Just before I began writing this book I was ensnared by a scammer and almost lost a good deal of money. Thankfully, I got out just in time and learned a valuable lesson that I am glad I get to pass on to you.

Aside from hooking up with someone in the Digidesign User Community (duc.digidesign .com) who has a used Pro Tools LE or M-Powered system for sale, there are two primary online locations to shop for a legacy system: eBay and craigslist.

eBay

eBay (www.ebay.com) is probably the world's largest auction site, where you can bid on used gear and often purchase new items from retailers and individuals. eBay is a reputable, stable, trustworthy company that provides a fantastic service. I enthusiastically encourage you to check it out. If you've never been to the eBay site before, you have to register to participate in the auctions. After you've done that and are ready, search for the items you're interested in or browse through the appropriate categories.

When you search, don't forget that you're setting up a studio. You can search for "Pro Tools," of course, but you might also be interested in scoring a used "compressor," "parametric EQ," "SM57," or "Les Paul." The category that I've found to be most applicable is the Pro Audio subcategory of Musical Instruments.

The key to eBay is to remember that you're in an auction. Other people might want the same gear you're looking at. It's a contest of demand, wills, and wallets. Decide beforehand how much you are willing to pay and where you're going to draw the line. Don't get suckered into winning at all costs, unless you can back up the "at all costs" part.

Finally, don't expect huge bargains. In other words, don't expect a 90 percent discount on something that is worth having in the first place. The people you're buying from normally know the value of the gear they are selling and can set the opening bid close to that, or they have reserves to protect their investments. In addition, your competitors are as savvy as you are, and I've found the demand for the gear that's available is sufficient to keep the closing prices higher than I would have originally expected for used gear. You'll pay less than you will at retail unless you get carried away or the gear you're bidding on has moved from merely being *used* into the highly sought after world of *vintage*.

craigslist

craigslist (www.craigslist.org) is a great resource that connects sellers with buyers all over the world. It's not an auction. It's more like placing a classified ad in your newspaper. People list what they have for sale, including the price and possibly some photos, and you contact them to buy it. Sometimes the prices are firm, and those cases are usually noted. Other times you can make your best offer and see what happens.

Take Five   If you are at a creative impasse and want to liven up a session in your studio, take a break and have some fun by visiting the best-of-craigslist at www .craigslist.org/about/best/all/. Be warned that the humor can be mature, rude, crude, and explicit. Of course, that's why it's interesting in the first place.

Protecting Yourself

When you go online looking for used gear, read any helpful information about security and how to detect and avoid scams that a site has to offer. eBay has a security center at pages.ebay.com/securitycenter/index.html. Read through their information and follow their guidance. Likewise, craigslist offers online help at www.craigslist.org/about/safety .html and www.craigslist.org/about/scams.html.

Aside from detecting obvious illegal activities, you should also be aware that people can rip you off without necessarily breaking the law. Here are some tips to help you out:

- If you see photos of an item, make sure it's the one being sold. If in doubt, ask.

- Pay careful attention to shipping. Many times people try to make extra money by charging you more for shipping and handling than is necessary.

- Confirm any software licenses that might be included.

- Read and understand the terms of agreement you are entering into and the payment method.

- If in doubt, don't buy.

Don't ever give your bank account number or credit card number directly to the person you're buying used gear from. That's like giving them the keys to your house. Don't do it. No gear is worth it, no matter what bargain you think you're getting. You might find your money stolen or your cards maxed out in the time it takes you to hook up an XLR cable to a mic.

Don't ever wire money. Never. Ever. Got it? Don't ever wire money using a service like Western Union or Moneygram. In and of themselves, those companies are legal and trustworthy. However, they the primary tools thieves use to steal money after they've trapped you into thinking they are legitimate. Would you send cash to someone you didn't know? There's no difference between doing that and wiring money to them. You'll send it, never get the gear, and never hear from them again.

It Happened to Me

This is embarrassing for me to tell, but I'll share it with you so you can spot the warning signs of an actual scam. This happened to me. It's not made up or embellished in any way, as my wife can attest.

I was bidding on some gear at eBay and didn't win the auction. I was comfortable with my final bid and could live with the fact that I didn't win the auction. A few days afterwards, I was contacted by another eBay user and told the winner had backed out and I could have the gear at my highest bid. The thing that fooled me into trusting them was the fact that they knew what my bid was. I was sort of suspicious that the user name didn't match the name of the person holding the auction, but when they knew my bid, I just thought they were using another account. Bad move. The truth is that when an auction is over, your bids become public information. Anyone can go to that closed auction and find out what you bid. The other bad move on my part was actually believing a person with a different account was the original seller. It seems very obvious now, but people can and will lie to your face. That's what these thieves do, and they're pros at it.

Next, I started getting e-mails that looked like they were officially from eBay. I was told I needed to follow the instructions exactly and wire money to England because this person was on a business trip. I had reservations, but because this e-mail looked like it came from eBay I proceeded to get the money to wire overseas. It didn't seem to matter to me at the time the names didn't match and the original seller had never sent me a message.

All the while, I was looking for some indication on the auction page or through my eBay account that the auction had been changed and that I had officially been given the chance to purchase the gear at my high bid. It never came. This is probably the thing that saved me. After I sent the money—yes, I actually wired the money—I was overcome by an intense feeling of doubt. Suddenly, I realized that this entire thing could be a fraud and that I had nothing to protect me. I quickly logged onto eBay, went to their security page, and sent them a copy of the original e-mail. Within minutes, they responded that it was a fraud. I had been had! I bought it all, hook, line, and sinker.

Thankfully, my story doesn't end there. I quickly went to the location I sent the money from and was able to cancel the wire before it was picked up. I was out the processing fee, but the bulk of the money was rescued.

Don't let this happen to you. It was worth it for me to learn my lesson, doubly so because I can share this with you, but don't let it happen to you.

 **Setting Up Your Studio**

I want to make this an informative chapter, yet not overly limited in how it approaches the task of setting up a studio. I don't expect you to be able to go out and contract a studio architect and start designing and constructing your dream studio after reading this chapter. I expect most of you are just starting out in your musical or audio engineering careers or have some experience but are new to Pro Tools. I say this because the range of what a studio is, where it can be, how it can be designed and furnished, and what you can do inside is tremendous. The only real limitations are your budget and time.

Given that, in this chapter I address setting up your studio from a "getting started" perspective but with an unlimited mindset. Use this information both to set up your studio today (the practical matter at hand) and plan for tomorrow (the unlimited mindset).

No matter what else I say in this chapter, I want to get this point across: do what you can with what you have. Great music or professional audio does not require a studio worth hundreds of thousands of dollars. The boom of home and project studios is a build-as-you-go boom. Get something small. Learn it. Master it. Have fun with it. Then move onwards and upwards.

Just What Is a Studio?

A studio is a place to make or produce music and other professional audio. I say "professional" audio because I mean just that. When you buy Pro Tools LE or M-Powered you're in the world of professional audio, whether you produce music as a hobby or distribute it nationally. Said another way, who buys *Pro* Tools to be an amateur?

I'm going to "ramble on" (sing that to Led Zeppelin) so you can think along with me about what a studio is and, more importantly, what *your* studio is going to be. Cross-reference your needs, dreams, and desires with how to fulfill them.

Ideas and Lists   I've written part of this chapter with an eye towards provoking thought. To that degree, I found that putting the information in lists and discussing each element helped me organize and communicate my thoughts. I see much of this as a starting point, where I introduce you to many aspects of putting your studio together.

Resources

How seriously do you want to pursue this? How much money (now and over time) are you willing to invest? How much of your life is this worth? Think about these questions when you are planning a studio. Not sure? Then start small and see how it goes. Build gradually. Is this a hobby that you want to pursue on the weekends, or do you think you'll get lost in it?

These questions aren't meant to scare you. They are to help guide you into making a firm assessment of what you want and help you budget your resources so that you can be on time and on target with your dreams.

- **Time:** Building a studio takes time: time to learn it and time to operate it. Most people I know see this as a calling in their life and devote a good deal of time to it.

- **Money:** You know it is going to take money: money to furnish your studio and to buy the gear. Sure, it would be nice to make money off this studio, but you can't always make money doing what you love. It's okay never to make any money off your studio. It can be entertainment and part of your lifestyle budget. No one I know expects to go to the movies, go bowling, dancing, or shopping and make money doing those things.

- **Energy:** Your energy is the beating heart of your studio.

Purpose

What do you do? What do you plan to do? That's a pretty important place to start. What a solo guitarist needs in terms of studio space is much different from the needs of a full-fledged rock band. Consider the following list of hypothetical purposes and what those purposes mean in terms of studio space:

- **Mix Master:** You're primarily interested in mixing, and you're really into audio engineering. You don't need a huge studio or a lot of gear for this task. Acoustics can be important, however. What you need is a good control room.

- **Beat Guru:** You are into making beats and need some space for a synth or keyboard. You can get by with a modest control room.

- **Solo Act:** Your work revolves around making your own music. You could be a singer, a guitar player, a jazz saxophonist, or a banjo player. Each instrument has its own requirements for space and noise levels, but unless you're playing a grand piano you don't need a lot of space. Because you're going solo, all you need is a decent control room and some isolation.

- **Electronica:** You need caffeine and the computer, disco lights, and headphones. You can get by with a couch, the top bunk of a bunk bed, or the passenger seat in someone's car.

- **Small Group:** You're one part of a team, perhaps a worship group or small band. Maybe you're a husband-wife (or significant other-significant other) team. You should probably seek out a larger room with enough space to jam and have your gear. Gobos are helpful here.

- **Big Band:** You've got a band, and you want to record yourself. Maybe you're making a demo or producing your own CD to sell. This is where home studios have a harder time coping with the task at hand. Ideally, a larger group requires a "great room" or space for a drum kit, and either iso booths or gobos to isolate guitars and singers. Unless you don't mind bleed between tracks, isolation allows for more creative editing, mixing, and overdubbing (the process where you go back and rerecord individual parts).

Notice the theme here? In almost every case, you can make do with one room, and not even a large one at that. Limitations arise mostly during recording. How loud instruments are (guitar amps on "eleven"), how large they are (drum kits and grand pianos being on the large side), and how many people you're trying to record (power trio or gospel choir) at one time all dictate the size your studio needs to be or the length to which you must work around problems.

Size
You can also look at studios based on size:

- **Desk-sized:** Part of a room, perhaps separated from another area with acoustic treatments or partitions. It could be a multipurpose room where you have a few computers, one of which is running Pro Tools. Essentially, this is a desk and chair. Very limited recording options, but mixing or composing might be easily done. Think of sitting on an airline with a laptop, Pro Tools, and your headphones. You could easily mix, edit, or work with MIDI.

- **Small to Medium-sized Room:** A dedicated room, which doesn't have to be large, but is one where you can shut the door and not bother other people. This can be an office or spare bedroom you've turned into a small studio. You can decide to purposely dedicate this room as your studio and put up acoustic material, partitions, and other studio gear without cramping everyone else's style.

- **Large Room:** A larger room with possible isolation areas or gobos to divide the room into functional areas. This could be a basement, garage, or loft.

Gobo   A gobo is a "go-between," or partition. It can be constructed out of any sound-absorbing material, such as 2×4s and plywood covered in carpet. Gobos are meant to be moved around as your needs require.

- **Big Time:** Multiple rooms, including a control room, a "great room" for recording groups or large instruments, and one or more isolation booths.

- **Studio Complex:** Two or more studios in reasonably close proximity. You have at least one large studio with a control room, large studio room, and iso booths, and at least one but potentially several smaller studios for mixing, mastering, and smaller projects.

What does the size of a studio tell you? Among other things it tells you how easy it might be to record larger projects and how expensive it is to own and operate. Larger studios almost always mean more time, more money, more people, and require much more business to stay afloat. The upside is that you can conceivably make far more money.

However, the fundamentals of what goes on in each studio, regardless of size, are the same. That's my point. Don't think you can't make a high-quality, upscale studio out of a small space.

Space

The last section started with size and moved to function. This section takes a look at existing spaces to see how you can transform them into a studio and what sort of studio you might get.

- **Spare Room:** This could be a bedroom or office that you decide to convert to a part-time or full-time studio. This is where many people start. I'm sitting in a spare bedroom right now, which is where I record my music at home. I can mix, record myself, create beats, work with MIDI, edit audio, and much more: all from one small extra room.

■ **Garage:** Here you have more potential. Garages are larger than rooms, and they are typically used for band practice. It gets the noise out of the house. A garage can be a viable medium-sized studio to record a small band, and if you decide to convert the garage to be a full-time studio, it can be very roomy. However, two considerations with garages are security and comfort. Both are less than optimal.

■ **Basement:** A basement is one of the best spaces to convert to a studio. Basements are typically larger than an upstairs room and are much more isolated from outside sounds than an upper room. However, if you have wood floors above, you could be in for sound transmission problems above your studio. Many people put a good deal of money into converting their basement spaces into pro-level studios.

■ **Loft:** I mention a loft because not everyone lives in a house with a basement, or perhaps you live in a large city. A loft could be a great place to set up a studio.

■ **Barn:** This is one of my dreams. I think it would be great to buy some property out in the country and have a large barn to be able to convert (over time) into a professional studio. Isolation and size are no problem.

■ **Warehouse:** I know a person who has bought or is leasing a warehouse in an industrial part of town and has converted this large space into a studio with several rooms. Awesome.

■ **Building:** Finally, you can always buy or build your own studio in its own building.

Control

Here are some things that you have some control over when you set up your studio:

■ **Size (within limits):** Larger rooms can be partitioned temporarily or permanently into smaller functional areas such as vocal, iso, guitar, or drum booths.

■ **Layout:** Where you put your desk, chair, monitors, and so forth. Not all layouts are amenable to good listening or recording.

■ **Reflective Acoustics:** You can control reflections with acoustic panels, foam, drapes, gobos, and blankets pretty easily. This is not the same thing as sound isolation, or soundproofing, which normally requires special techniques.

■ **Isolation:** Keeping sound out and within. This is much harder to control than reflections and ideally requires you to build your facility specifically with this in mind.

- **Power:** Although you might have to hire an electrician, you do have some control over your power situation. By that I mean grounding and isolating your supply to a different circuit than other rooms (especially the kitchen and laundry facilities).

These are the things that are pretty much beyond your control:

- **Location:** Most of us make do with what we have. However, if you are able to scout for your ideal location, make sure it's not next to any train tracks, beside an airport, near heavy industrial activity, or underneath power lines.

- **External Noise:** This is tied to location and what's going on. If you live in the country, you are far better off than those living in a busy, noisy city. You can't control this from the outside, but you can modify your structure to mitigate the transmission of noise inside your studio. That's a needlessly fancy way of saying you can build it better.

- **Interference:** Related to noise, only of an electronic variety. Cell towers, radio interference, and other strong electromagnetic signals can wreak havoc with your computer and audio gear. Having clean power helps, as does shielding instruments like guitars and basses.

- **People:** If you've got a noisy neighbor, or a person nearby who drives a loud vehicle (like I unfortunately did), that person can often interrupt your sessions. Try to work it out as civilly as possible.

Mobile Studio

I don't want to leave mobile studios out of this equation. Pro Tools LE and M-Powered are in many ways very mobile systems. You might be building a studio that you can take on the road with you to record live sound in many different types of locations. In these situations, you have very little control over the environment.

You still need to learn about aspects of recording such as how to isolate instruments and vocals from each other, but instead of practicing these techniques in your own studio, you can do them in someone else's garage, house of worship, basement, or club. These venues can be large or small. After tracking on location, you'll need to edit and mix your material, master it, and publish it. More than likely, that part will take place at your "home base" studio (although outsourcing mastering and publishing is a viable solution).

My list of things for you to think about is as follows:

- **Storage:** Where are you going to store the gear you take on location? Are you going to set it up and use it in your studio?

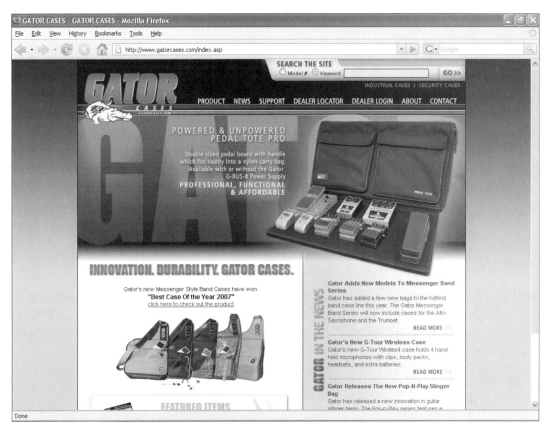

Figure 3.1 Gator Cases protect your investment.

■ **Protection:** Every time you pick something up and move it you risk damaging it. Good travel cases are an important investment. Figure 3.1 shows the Gator Cases website, a manufacturer of portable racks and all sorts of cases.

■ **Transportation:** This depends on how much gear you're transporting and its size. It could range from your car, truck, or van up to a large moving-type truck.

Be the Master of Your Domain

What's the most important piece of gear you can put in your studio? You. That might sound overly corny, but it's true. You are what can't be replaced. You're the brains, the intuition, the musicality, the drive, the passion, the craziness, and the soul. And each one of you is different.

Cynics say that anyone can be replaced, that no one is unique, that the music business is a ravenous beast that eats people alive, and that no one can succeed, especially in this age of the Internet where CD sales are dropping, studios are closing, and the competition is fierce.

I've literally been shown the door and told that I'm not worth the time, that the music business is dead or dying, and that I shouldn't try because this is all a pipe dream.

If you meet someone like that, ignore them, and do what you want to do. Shake the dust off your feet as you walk out. Be the master of your domain. When they lay me in the grave, I want to have at least tried—and not given up when haters hate and whiners whine. It's true: the music industry and traditional studio system is changing, but I am a fierce believer that there's room here for continued success and that I—and you—can be a part of it.

Setting Up Your Studio

I think it's time to set up a studio. What about you?

Here are some general steps you can follow to help you through the process. These aren't in any absolute order; these are just my thoughts. I've put personal or anecdotal notes with these steps to try to illustrate problems you might encounter or stimulate your imagination.

1. **Determine your purpose**: This helps you identify your needs. Be honest with yourself, but realize that purposes can change over time. Identifying what you need to do now does not lock you into that forever. It helps you get started today.

2. **Find a space**: Ideally, your space will meet all your needs. Most often, you must compromise. Sometimes this is, by necessity, the only space you can use. That's okay. Get started anyway. Remember, not every studio needs to be huge.

3. **Evaluate acoustics**: Even now you should be thinking of how sound is going to be bouncing around in the space you choose. You might not have a choice, of course, but setting up a mastering studio in a room with bare concrete walls and a noisy heating and cooling system is going to affect the quality of your work. Identify problems and begin thinking of solutions.

Room Tuning   Some debate exists over which room tuning method is best to use—electronic equalization (EQ) or acoustic panels. Both techniques first involve determining a room's frequency response by playing pink noise from the monitors and measuring the result with a reference microphone (which is connected to an armed track that has a spectrograph plug-in on it) located where you head would be. Electronic EQ then addresses the problem of peaks or valleys in the response curve by placing a dual-channel EQ in the signal path before the monitors and selectively raising or lowering the gain at those "problem frequencies" to achieve a flat response. Acoustic panel advocates fix the problem with acoustic panels that are designed to control various frequency ranges in strategic spots in the control room to control reflections. I would go with both. Use panels for the most part but use EQ to perfect the sweet spot where you sit.

4. **Test the power:** Check for grounding. Ungrounded power is not safe to use and could kill you. With mobile studios you should be especially careful when visiting a venue for the first time. Test the outlets you intend to use with a nifty tester. If necessary, find a grounded outlet in another room and run a heavy-duty extension cord until you can get the situation fixed. Yes, it stinks having a heavy-gauge gaudy orange power cable running through the middle of your house. But I've had to do it, and it works well. Power is a real problem in home and project studios, and one of the main causes of electronic noise.

Living in a World of Yes   Although technology has progressed to the point where you and I can create astounding digital audio creations from the comfort of our own homes, large studios still have a major advantage—money. You live in a world of duct tape and compromise, whereas they live in a world of "yes" (until they go out of business, that is). If your power stinks, you might be forced to compromise for some time, until you have the money to address the problem with "industrial strength" power conditioners. Large studios just go out and buy them.

5. **Evaluate isolation:** Find out if you're going to be battling noise from the outside. Because sound travels in all directions, remember to check if the sound level you are going to be working at is going to be a problem for others. Lower frequencies are the hardest to stop, and studio architects and builders go to great lengths during design and construction to build walls that attenuate these "problem frequencies" the most. You might not be able to build a double-walled acoustically isolated studio with a double ceiling, floating floor, and air locks in your spare bedroom. One of the greatest misconceptions people have is believing that foam or acoustic panels have anything to do with isolation. They don't. They are designed to battle reflections, not isolate a structure. If you set up in a basement, you're going to be more isolated than if you set up in your dining room with bay windows. Try to find a space that has as few windows or openings as possible, or if you can, cover them up.

6. **Consider floor plan:** Decide where things are going to go. Put your desk facing the narrow wall of a rectangular room so the sound doesn't bounce off the wall behind your head. Give your gear some breathing space, and don't get too close to a wall, either.

7. **Add furnishings:** You're going to need at least a desk or table, a chair, possibly a rack for outboard gear, and who knows what else. Take it from me—try to get the best chair you can afford. I've sat for hours on some pretty cheap chairs of both the folding and nonfolding variety, and was barely able to stand up when I was done. Your back can hurt, and it can hobble you for days. Don't forget the lava lamp, and find some furniture for your guests and artists. A couch is a must. Even if you have to go to the Salvation Army or Goodwill (or another charitable location where you live that sells donated items inexpensively) to get it, an artist couch immediately tells people they're in a studio.

8. **Install equipment:** This is where you bring in Pro Tools, your computer, monitors, and other gear that comprises the engine of your creativity. Set things up, run cables, and test everything out.

9. **Secure your studio:** All this stuff is expensive, and people might be inclined to steal it if you give them a chance. Don't even tempt them. Limit access to your studio. Keep it locked. Don't go showing off your $3,000 Pro Tools rig to everyone at the bus station. Either have a lockable microphone case, cabinet, or closet, or keep your gear somewhere else secure. Maintain an inventory and check it every session. If your studio is in the garage, make sure you have a sturdy garage door and reinforce any other doors or windows. My father-in-law had someone break into his garage to steal a snow blower (of all things). They broke the glass on the window and just reached in to unlock the door. A door or window that isn't sturdy can easily be forced open just by bumping into it. Remember to insure your studio and all its belongings. Talk to your insurance agent about the best policy for you. Take photos of all your gear, write down any serial numbers, and store that inventory offsite. If your studio is in your house, be especially careful to protect your family from anyone you might not know. Consider a home security system or alarm.

It Takes a Thief   There used to be (I think it's in reruns now) a show on the Discovery Channel called *It Takes a Thief*. These two guys would pick a house out they thought they could rob. They would contact the owner beforehand, who got to sit in a van and watch on closed-circuit TV. I was astounded how easy it was for one guy to quickly and efficiently break in, ransack a house, and load all the valuables into a getaway van. Evaluate your studio or home from that perspective.

The Great Studio Gear List

I don't mind repeating the fact that setting up a studio is a pretty daunting prospect that gives you a lot of things to think about. So many, in fact, that it's easy to lose track of them all. Use this list to orient yourself as to what you might want to include in your studio—today or down the road. I've included some helpful thoughts with each entry.

Add On!   I've tried to be comprehensive in this list, but I admit that I might have missed things. Start here. Add on. Make it yours.

And, by the way, I've left the order of this list as a semi-random, brainstorming thought process. It's like I felt when I wrote it—fun and spontaneous.

- **Computer:** Yup, got to have one of those.

- **Pro Tools:** This is *Your Pro Tools Studio,* after all.

- **Microphones:** Might not be required, depending on your purpose. Useful for recording, however.

- **Microphone Stands:** Get a variety of these, so you can mic a kick drum or guitar amp with a small one and a standing vocalist with a taller one. Cheap ones are cheap. You'll hate them because they won't hold a heavy mic up where you want it.

- **Quick-Release Microphone Connection:** Cool time-savers you screw into the mic stand once and then pop the mic on and off with a quick-release (see Figure 3.2).

- **Pop Screens:** To stop pops from vocalists who spit all over the place and have plosive P's and B's.

- **Foam Microphone Windscreen:** Reduces heavy breathing, hissing, and obviously wind noise if you're outside.

- **Gobos or Partitions:** Standing structures to block sound and isolate band members.

- **Blankets or Moving Pads:** Padding to muffle sounds or block reflections. I've used pads on guitar and bass amps, on pianos, and around drum kits.

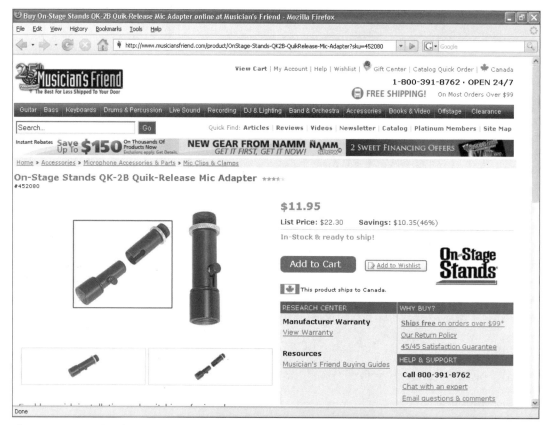

Figure 3.2 Quick-release mic adapters: These little guys are incredible time-savers.

- **Drum Rug or Platform:** To place a drum kit on to isolate it (a bit) from the flooring and everyone else.

- **Drum Shield:** These puppies are expensive, but block and contain the sound from a drum kit. (See Figure 3.3.)

- **Microphone Cables:** In a variety of lengths, from short to long. If you need a lot, try buying the cable and connectors in bulk and making the connections yourself with a soldering iron.

- **Instrument Cables:** Ditto, only these are 1/4-inch unbalanced cables.

Get Good Cables Don't believe anyone who says good cables don't make a difference. I had a situation where I was fighting interference and noise with my guitar and went round and round with it for ages. I had the guitar shielded,

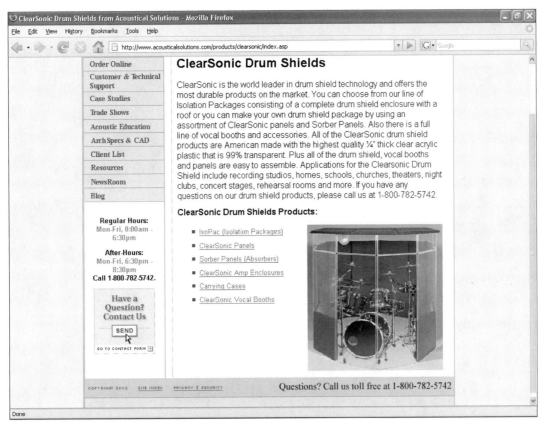

Figure 3.3 Put your drummer in one of these.

looked at the power and grounding in the room, the amp, and everything else in the signal chain. It came down to my cheap (which I thought was good enough at the time) instrument cable. Expect to invest heavily in good cables.

- **Patch Cords:** It doesn't hurt to have a few around in case a guitar or bass player needs an extra.

- **Digital Cables:** In case you have digital runs. Not *the* digital runs, hopefully.

- **Cable Tester:** This can save you a lot of time and frustration when something isn't going right and you don't know what. Test the cables in question.

- **Hum Eliminator:** I've got one of these from Ebtech (see Figure 3.4), and it works wonders for eliminating hum caused by ground loops. The number-one problem is correctly identifying the problem. If it's not a ground loop hum, this product won't

Figure 3.4 Fighting hum.

help. It does, however, convert back and forth between balanced and unbalanced lines if you need that in a pinch.

- **Additional Headphone Amp or Distribution Box:** If you've got a number of band members, one headphone out on a Pro Tools interface might not be enough. Route that (or another stereo pair) out to a headphone amp or a distribution box (see Figure 3.5).

Taking Things Back   If a store has a return policy, don't be afraid to use it. It's your money, and you often have no way of knowing beforehand if the gear in question is right for you and is going to work out. If I knew of any other way I would try it, but no matter how many reviews and opinions you get, yours is the one that counts. Don't let a salesperson embarrass you into keeping something that you don't want. I've taken back about as much as I've kept, which can raise eyebrows, but the guys and gals I deal with know I keep coming back.

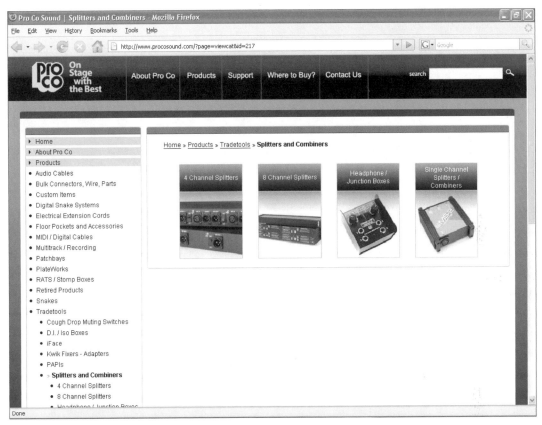

Figure 3.5   Pro Co headphone distribution boxes are sturdy and convenient.

- **Desk or Table:** To put your computer monitor, keyboard, and mouse on. I'm using one of those tables that you commonly see in churches, only it's white PVC, I think. I got it at Sam's Club for $39.99. It's spacious, and I can adjust its height. Specialty desks (see Figure 3.6) are pretty expensive, but very cool.

- **Outlet Tester:** These handy little gadgets (see Figure 3.7) are lifesavers. Literally. Plug it into an outlet, and it tells you if it is wired properly and grounded or not.

- **Powered Nearfield Monitors:** These take a line-level signal coming out of Pro Tools or a mixer and require no additional amplifier (see Figure 3.8). Plug them in and turn them on. If you have the budget, get two different sets so you can A/B between them and compare. Subwoofers are an attractive addition to a home studio because they make up for the bass frequencies smaller nearfield monitors have difficulty reproducing. Look at the specs carefully (frequency response is an interesting

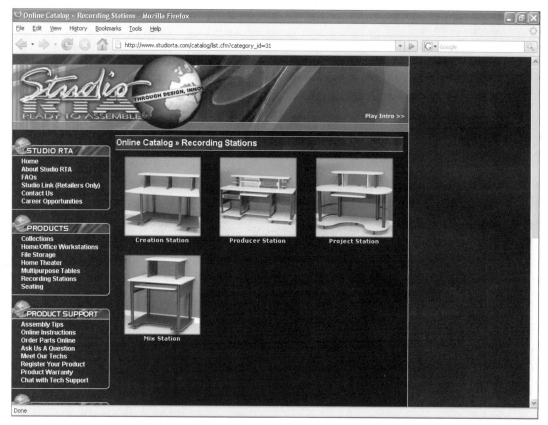

Figure 3.6 Desks come in many sizes and shapes.

comparison), and take note of whether you can tune the monitors. They are also known as active monitors.

Monitor Pricing Oddness   Double- and triple-check the price of the monitors you are interested in to see if it's "each" or for a pair. I find this very troublesome, and it's easy to get confused. If in doubt, contact the retailer and specifically ask. Notice in Figure 3.8 at the top it says *Yamaha HS80M 8" Powered Studio Monitor – **Each***.

- **Monitor Stands:** These support your monitors and allow you to position them more precisely to your needs than just placing them on your desk.

- **Monitor Isolation Pads:** Auralex sells great pads to put monitors on.

Figure 3.7 Save your life and buy one of these outlet testers.

- **Artist Couch:** A studio staple.

- **Lava Lamp:** For the mood, as shown in Figure 3.9.

- **Music Stands:** Don't forget these if you or the artists you are recording bring in sheet music.

- **Pens, Pencils, Paper:** For note-taking.

- **Snacks:** Healthy or otherwise. If people get the munchies, having a snack can keep the vibe going. Nothing kills a fantastic recording session faster than everyone getting hungry and taking a two-hour lunch.

- **Refrigerator:** I say this with some trepidation, as a refrigerator motor cycling on and off can cause electrical interference. However, they are nice to have outside your studio proper (and on another power circuit) for clients and artists. If you're in your

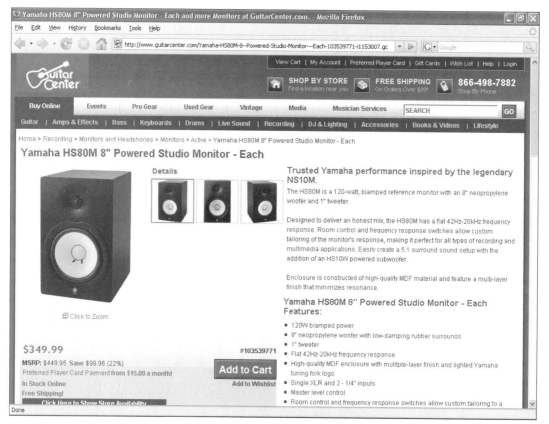

Figure 3.8   Yamaha nearfields are an industry standard.

own home, a studio fridge keeps people from walking around your house looking for refreshment.

- **Sodas, Coffee, Bottled Water:** Total service.

- **Open-Back Headphones:** For vocalists and other band members, mostly.

- **Closed-Back Headphones:** For drummers, although some like open headphones. (See Figure 3.10.)

- **Headphone Cable Adapter (1/8-inch TRS to 1/4-inch TRS):** Most headphones terminate in an 1/8-inch stereo plug, but for some reason most headphone jacks on gear are 1/4-inch stereo. Go figure. I've got several of these.

- **DI Boxes:** For recording guitars and basses directly (see Figure 3.11).

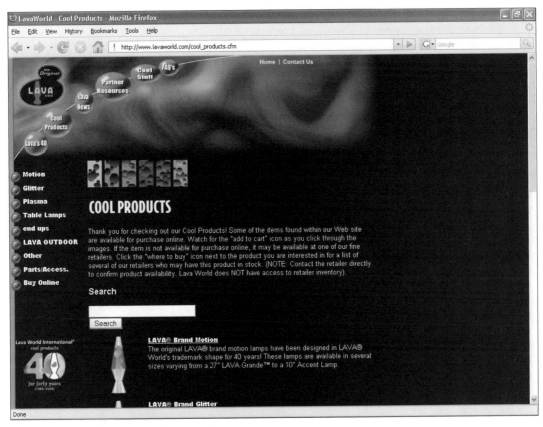

Figure 3.9 Hot lava to set the mood.

- **Power Attenuator or Load Box:** To record a tube amp at lower volume but high power.

- **Mixer:** Not required, but I wouldn't give my Yamaha mixer up.

- **Power Conditioner:** After it is captured by a microphone or pickup or generated by a synthesizer, sound is nothing but electricity. Power conditioners (see Figure 3.12) theoretically clean and condition your power supply, in addition to providing some surge protection. Cheaper units are barely more than a power strip. More expensive units deliver on their claims.

- **Stomp Boxes:** Over time, you might want to have a collection of stomp boxes for guitarists to try.

- **Extra Instruments:** Same theory. This can set you apart from those engineers who don't have them.

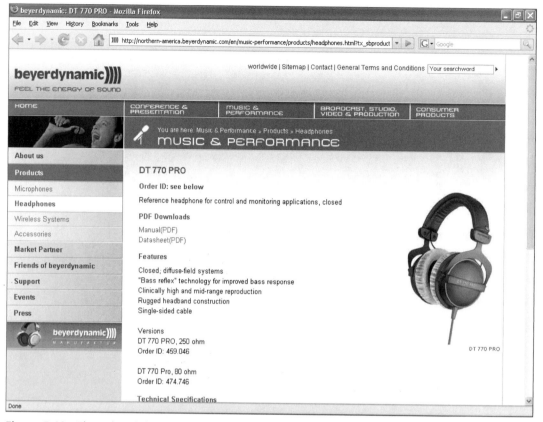

Figure 3.10 These headphones are what I use.

- **Patch Bay:** If you run a lot of outboard gear or have a multitude of connections you switch around constantly, try getting a patch bay.

- **Writeable CDs:** To burn CDs of preliminary mixes that artists can take home.

- **Tuner:** You can use a plug-in for this, but having a standalone tuner is also nice.

- **Metronome:** You can use a plug-in for this, too, but you never know.

- **Drum Tuner:** Most good drummers have this, but just in case, you can come through in a pinch.

- **Tape:** To tape cables down if you need to or for general use. You might need tape to get a handle on a rattling drum head as well.

- **Extra Guitar and Bass Strings:** Clients come back to a full-service studio.

Figure 3.11 Radial direct boxes are very good.

- **Extra Batteries:** For active pickups, DI boxes, stomp boxes, and anything else that might need a battery. The most popular format is 9V.

- **Acoustic Panels:** Bass traps and panels (see Figure 3.13) to treat the acoustics of the room you're in.

Stay Focused

If you get bitten by the gear or studio improvement "bug" and spend all your time "keeping up with the neighbors," it's going to drive you crazy. You end up being more concerned with what you don't have than using what you do have. A corollary to this is that you'll always be scared to make a decision because one person says a piece of gear is the "bee's knees" while another flames you for even thinking about it. How do

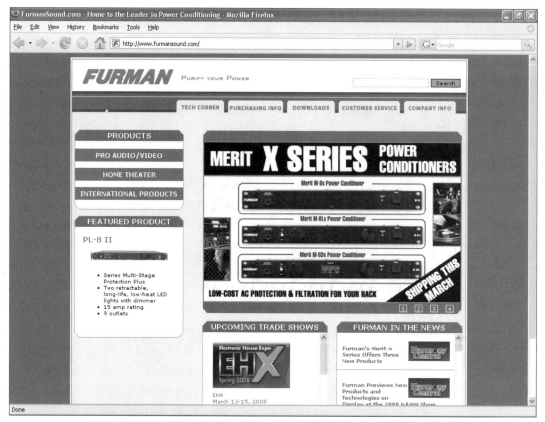

Figure 3.12 Furman is a standard in power conditioning.

you know who is right? What gear should you get? Is your studio ever going to be good enough?

You can spend hour upon hour researching every fuzz box in existence, every homemade mod to current and classic models. You can look at cheap ones, expensive ones, new ones, used ones, troll forums and read post upon post about which stomp box should be proclaimed the undisputed King of All Fuzz Boxes—and *never make any music*!

Sure, undoubtedly a difference exists between certain stomp boxes, EQs, compressors, and other gear. Some plug-ins look cool, and some are ugly. You're entitled to your opinions and favorites. I have them! *Vive la différence* (that's French). Sure, there's a difference between recording at 44.1 kHz and 96 kHz sampling rates. Sure, there's a difference between my $150 guitar (with $229.98 worth of pickups) and $479 amp (15W tube) and a vintage '59 Les Paul being played through a 1970:s-era Marshall Master Volume amp. You get no argument from me there.

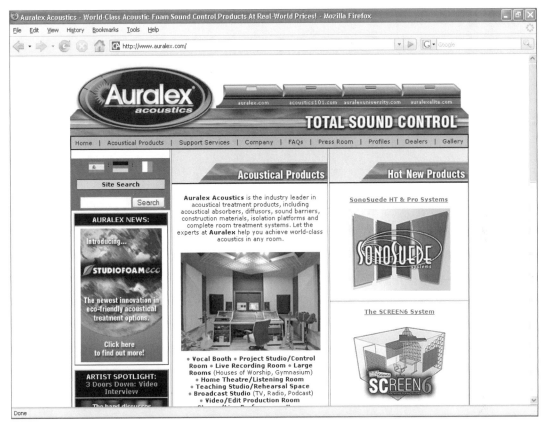

Figure 3.13 Many people use Auralex panels.

Being overly concerned with gear or fretting that you don't have the perfect studio can be a large distraction, especially when you're starting out. How do you get past it? Get something and start using it. Learn it and figure out why you like it or don't like it. Call that desk your studio and be an audio engineer and music producer today. As you get more, your experience can tell you when you've outgrown your current gear and/or digs and what you need next.

4 Preparing to Install

Who wants to prepare? I mean, let's just rip that box open and start plugging things in! No, wait. Thing is, you're not installing a toaster. Pro Tools is professional audio gear that requires a professional to run it, whether you're doing this in your spare time as a hobby or making money off it. Computers alone are incredibly complex pieces of machinery that need their share of grooming to run well. That grooming, and the knowledge and experience you gain from it, is often the difference between throwing your system out the window and being able to record your music with it.

Preparing to install is something that takes place before you start. In fact, it's critically important that you do this before opening that new piece of gear. Give yourself time to do this. Allowing yourself that time might not always be possible, but if it is, schedule your prep time when you don't have to be productive and aren't on a deadline. Then, you can move more smoothly, and successfully, onto installing the hardware, software, and getting busy with it.

Installation Workflow

Pro Tools is a system of components that have to work together to work at all. You've got the hardware, which has to be installed correctly to communicate with your computer system. Then you've got the software, which has to run properly in and of itself, but also has to communicate with the hardware. It's a veritable square dance of electrons. In the end, it all relies on your computer to function.

Having a game plan helps take some of the mystery and fear out of maintaining a computer. Including an orderly installation process is effective and saves time. Think of your installation as a journey of several discrete stages.

General Digidesign Installation Flow

The Digidesign journey is actually pretty simple. Here it is:

1. **Prepare:** Get your work area ready, the computer, hardware, and so forth. That's what this chapter is about.

2. **Connect the hardware:** Windows users will connect the interface to their computer with the USB or FireWire cable. Mac users will install Pro Tools LE first, then come back to this step. I cover this and the following steps in the next chapter, Chapter 5, "Installing Pro Tools LE," where I talk about Digidesign gear specifically.

3. **Install Pro Tools LE:** The point of the whole show.

4. **Launch Pro Tools LE:** The first run authorizes the software.

5. **Test:** Before you get involved in extensively configuring Pro Tools, make sure Pro Tools LE is installed correctly and it works with your hardware. Perform a minimal recording check.

6. **Configure Pro Tools LE:** Make it your own.

7. **Integrate Pro Tools LE fully into your studio:** Make all the final audio connections and stabilize your workflow.

Installation on USB Ports   Decide carefully what USB ports you want to use for your USB audio devices such as the Digidesign Mbox 2, M-Audio MobilePre USB, iLok, and USB-capable MIDI keyboard. Once you connect them and install the hardware drivers, you may be locked into using that port every time you want to use that device. I have two convenient USB ports on the front of my computer, and I used one to connect things as I installed Pro Tools. I had to constantly switch configurations and devices while writing this book, and when I tried connecting my USB gear to a different port, a "Found New Hardware" message popped up (Windows), asking me to install new hardware drivers. To get the device working I had to switch it back to it's original USB port. I should have spread them out and devoted a unique USB port to each device the first time.

General M-Audio Installation Flow

Here are the slightly more involved steps to take when installing M-Audio gear and Pro Tools M-Powered:

1. **Prepare:** Check.

2. **Install the hardware drivers:** Roger that. This step and the ones that follow are covered in Chapter 6, "Installing Pro Tools M-Powered."

3. **Make the audio connections:** Run your cables. I suggest connecting just one in and two outs and leave the rest for later.

4. **Initial test:** Because M-Audio gear is compatible with other digital audio workstations (DAWs), I like to make sure the hardware works at this stage before going on. I use another DAW on my system and record with it. In fact, you might decide on an M-Audio audio interface and install it before purchasing Pro Tools M-Powered.

5. **Install Pro Tools M-Powered:** Bring out the big dog.

6. **Test again:** Make sure Pro Tools M-Powered is installed correctly and that it works with your hardware.

7. **Configure Pro Tools:** Enough said.

8. **Integrate Pro Tools M-Powered fully into your studio:** This is when you know it works, and you can make all your connections and get down to making music.

I go to this much trouble to protect myself and to make sure I get what I want. I want something that works. I want to make the process go as smoothly as possible and be able to repeat it if I have to. This might not be the only time you have to install this stuff. If you get a new computer, want to update the drivers, upgrade your hardware, or any number of other scenarios, you might have to uninstall and reinstall everything.

When Things Go Wrong My own experience is that installing gear is often the hardest and most frustrating part of audio engineering. Things often go wrong. When they do, you must clear your mind of the frustration you feel. Think clearly, logically, and confidently. You're the sentient being with opposable thumbs. You can do it.

Typical M-Audio Hardware Installation Flow

Regardless of the interface type (USB, FireWire, PCI/PCIe card), M-Audio hardware installation typically follows the same general steps. This is a general flow to help you get the big picture. This does not obviate the need to read the M-Powered installation chapter in this book, where I go into much greater detail with representative hardware.

1. Download the latest drivers off the M-Audio web site (www.m-audio.com).

2. Install the hardware drivers *before* the hardware is connected or powered on.

3. Shut down the computer.

4. Connect or physically install (e.g., internal cards) the hardware.

5. Turn the computer on.

6. The computer will recognizes the hardware and finish installing the driver and/or control panel.

7. Now you're ready to install Pro Tools.

The reason I want to give you a bigger picture is that I can't cover every conceivable installation with all possible hardware in this book for both Macintosh and Windows platforms. That's what the detailed manuals for each system are for. However, I want to get you into a comfort zone where you have some idea of what's coming and how to prepare for it, which can hopefully make your installations go much more smoothly. I wish I had this help when I was trying to figure out how to set up a digital home recording studio.

Computer Issues

At one time computers played no role in music production. You recorded through an analog console and onto analog tape. If anything was digital, it was the reverb unit or some other special effects gear. People might not have even had a computer in their studio. Not so anymore. Computers are now an integral part of most studios, from the upper echelon pro houses to garages. It's the lower end that's gotten much more affordable and powerful in recent years. I'm benefiting from this trend, and you can, too.

But, and this is a big *but,* introducing computers into the audio world has not been without growing pains. I can't point you to any one system or configuration that's an infallible setup where you make no decisions and take no risks. Computers aren't toasters, and until they are, you've got work to do.

Upgrading or Buying a New System

The first step is to determine if your computer can run Pro Tools at all, and whether or not it can deal with the workload you're going to put on it. Please visit Digidesign's and

M-Audio's websites to check for the latest specs on the specific gear and software you plan on purchasing and installing.

System Requirements Links   For the most current system requirements and compatibility information, visit www.digidesign.com/compato (for Digidesign hardware and Pro Tools LE/M-Powered) or www.m-audio.com for M-Audio hardware. After you arrive at M-Audio's website, navigate to a specific product page and you can easily see the System Requirements link.

Here are some things to look for as you consider upgrading or buying new computer equipment:

- **Processing power:** More is better. Get more. Get dual- or quad-core technology, available in Mac and Windows computers. You won't be sorry.

- **RAM:** Ditto. I'm using 4 GB. I remember my first PC. It had 4 MB (yes, four *megabytes*) of RAM and no CD-ROM. This was before CD-ROMs were used with computers (the year was 1992). It was a PC with a 486DX chip in it that ran at 33 MHz. I scrimped and saved to upgrade to 16 MB, which cost about $300. Get more RAM. It's ridiculously cheap compared to the old days.

- **Hard disk drives and storage space:** High-quality pro audio takes up space. The more you record, and the higher the quality, the more space you need. Fortunately, the average price per gigabyte seems to keep dropping, and you can buy huge capacities for very little extra money. Don't skimp on this. I have four hard drives: three internal and one external USB. I allocate one of each internal for my system, audio, and backup. I use the external drive for mobility and longer-term archiving.

- **FireWire and USB ports:** You need enough FireWire and/or USB ports to connect the things you have and the things you're going to get. If you're running Pro Tools LE with an Mbox 2, for example, you might need two open USB ports: one for the interface and one for an iLok if you purchase additional plug-ins. If you're already close to maxing out, consider getting an extra internal card that has more.

- **Monitor(s):** Don't let the fact that you're going to be working in audio (as opposed to playing video games) make you think you don't need a good monitor, or more than one. I've worked on dual-screen monsters running Pro Tools HD with the mix and edit windows on separate screens and loved it. At home, I have a 21-inch widescreen digital flat-panel display (with a "souped" up graphics card with 512 MB RAM) that maxes out at a resolution of 1680×1050. It's very comfortable to use, and

I can see a lot of tracks at once. It can get old constantly scrolling up, down, and sideways when you're editing. If your system is up to date but you've got a small monitor, consider upgrading. Don't forget to look at your graphics card in conjunction with a new monitor to see if you have the power to fill all those pixels.

- **PCI/PCIe (PCI Express):** Finally, consider what internal cards you need and whether your computer has the space and is compatible. M-Audio's Delta 66 is a PCI card that has to fit in my computer alongside another sound card and a card with extra USB ports. You might have other cards and needs to consider. That's what this is about. Plan beforehand.

My First Mac   My first Mac was a Mac 128K—the original. I was a student at the USAF Academy in the mid-1980s and bought it used for writing my papers. Everyone else was using PCs, and I wanted this thing that looked like something recognizable, not a black screen with green characters on it. Sadly, one day the logic board died, and I tossed it unceremoniously out instead of lugging it around.

Generally speaking, if your system is relatively new (within a few years), you should be okay running the latest software. The audio hardware isn't so much of an issue, as all you generally need is a USB or FireWire port to use it, and the hardware is designed to have a far greater practical lifespan than the software. Software is updated more often, and the capabilities that keep being added are what pushes your system to the limit. Think of it this way—the Mbox is on its second revision (that is, Mbox 2), but Pro Tools LE is up to version 7.4.

Mobility

Another important consideration is mobility. Should you get a laptop or a desktop model?

Time Warp   Someday, the decision won't be between a laptop or a desktop. You'll look back at that and laugh because you'll be choosing between headset or keychain models.

This might seem like an obvious decision. If you need to be mobile, you're going to have to have a laptop; that is, unless you're willing to truck a desktop computer around and set it up at gigs, rehearsals, or other venues. My advice would be to start with the power you need at a given price and work backwards. It makes no sense to get an underpowered laptop that can't do the job (laptops tend to cost more for the same capability than desktops) because you can't afford the tricked-out version, no matter how portable it is. See what I mean? It's all tied together. Needing or wanting to be "more mobile" is not the only criteria you should consider. Laptops are also less easily upgraded than desktop computers and more easily stolen. You get what you get, and that's basically it. Mobile is also in the eye of the beholder. I know many live sound guys who take huge consoles, monitors, lighting, cables, and other gear to every show. If you're working at that scale, the difference between a laptop and a desktop's portability is less than if you have to toss it in your backpack and go.

System Flavor

By flavor, I mean deciding whether or not to buy a PC-compatible computer with Microsoft Windows as the operating system (OS) or a Macintosh computer from Apple.

In the audio realm, Macs have a performance leg up (mostly using other DAWs besides Pro Tools) on Windows because of their audio driver architecture. It's called Core Audio, and it's awesome. The best non-Pro Tools audio drivers Windows has are ASIO, which introduces a continual latency battle. This is not so much of a problem that I wouldn't recommend using Windows (I use it), but it's a known issue when using Windows versus Macintosh.

In other factors, such as overall system speed and the ability to upgrade individual components, PC architecture comes out on top. PCs are cheaper, and you can have a faster system for the same price as you would if you bought a Mac.

Operating Systems and Versions   Be very careful when buying a new computer or deciding to upgrade your operating system. In general, programmers of audio applications, Pro Tools in particular, are more interested in stability than they are in quickly deploying a new version to be compatible with the latest Windows or Mac operating system. Check the Digidesign website to ensure that the OS you are considering is supported before buying it. This is one case where it pays to be patient.

In particular (for PCs especially), pay attention to the OS when you buy a new "prebuilt" computer (as opposed to buying the individual components and putting it together yourself) and see if you have any options.

Part of the decision on what operating system to buy might depend on what you use now and what you're comfortable with. Do you want to have to learn an entirely new system, be it Windows or Mac, or go with what you're familiar with?

The bottom line is that you can record and mix professional audio with either a Mac or Windows machine. Both have their strong points and followers, as well as their weak points and detractors.

Audio Interfaces

You should know what interface you want before you buy that new computer. Are you planning on getting the Digidesign Mbox 2 Pro? If so, you must have a FireWire port available to use on the computer. If you run other FireWire gear, such as external hard drives, you might have to add FireWire ports. This requires either getting a new motherboard (the overkill solution) or installing an internal PCI/PCIe card with more FireWire ports. The interface you choose will often affect other things down the line. Be aware of that when you are looking for a new computer.

Laptops and I/O Ports   Some PC laptops do not have any FireWire ports, and the new Mac Air doesn't have any either. The MacBook and MacBook Pro that are currently available do, however, as well as many PC laptops from companies like Dell. Make sure you have them if you need them!

If the interface you are going to get uses USB, the only problem you might have is running out of ports. At one time or another, I've had so many USB devices I could hardly count them: mouse, keyboard, joystick (got to have one of those), scanner, printer, and external hard drive. That makes six. I had an external DVD-burner with USB, so that made seven. Add in the audio interface—a MobilePre USB—and I needed eight ports. Throw in an iLok, and that's nine. That's a lot, and because most hardware and software specs steer you away from using USB hubs (the things you plug into a USB port that add more USB ports), I had to go the internal card route to add more USB ports.

When I bought my M-Audio Delta 66, I had to ensure my computer had enough internal slots of the right type. It did, but they were all being used. I had to ditch one of the USB/FireWire cards to fit the thing in.

Another odd but important task is to make sure your I/O ports are active. On Windows machines, for example, you can turn off the motherboard's USB and FireWire ports in the BIOS Setup routine during bootup. Check this before you start installing gear and software; otherwise, you might be pulling your hair out trying to figure out what's wrong. If you've got another device that uses the same bus architecture, plug it in and see if it works. If it does, you're in business!

Latency

Latency is the difference in time between making a sound and hearing it through your audio interface. Large latency values make it impossible to play anything coherent because you're hearing an echo through your headphones (or monitors) as opposed to a low- or no-latency signal.

Samples and Latency   You often see latency measured in samples, which is not wrong, but is potentially misleading if you want to know how much time is involved. If I am recording at a sampling rate of 44.1 kHz with a latency of 1024 samples, the time value of the latency is 23 milliseconds (ms), but if I am recording at 96 kHz, the same latency as measured in samples comes out to only 10 ms.

I'm not going to get into this too deeply here, but the most critical factors affecting latency in most DAWs are 1) the audio drivers you choose, 2) the audio interface-software configuration, and 3) the computer. Pro Tools doesn't allow you to choose different drivers, so that's a done deal. Buffer settings rather than drivers are what controls latency in Pro Tools LE and M-Powered (larger buffer settings allow you to increase the processing load on your CPU but also increase latency; smaller buffer settings lower latency but at the price of less processing power). Although there are three different types of audio interfaces—via USB, FireWire, or internal card—assuming your computer is working properly and these busses are transmitting data at the speed they are supposed to, this is out of your hands, too. So your computer is the important remaining piece of the puzzle, which is why you should maintain it properly; have an updated, fast machine with plenty of RAM; and record to a hard drive that is not the same drive your system is on.

Here are some variables that have an impact on latency:

- **Tracking:** This is where latency is most problematic, because your cue mix cannot lag very far behind your musicians or it throws everything off. Given the design of the hardware, tracking latency is most often caused by using the wrong settings in Pro Tools, trying to do too much at one time, and putting plug-ins on tracks you are recording.

- **Mixing:** Latency is less of a problem here because you aren't working in real time. Plug-ins, MIDI instruments, and a high track count are the predominant causes of mixing latency. Unlike other applications, Pro Tools LE and M-Powered limit the number of tracks you can work with at one time to help set a reasonable operating envelope for the hardware and software.

- **Audio interface:** Essentially a static variable in the latency equation because the hardware is designed to do what it does and only that. This is why many Digidesign and M-Audio audio interfaces that run Pro Tools LE and M-Powered have only a limited number of inputs.

- **CPU/system:** This is highly variable, and the faster the better. CPU speed is not so much a problem in tracking as much as it is in mixing, because the CPU performs all the Real Time Audio Suite (RTAS) processing. This is one of the main differences between Pro Tools HD and LE or M-Powered. HD uses dedicated audio processing cards called DSPs (which run off a time-division multiplexing, or TDM, bus) that take the load off the computer. It is only recently that affordable computing power has caught up with the demanding world of audio processing and allowed you to put the load back on the computer itself.

- **Pro Tools:** This depends on how you have it configured. A number of settings within Pro Tools allow you to configure how Pro Tools runs and optimize it for your current task. I cover these in Chapter 7, "Configuring Pro Tools."

- **Monitoring setup during tracking:** Assuming everything is set up and optimized correctly, you can still fight with latency if you choose to monitor the main output of Pro Tools as you play. Often, what causes this latency is having a lot of tracks and numerous plug-ins. It's just too hard for Pro Tools to record the audio coming in in real time, then use electronic equalization (EQ) and compress the audio, put some reverb on it (while playing back and processing ten other tracks), and then output it all to you with no discernable delay. This is why professional studios spend hundreds of thousands of dollars on the best possible gear with the most power and lowest possible latency. Even then, I've stressed HD systems so much that they've had a hard time keeping up. The only real way to get no-latency monitoring is by monitoring the incoming signal before it goes to the computer and mixing it with the main outputs. Even then, if you have too much going on, your system won't be able to handle it without delays.

- **You:** One of the squirrelly variables.

Computer Maintenance

Computer maintenance is actually one of the most important steps in this entire process. Would you put some awesome wheels on a car that doesn't run, or one that coughs, chokes, and spits down the road? No, neither would I. Pimping a ride is still about the ride. Accordingly, Windows and Mac users alike benefit from routine maintenance.

Mac users should perform regular disk checks and repair permissions using Disk Utility. If you have a complete system maintenance and optimization utility like OnyX or

MacJanitor (both freeware), you have access to more robust tools that dig deeper into the system to ensure it runs smoothly. The great advantage of these tools is that you don't have to go spelunking around your system from the terminal.

Foot Stomper   This is so important I'm going to repeat it as a strong caution: start this kind of thorough maintenance and optimization before you install audio hardware and Pro Tools. Give yourself time to complete it and make sure your system is stable before proceeding to the fun stuff.

It's very important that you clean up your system, upgrade your software and hardware, uninstall unneeded applications, and otherwise mess with it well before you install any pro audio gear and Pro Tools LE or M-Powered. Do it on a day when you don't have to make music, don't need to be productive, and have the time to resurrect your system should it turn totally against you. I've worked extensively with Mac and Windows systems, and I don't know for the life of me why this can't be made any easier. At the moment, Macs seem to have the upper hand versus Windows in regards to the ease and possibility of successful computer maintenance.

Virus Scan

First, make sure you perform a virus check with all the Internet spamming detectors turned on, as shown in Figure 4.1. Then, turn that puppy off and never go on the Internet with this computer again.

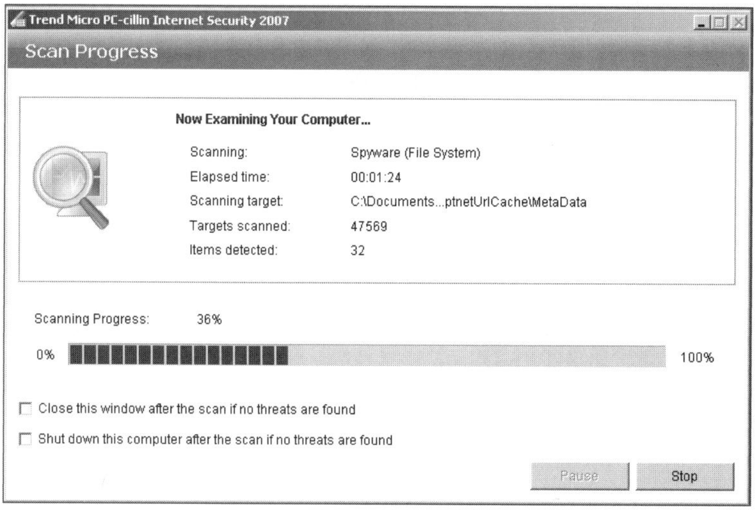

Figure 4.1 Get a clean bill of health before installing.

That's probably an unrealistic expectation. However, seriously scan your system as the first step in this process so you can be certain nothing nefarious is hanging around, especially if it causes a system slowdown.

When to Disable Your Virus Checker   For the best result, disable any form of virus checker before you install any hardware drivers and Pro Tools LE or M-Powered. You should also disable it when recording or mixing. If you need to be certain of security while you are making music, disable your Internet connection or unplug the cable for the ultimate in protection.

Uninstalling Old Software

It's really nice to be able to have a computer devoted solely to making music. This is the ideal, and in this scenario you don't install anything that isn't directly related to your gear, Pro Tools, and making music. A single-purpose computer prevents many of the problems that crop up over time as you use your computer for various things. System sludge, slowdowns, hiccups, and other nasty problems are more likely in an environment where you're constantly installing the latest game, software application, productivity suite, and surfing the net on MySpace and Facebook every day.

My Routine   I've found that I like a clean computer, and the only effective way for me to have it is to wipe the system drive and reinstall everything at least once a year, and sometimes twice. I configure my computer and store my data in such a way that everything I need is on another drive, so I can proceed without days of backing up and preparing. I make sure all my data is in its place and safe, copy over whatever might be on the system drive to a backup drive, and wipe it. Try it. It's scary the first few times because you really don't want to mess up, but you are rewarded with a "new" computer a few times a year.

The problem is that most people don't have a computer dedicated solely to audio. I don't. I write books, work on photos, create art, browse the Internet, create web pages, and e-mail on one computer. My kids play games on the Internet, and I have installed some of their favorite games (Sonic the Hedgehog and the Teenage Mutant Ninja Turtle games) on my system. I know that's not ideal, but it's real.

The balance I strike is to clean house every once in a while. I uninstall unneeded or unused programs regularly (Figure 4.2), and before I install a new piece of gear I give my system a very careful once-over.

Just because I do it one way doesn't mean there aren't other workarounds. Find what works for you. You could run multiple user accounts, hardware profiles, or dual-boot into different operating systems. If you're running an Intel-based Mac with OS X Leopard, you can use the Boot Camp feature to run Windows and Mac on the same hardware (make sure to check for compatibility with Pro Tools before you jump into something like that, however).

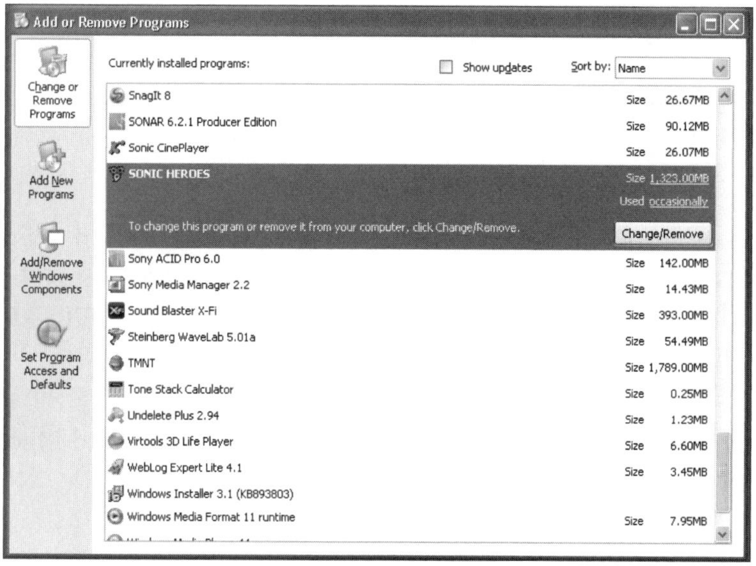

Figure 4.2   Clean up unnecessary applications.

Checking Disks for Errors

Windows users should regularly scan their disks for errors using Scandisk. Right-click on a drive icon from the My Computer window and choose Properties, then navigate to the Tools tab. Press the Check Now button from the Error checking section, and Windows will run Scandisk on that drive (see Figure 4.3) or schedule it the next time you reboot. I've selected the option that automatically fixes errors, but because I don't want to spend a day and a half doing this, I've left the bad sector recovery option unchecked.

Mac users should routinely run Disk Utility to check their disks for errors.

Defragmenting

Defragmenting is a process whereby your computer is forced to rewrite all of its data sequentially: nice and neat. Originally, computers looked for open space, no matter how large or small, and wrote data on a "first come, first served" basis. If the space was too

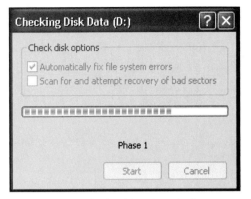

Figure 4.3 Disk checking in Windows.

small for a given file, the system broke that file up and stored a bit over here and a bit over there. That's called fragmentation. It's not so bad when only a few files are scattered all over the hard drive, but when a certain "critical mass" is reached, the computer starts to bog down tremendously. It has to do so much work finding pieces of files that you've got to stop and defragment the hard drive.

As operating systems have evolved, this situation has improved, but Windows and Mac users still benefit from the occasional defrag (see Figure 4.4).

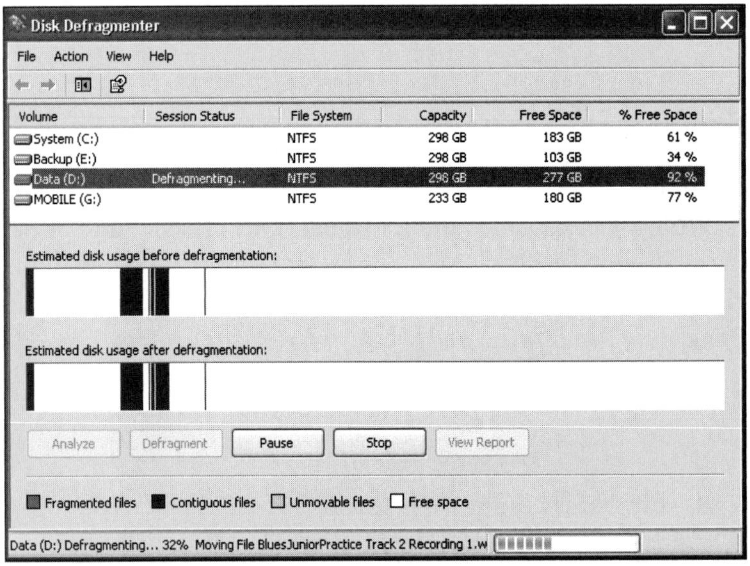

Figure 4.4 Defragging is mesmerizing.

Organizing Your Hard Drives

Let me say from the outset that if you don't have a second drive in your desktop system to use as an "audio only" drive, go get it now, install it, and then pick up right here when you're ready. This advice is just too valuable to ignore, especially with today's very low cost per gigabyte. Not only that, but a separate drive is often required to use Pro Tools effectively.

Figure 4.5 shows my setup. I've got four hard drives. I use the first exclusively for the system and programs. I use the second drive for audio. This is where I save my Pro Tools sessions and where I store all the audio data. It's easier to take care of this drive with frequent disk checking and defragmenting, and most importantly, the system can write to this drive without interrupting other system tasks. I use the third drive for backups, and my external drive I use to network and for longer-term storage.

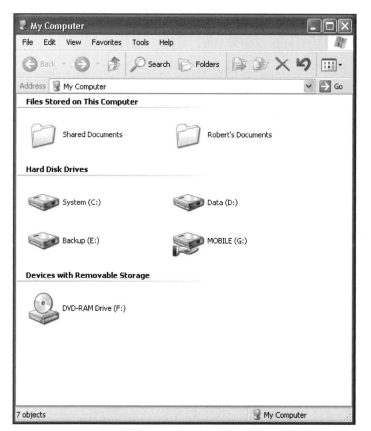

Figure 4.5 My functionally organized hard drives.

Preparing Your Studio

Buying new gear is like bringing home a new baby. You wait with anticipation and then bring it home and begin a life of sleep deprivation. Sometimes you're ecstatic, and sometimes you pull your hair out. I've brought home four kids, and it's been terrifically exciting (and scary) each time. Remember, you don't bring home kids and just toss them on the couch. No, you prepare a place for them.

Mister Obvious   I know some of this seems obvious. I do. I don't think you're an idiot, either. The thing with successfully making music with pro audio gear and a computer is that, taken as a whole, the process is involved, complex, and very challenging. Sometimes you have easy steps, like this one. Prepare a spot on your desk. Think about where you want the gear. Make sure it all reaches and the cables are long enough. Okay, that's not brain surgery. I'm sure you get it. However, with so many things to do, it's easy to lose sight of some of them. My job is to help you set up your Pro Tools studio. You're paying me to do that by virtue of buying this book. I take that very seriously, and one way I want to ensure I do my job is to get as much as I can down on paper for you, even the easy stuff.

---

iLok

An iLok is a hardware "dongle" that stores software licenses. You plug it into your computer through a USB port. Having an iLok and the appropriate authorizations effectively proves you're a legitimate owner (that is, licensee) of the software you have installed. The storage capacity is limited, so you might need to go buy more iLoks to keep up with your software appetite.

Software vendors have searched for effective yet nonintrusive protection schemes since home computers have existed. These have ranged from serial numbers (easily copied) to manual queries ("What's the third word of paragraph 2 on page 142?"). So far, not many companies have had the guts to enforce a hardware solution, which is pretty intrusive.

Digidesign, however, has. It's effective and hard to defeat. It's not going away, so you have to deal with it.

Total Security   Taken together, the fact that Pro Tools cannot run with a non-certified audio interface and that you often (not always—see later in this chapter) need an iLok for authorization means this system is about as secure as you can get without having to physically go to a Digidesign studio to use their gear.

Who Needs an iLok
Today, users of the following Pro Tools software must have an authorized iLok for the application to run:

- Pro Tools HD 7

- Pro Tools M-Powered

- Pro Tools Academic (for M-Audio interfaces)

The good news for these users is that a pre-authorized iLok comes with your package. Use this during your installation. In addition, many of Digidesign's optional software packages, such as the Music Production Toolkit, DV Toolkit, the DV Toolkit 2, plus third-party plug-ins, require a valid iLok (either sold separately or shipped with the product). All versions of Pro Tools LE use a serial code for verification.

Purchasing and Registering
You can purchase an iLok from its makers, PACE Anti-Piracy, Inc. (www.ilok.com); Digidesign's store (store.digidesign.com); and most audio vendors such as Musician's Friend (www.musiciansfriend.com) and Guitar Center (www.guitarcenter.com). They're around $40. Make sure to buy the Dongle Buddy (a questionable name if I've ever heard one). It really helps and makes me feel confident I won't knock into the thing and break it off.

If you want to buy an iLok from PACE, you have to create an iLok account and log in to see the purchasing area. That's normally a pain, but in this case you have to create an account with iLok anyway to manage your iLok(s) and licenses.

Here are the steps to create an account and get started:

1.   Go to www.ilok.com and sign up for a free account (see Figure 4.6).

2.   Follow the Signup link to register and build your profile (see Figure 4.7). You also choose a user name and password here.

3.   Log in (at this point you can click the Buy iLoks and Buddies link to purchase, as shown in Figure 4.8).

4.   Wait. You will get your new iLok in the mail and can then set up the client software and manage your iLok.

Setting Up the iLok Client Software
You only have to set up the iLok Client software on the machines from which you are going to manage your iLoks. The client software is distinguished from the iLok driver in

Figure 4.6 Sign up for a free iLok account.

that you use the client to manage the iLok on the web and the driver handles the connection from the iLok to your computer and audio application. Most times, you won't need to install the iLok driver.

To set up the iLok client software, follow these steps:

1. Plug in your iLok.

2. Go to www.ilok.com and log in.

3. Download the iLok client software (see Figure 4.9). This is what allows you to connect to the iLok website and manage your iLok online. You only need the iLok driver if for some reason you need the latest version of the driver. Otherwise, Pro Tools automatically installs an iLok driver if necessary.

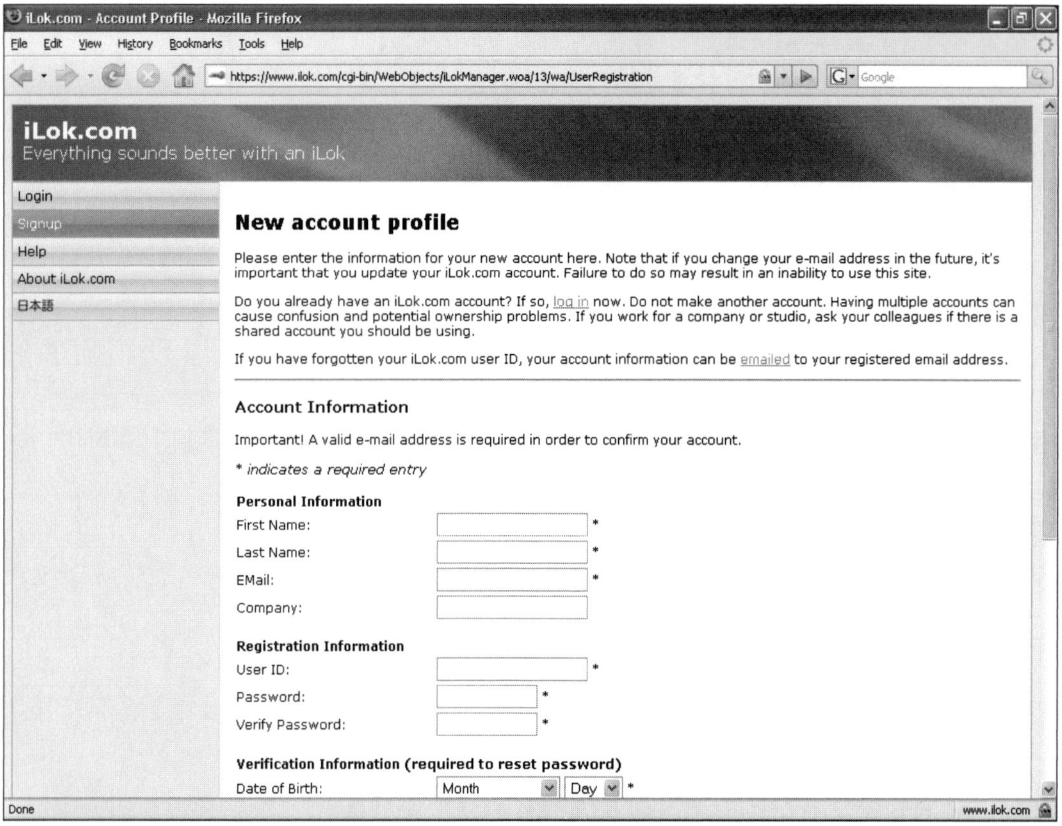

Figure 4.7   Just don't choose iLok for a username and password.

4.   Run the client file that you just downloaded to install the software. Follow the instructions (they're very simple). The one quirky thing is that when you are prompted for a User Name and Company Name, you must put text in both fields (see Figure 4.10).

5.   At this point you might want to see what licenses you have on the iLok, transfer authorizations from one iLok to another, edit the name and description of the iLok, and so on. I cover all those fun things in the next section.

Managing Your iLok and Licenses

Managing your iLok is fun and rewarding. Nope. Just kidding. However, it is critically important. You bought the licenses with your hard-earned (I'm assuming) money,

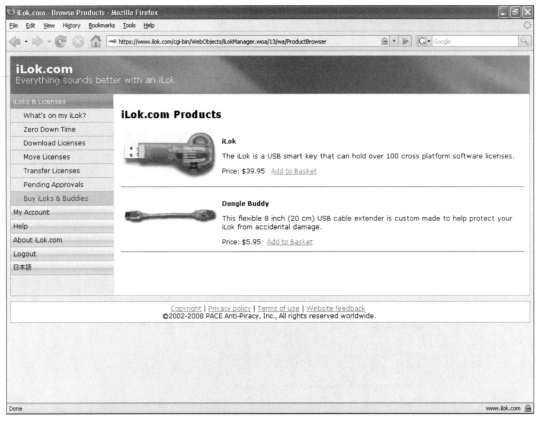

Figure 4.8   The iLok and its Dongle Buddy.

and they could all go "poof" if you don't treat your iLok and the management of it with care.

iLok management takes place on the web. You need a valid iLok account that you are currently logged in on and your iLok, and you need to have already successfully installed the iLok client software.

The important tasks are listed on the menu located on the left side of the screen, as shown in Figure 4.11.

The following list reviews some of the more important items:

- **What's on my iLok:** Shows you the licenses currently installed on each iLok you currently have inserted into your machine (see Figure 4.12). You can have more than one iLok inserted and identified.

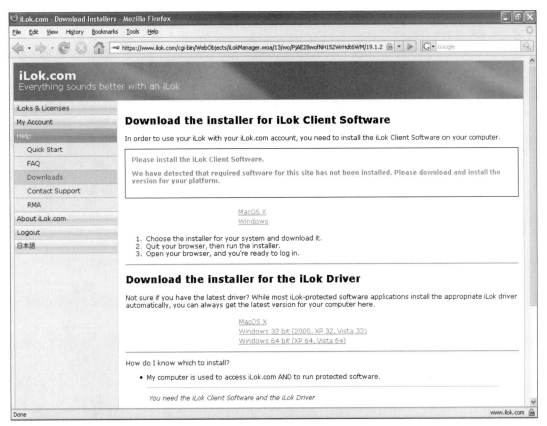

Figure 4.9 The client is what allows you to manage your iLok from this computer.

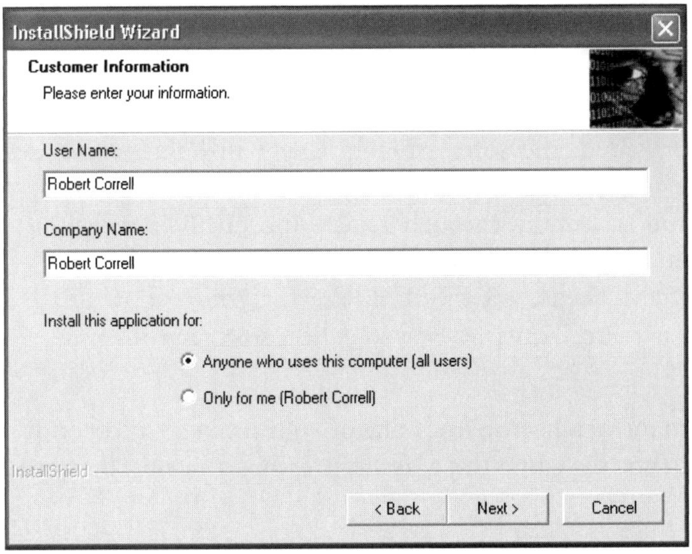

Figure 4.10 Install quirkiness: you must input a company name.

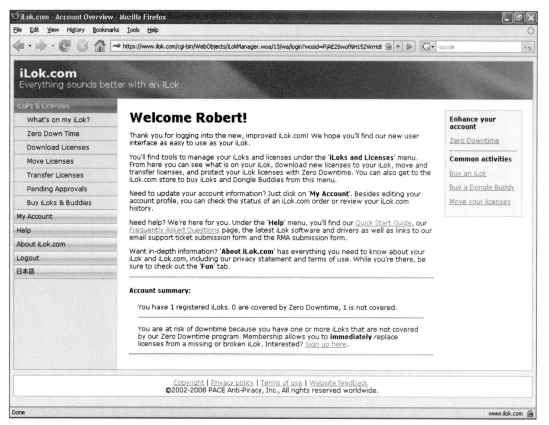

Figure 4.11 Current iLok administration menu.

- **Download Licenses:** If you've bought third-party software that requires an authorized iLok that isn't provided, the software company will have procedures for downloading the license to your iLok. You must first establish your identity with the company in question (normally through registering on their website) and provide them your iLok ID (which is your iLok User Name). After they verify this, they will deposit the license on the iLok site for you to download. I'm preparing to download my Pro Tools M-Powered license to my iLok in Figure 4.13.

- **Move Licenses:** Allows you to move a license from one of your iLoks to another. It's important to note that this is not the same thing as transferring a license between different users.

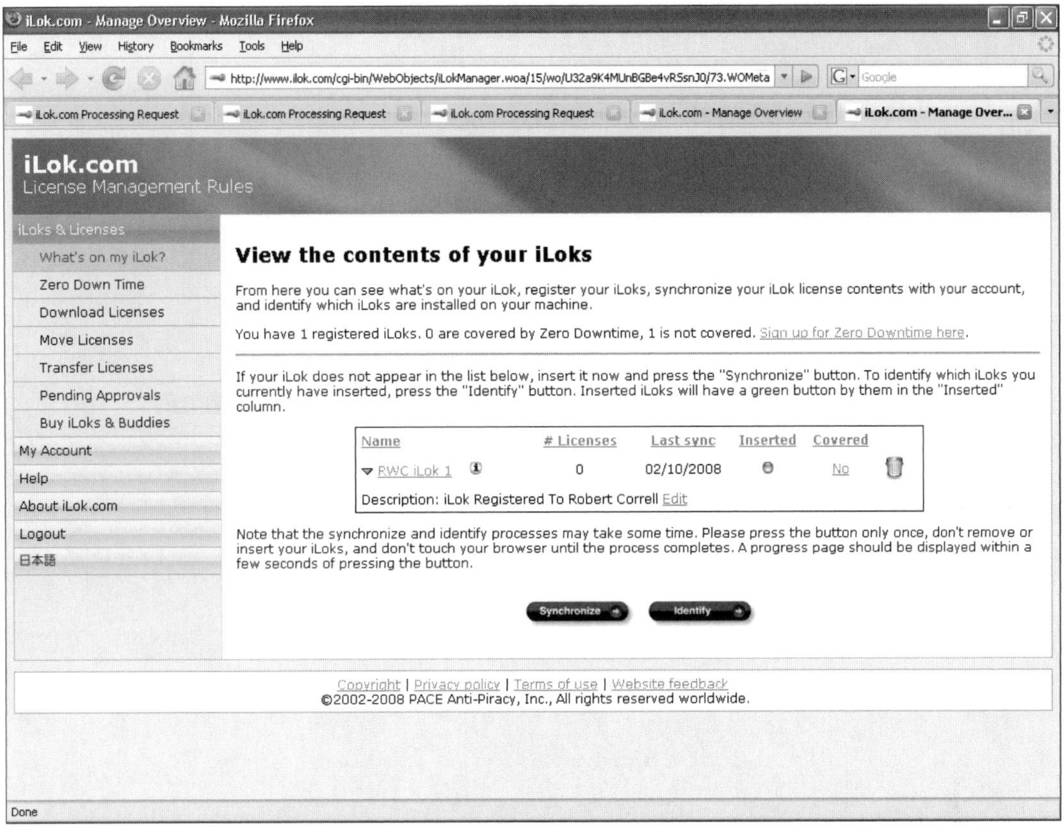

Figure 4.12 My empty iLok.

- **Transfer Licenses**: Allows you to transfer a license to or from another user.

- **Pending Approvals**: Sometimes companies have to approve license transfers. If you're in that situation, come here to see the status.

Two commands that appear in several places bear some explanation. They are the following:

- **Synchronize**: Makes sure your licenses are on your iLok.

- **Identify**: Identifies a given iLok.

Both launch an external application that runs on your computer. First, as shown in Figure 4.14, it asks permission.

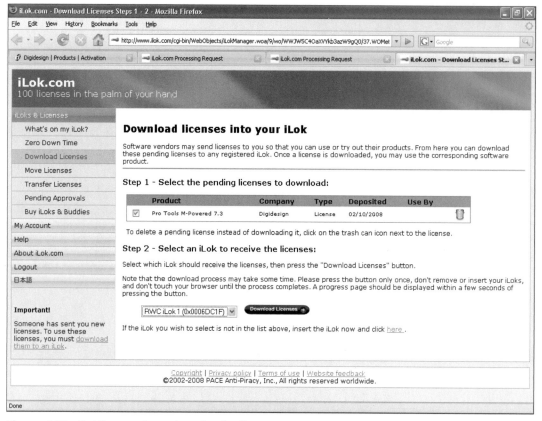

Figure 4.13   Getting ready to download a license.

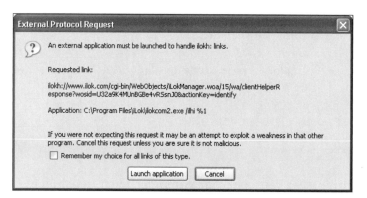

Figure 4.14   iLok runs an external program to identify and sync.

Figure 4.15 Accessing your iLok.

Following this, you will see a new web page show up that indicates the status of the current operation (Figure 4.15). Don't mess with this while it's running and leave your iLok alone.

Using Your iLok
Plug it in. Run Pro Tools. It couldn't be any easier.

5 Installing Pro Tools LE

I've worked with a lot of Digidesign gear and have yet to be disappointed. Before you get to work with it, however, you have to install it. The home and project studio boom takes place in a land of "do-it-yourself." You should take that seriously, but also enjoy it. At home, you don't have a studio manager looking over your shoulder when you do this. It's just you. It's on your shoulders to get things running. One of the most important items in ensuring your success is correctly installing your gear and software.

Installation Workflow Review

Here is a quick review of the steps you need to take to install your Digidesign hardware and Pro Tools LE. I've divided them into Windows and Macintosh lists. Here is the Digidesign journey for Windows users:

1. **Prepare:** Get your work area ready, the computer, hardware, and so forth. This was the subject of Chapter 4, "Preparing to Install."

2. **Connect the hardware:** Connect with the USB or FireWire cable.

3. **Install Pro Tools LE:** The point of the whole show. You restart after this step.

4. **Launch Pro Tools LE:** The first run to authorize the software.

5. **Test:** Before you get involved in extensively configuring Pro Tools, make sure Pro Tools LE is installed correctly and that it works with your hardware. Perform a minimal recording check with basic audio connections.

6. **Configure Pro Tools LE:** Make it your own.

7. **Integrate Pro Tools LE fully into your studio:** Make all the final audio connections and stabilize your workflow.

And for Mac users:

1. **Prepare:** Get your work area ready, the computer, hardware, and so forth. This was the subject of Chapter 4.

2. **Install Pro Tools LE:** This order is different than for Windows users. After you install, the computer restarts.

3. **Connect the hardware:** Plug that thang in.

4. **Launch Pro Tools LE:** The first run to authorize Pro Tools LE.

5. **Test:** Before you get involved in extensively configuring Pro Tools, make sure Pro Tools LE is installed correctly and that it works with your hardware. Perform a minimal recording check.

6. **Configure Pro Tools LE:** Make it your own.

7. **Integrate Pro Tools LE fully into your studio:** Make all the final audio connections and stabilize your workflow.

Mbox 2

Many of you no doubt are buying and installing the Mbox 2. It's the "sweet spot" in the Pro Tools LE lineup. The Mbox 2 has very powerful capabilities for recording and mixing, yet is very affordable if you're on a budget (and who isn't!). I can't stress enough (and you'll find out soon enough if you don't know this already) that the interface is only one component out of many that you'll need to succeed in the pretty pricy world of professional digital audio. Other components might or will be cables, monitors, headphones, the computer, and possibly instruments and other outboard gear. Not having to spend an arm and a leg to get in the door gets you in the door. It's like getting into a trendy nightclub. After you're inside, you're inside. You can learn, grow, and build from here.

Digidesign sent me an Mbox 2 to install and work with.

Vendor Support   I've been blessed to receive great support from both Digidesign and M-Audio for this book in a variety of ways. I accepted their help in the form of "loaner" hardware not because I had to have it (shoot, I own two M-Audio interfaces right now with Pro Tools M-Powered and have worked with all levels of Pro Tools from LE to HD and HD I ACCEL, from the original Mbox to the Control I 24, 24-fader ICON D-Command, and 32-fader ICON D-Control), but because I wanted to put myself in your shoes and get something that I had to open new, install, and work with from scratch. Digidesign and M-Audio had no say in the content of this book and are not in any way involved in the writing or approval of the manuscript. If I don't like it, I have the total freedom to say it.

Unpacking

The Mbox 2 box looks really pretty. I love the blues and reds with the nice photos on the side and bottom of the box. I appreciate good design. It makes me hopeful that what's inside is as well put together as the packaging. That's not always the case, which is why I remain calm, follow a set of general installation guidelines, and pay attention.

First, cut the plastic seal that holds the box shut. It's underneath in the front. You can try with your fingernail, but I quickly resorted to scissors. Pull the flap out and up to reveal the inner workings of the box. This flap is a little easier to deal with than the M-Audio FireWire 410 box is.

Cool. Looks like there's a carton within the box to protect the hardware and a tray on the top that has lots of goodies and software. Take a look at what's on the top.

The Registration ID is a postcard-sized card. It's pretty important. If you lose this, you won't be able to register your gear with Digidesign. Don't confuse this with the authorization number. This is optional whereas the other number is a must have.

Next, I come to the Pro Tools Ignition Pack 2 (with large flyer). Oh, I love this stuff—lots of CDs with great plug-ins, instruments, and other things on them. Here's a list of what you get (sadly, the Mbox 2 Micro doesn't ship with the Ignition Pack):

■ **AmpliTubeLE:** Guitar/bass amplifier and effect modeling. I've used different versions of AmpliTube off and on and have come away impressed with the sounds you can get out of it.

■ **Analog Factory SE:** Virtual instrument. It's critical to have these if you're planning on using MIDI. Install and try it out.

■ **BFD Lite:** Virtual drums. This is very cool to have. It turns so-so MIDI into a rocking set.

■ **Live Lite 6 Digidesign Edition:** By Ableton of Ableton Live fame. Sampler/sequencer.

■ **Melodyne Uno Essential:** Sample editor. Looks promising.

■ **Ozone 3 Lite:** From iZotope. Useful for mastering.

■ **Reason Adapted 3:** This awesome virtual rack and sequencer comes to Pro Tools. A must have.

■ **Spectron Lite:** From iZotope. For adding spectral effects.

■ **TimewARP 2600 Lite:** Emulates the ARP 2600 analog synth.

■ **Thrash Lite:** From iZotope. For amp tones and effects.

- **Xpand:** A virtual instrument that I've played around with quite a bit and like a lot. Definitely worth the price!

- **ProSessions SE:** Collection of samples. Great to have in your library.

- **One-year membership to Broadjam.com:** Promote and sell your music online.

- **One contest entry at GarageBands.com:** Compete with others.

- **One-year membership to Sonicbids:** Promote yourself within the music industry.

- **Pro Tools Method One Instructional DVD:** Of course, you won't be needing this because you've got me. Actually, I would encourage you to open this up, including all the documentation that comes with Pro Tools, and learn everything you can from everyone you can.

A Pro version of this pack adds a few more freebies. If you get the Mbox 2 Pro Factory, 003 Factory, 003 Rack Factory, you get the Pro pack.

Next is a Health and Safety Guide. Make sure not to use Pro Tools LE in the rain, lighting, in lava pits, while under the influence of anything that could influence you, or while driving (I know people who have).

Finally, you have Pro Tools LE, which is packaged with a Getting Started manual and a separate software updater DVD (for example, if you install 7.3 you might have the 7.3.1 update on another DVD).

Now, pull the top of the carton off and peek inside. There it is. The Mbox 2 in plastic wrap. Take it out and set it aside for a second.

Underneath, you will find the USB cable and a doohickey-gizmo that replaces the handle of the Mbox 2 with a different (closed) plate. If you want to experiment with this, now is the time. Do it before you make all your connections. If you think you want to stand your unit up, I would keep the larger handle on, because it provides some stability against tipping over (this is one of those things I don't like). If you're going to lay the unit down, either the handle or the plate seems fine. However, the larger, open handle makes the Mbox 2 sit up more so you can read the labels and access the knobs and buttons more easily. If you want to swap things out, find the small hex driver (Allen wrench) that's included in the box. This fits the screw that holds the handle in place. That screw is located on the right side of the Mbox 2, around the corner from Input 2's mic/line switch.

Carefully take the plastic wrap off the Mbox 2 and set it aside. Keep everything, just in case there's something wrong and you have to repack the unit and send it back. I keep everything anyway, to pack up if I move, or if I ever sell it.

Warning   Don't eat the silica gel inside. Like it says, throw it away. If you've got kids or pets, throw it in a trash can they can't reach inside of (or that has a lid). Our youngest son, Sam, is getting old enough now that he's very interested in what goes in the trash. He likes taking things out of the trash, so we have to pay attention to things like this.

Look your hardware over. This is your chance to inspect it for damage, find loose knobs, or anything else that might be a problem. Push all the buttons and turn the knobs to make sure they work. Look at all the labels on the front and back. Become acquainted with what everything is and where it's located.

If you're familiar with the original Mbox, you've undoubtedly discovered the Mbox 2 is very different. First, it's meant to sit differently on your desktop. That can be unsettling at first, but you can also stand the Mbox 2 on its end if you like (although it would seem less stable that way). Second, the Mbox 2 has one more knob and a few more buttons on the front. The difference in knobs is that the Mbox 2 has a Monitor control that directly controls the Monitor Out levels. The buttons basically do the same thing, but you've got a dedicated phantom power button on the front of the Mbox 2 (rather than the back) and pads on each input, which are new.

After a quick check you find no warnings of any kind, nothing telling you to do things in a particular order or the unit will fry. That's good. USB always seems more forgiving than FireWire in that regard, and plugging in a USB cable is far easier than cracking open the case and installing a PCI/PCIe card.

Notice you find no power supply or power cable for the Mbox 2. That's because it is powered by the USB bus. That's one less thing you have to worry about.

Read through the Getting Started documentation for the Mbox 2 to make sure you install things correctly and in the proper order. Optimize the system. Check. Don't have a bunch of crap running in the background. Check. It's time to plug the unit in (if you're running Windows, that is; if you are running Mac, install the software first).

Connecting the Unit

Windows users should complete this section before installing the software, while Mac users should install the software first.

Go back to the box and get the USB cable out now. Take it out of the plastic wrap and remove the twist-tie. The small end goes into the back of the Mbox 2, and the large end connects to your computer.

Which end should you connect first? It depends.

Which End First?   The manual says go for the small end first, but I think it depends. If you have to reach around to the back of your computer, especially if it's under the desk or something, make the computer USB connection first (it is the larger one) and run the cable around to where you can grab it up top. Sit back down and connect this end to your Mbox 2. I can't think of any technical reason why which end you connect first should matter.

After making the USB connection, your computer recognizes the new hardware, and after a few moments, you see the Found New Hardware Wizard (Windows only), as shown in Figure 5.1.

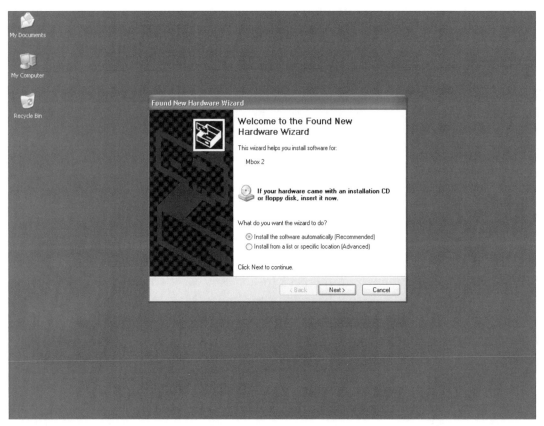

Figure 5.1   For God's sake—ignore this!

Here's where it pays to read instructions.

Do not, I repeat, do NOT click Next. It's calling on you to. I know it. I feel it. Resist the urge. I'm telling you! Drag the dialog box off to one side of your screen so you won't be tempted to click on it. Just ignore it.

Installing Pro Tools LE

Mac users should complete this section before connecting the hardware, while Windows users should have connected the hardware prior to this section.

Unlike when you install M-Audio gear (covered in the next chapter), you really have no separate hardware driver to install for the Mbox 2. Digidesign hardware installs its drivers when Pro Tools LE is installed and not separately. If you wanted the unit to work with other DAWs, you would install the standalone drivers that ship with the unit separately.

The big difference between installing to a Mac versus Windows is which order you connect the hardware and install the software (for more Mac/Windows installation differences, see Chapter 6). For Windows users, it is in that order, but for Mac users it is reversed. Any way you slice it, here are the steps I used to install Pro Tools LE 7.3.1 that came with the Mbox 2.

Continuation   Even though these steps start at number "1," they are a continuation of the entire installation process and not meant to be jumped into willy-nilly. Read about what you need to do before you do this.

---

1. Open up the Pro Tools LE software package (I used a guitar pick to slice through the plastic), get the Pro Tools LE 7 DVD out, and put it into your DVD drive. Take the Getting Started manual out and set it aside in a safe place. The authorization number is located on the inside of the Getting Started manual. This is what authorizes you to use the Pro Tools software (unlike the iLok and Pro Tools M-Powered).

2. Display the contents of the DVD in an Explorer window, as shown in Figure 5.2.

3. Navigate to the Pro Tools LE Installer folder (Figure 5.3).

4. Locate the setup program (the one called setup.exe) within that folder and run it by double-clicking its icon.

5. The Pro Tools LE installer runs and welcomes you (Figure 5.4). Press Next.

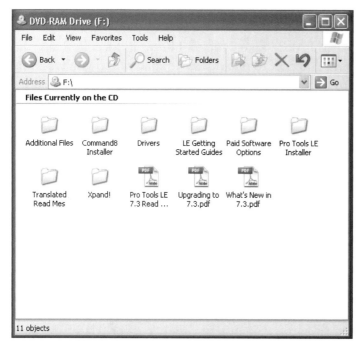

Figure 5.2   The Pro Tools LE DVD.

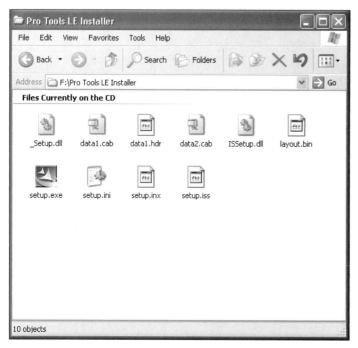

Figure 5.3   Navigate to the installation folder.

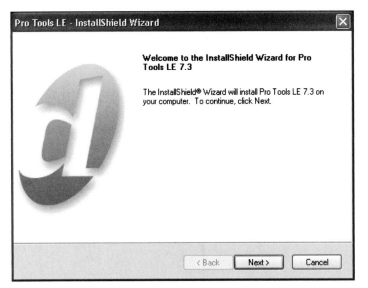

Figure 5.4   Welcome to pro audio.

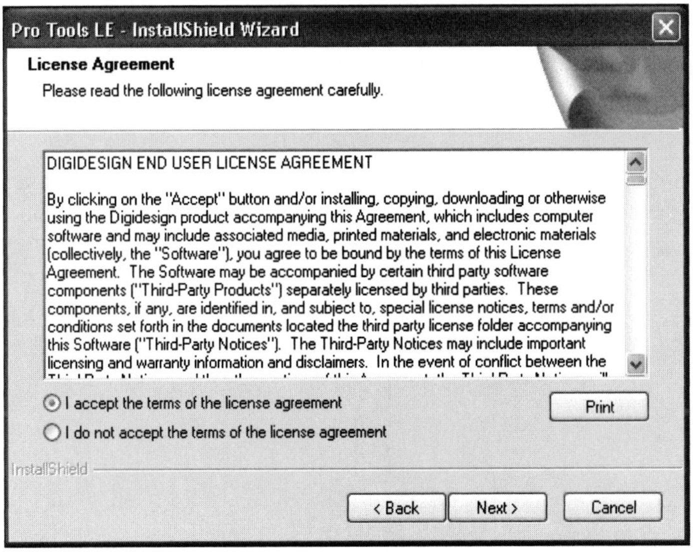

Figure 5.5   Software is licensed, not sold.

6.   Agree to the license agreement (Figure 5.5), which states you don't own squat, but are rather paying money to use the software on your computer. Click the Agree button and then Next.

7.   Take a look at what you're going to install (see Figure 5.6), and check or uncheck things you want or don't want. Unless you have reason not to,

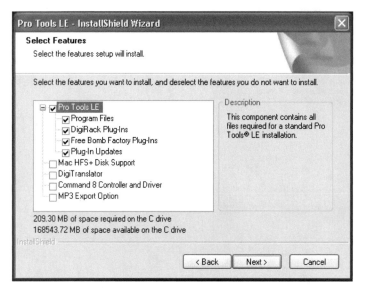

Figure 5.6   The default options are shown here.

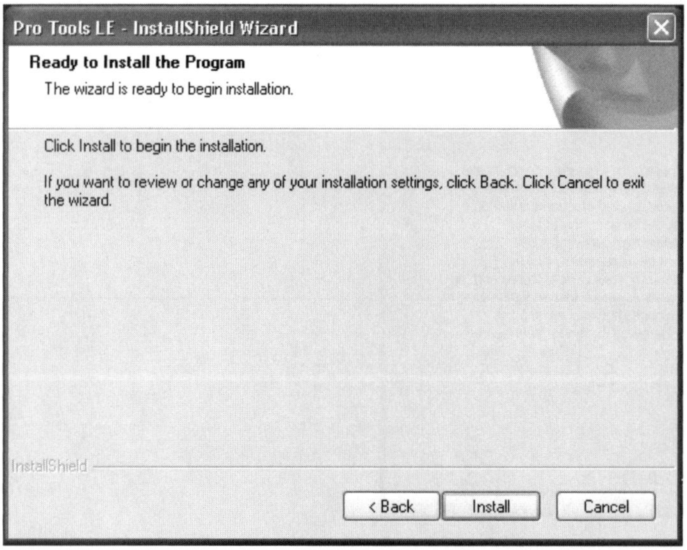

Pro Tools LE - InstallShield Wizard

Ready to Install the Program
The wizard is ready to begin installation.

Click Install to begin the installation.

If you want to review or change any of your installation settings, click Back. Click Cancel to exit the wizard.

InstallShield ————

< Back   Install   Cancel

Figure 5.7   The wizard is ready to begin installation, and I'm ready, too.

accept the defaults. The MP3 option, despite its being included here, works only if you've paid extra for it. Click Next to continue.

8.   You're given one last chance (Figure 5.7) to change your mind or go back and change the options. Click Install to get going.

9.   Pro Tools LE installs to your computer. When the installation initiates, you're warned (see Figure 5.8) that you might see dialog boxes that tell you the hardware has not passed the Windows Logo Test and that you should ignore those boxes.

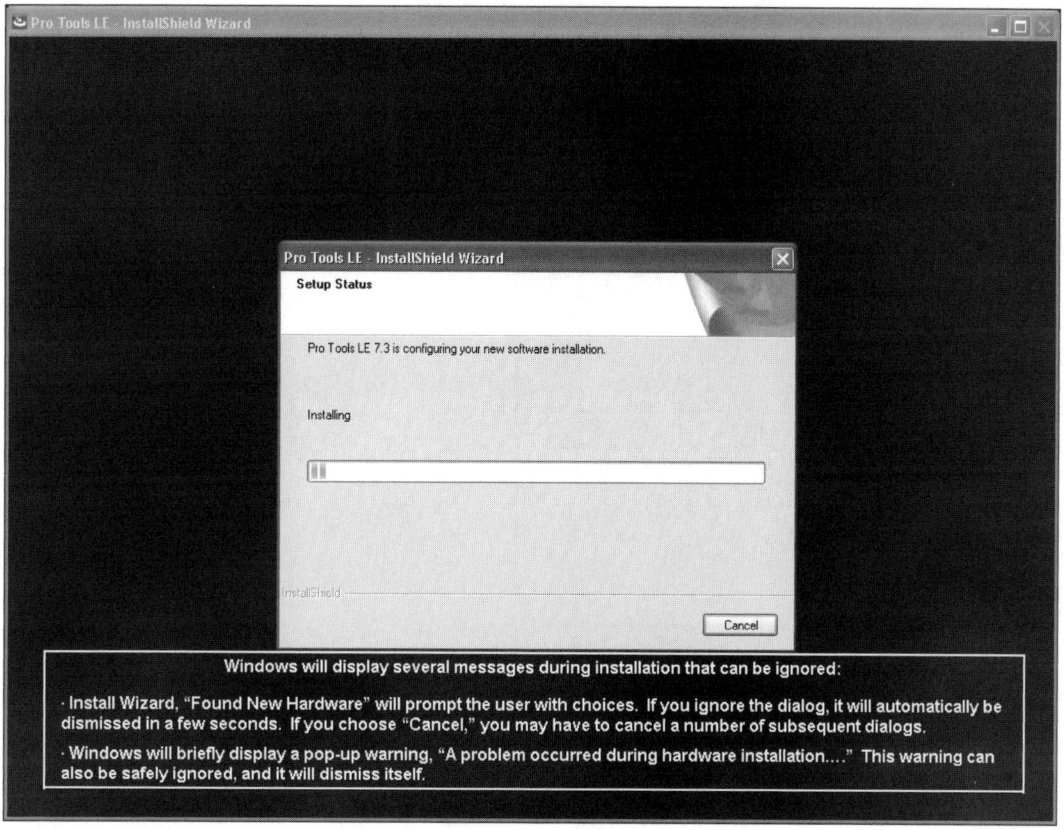

Figure 5.8   Telling you to ignore Windows.

10.   Next (Figure 5.9), you're told to connect the hardware (mine was already, but that didn't seem to mess things up) and click OK.

Figure 5.9   Press OK to launch missiles.

11.   Now the hardware drivers are installed (Figure 5.10).

Figure 5.10   Installing hardware drivers.

12.   This is when you see the dialog boxes (Figure 5.11) asking if you want to continue. Ignore them. If you try and click them away, you end up having to click about 50 times when you don't have to.

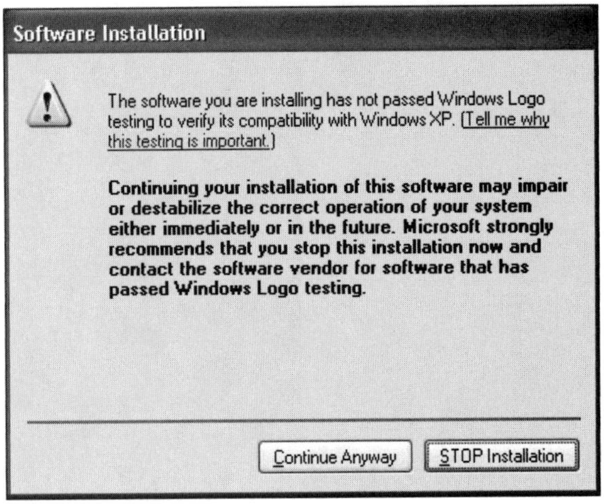

Figure 5.11   More ignoring to be done.

13.   Finally, when everything is installed, you are prompted to Restart your computer (Figure 5.12). Do not say "No" and then go out and try to run Pro Tools LE. Just restart your computer.

After your computer restarts, it's time to test the installation.

Testing the Installation

I refer to this as a test because I advocate making a few minimal audio connections and seeing if the hardware and software works before you route all your cables and get settled in. If you have problems, you want to know it now.

You can pick up after the restart. When you come back, you've got a nice Pro Tools LE icon on your desktop, as shown in Figure 5.13. Check in the next chapter and you can

Figure 5.12 Restart to finish the installation.

see that the Pro Tools LE icon is different from the Pro Tools M-Powered icon. LE is gold and silver while M-Powered is red and silver.

1. Make sure your interface (the Mbox 2 in this case) is connected to the computer and the power light is lit (if applicable). If you're running the 003, you should follow the procedures for startup and shutdown listed later in this chapter.

---

iLoks and Pro Tools LE   Pro Tools LE is authorized via an authorization number and not an iLok. However, if you already have licenses on an iLok or have the additional software packages that include an iLok, make sure your iLok has the proper licenses and is plugged into a USB port on your computer. Chapter 4 has more information on iLoks.

---

2. Run Pro Tools LE by double-clicking the icon on your desktop. You then see the interface launch and Pro Tools "boot up," as seen in Figure 5.14.

3. Authorize Pro Tools LE by using the authorization number on the inside front page of the Getting Started manual and entering it in the text field (see Figure 5.15). Click Validate to continue.

4. Next, take a look at the hardware by selecting the Setup>Hardware Setup menu. You should see the Mbox 2 (or whatever it is you are installing),

Figure 5.13 Pretty paper, pretty icons.

as I do in Figure 5.16. If you don't see it, make sure the unit is connected, receiving power, and not dead. If necessary, close Pro Tools and reboot your system again. You might try using a different USB or FireWire port.

5.   Create a new project by selecting the File>New Session menu (Figure 5.17) so you can test the installation.

6.   Find a convenient place on a secondary (not your system) drive to save the file, name it, and select the bit depth and sample rate you want to record at (Figure 5.18).

7.   Now, make sure you're looking at the Edit window (if not, go to the Window menu and choose Edit). Select the Track>New menu (Figure 5.19) to create a new mono audio track.

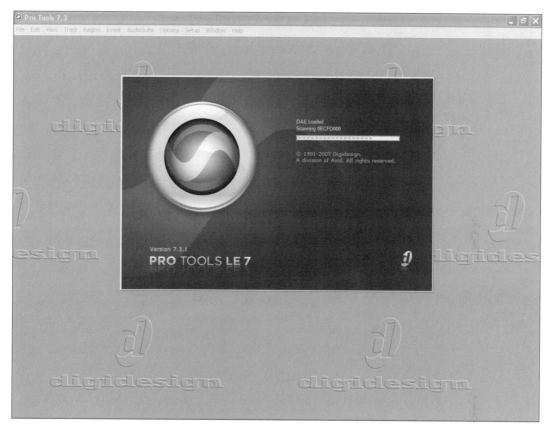

Figure 5.14   Pro Tools LE launching.

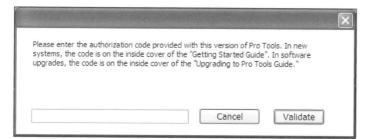

Figure 5.15   Pro Tools LE requires an authorization number.

Do It Your Way   I play guitar. It's easy for me to hook that puppy up and test something out very quickly. You might be a vocalist or want to hook up your keyboard in stereo and test it that way. Go for it! If you go for stereo, change Mono to Stereo when you create the track, and you're off. In that case, of course, you need two inputs going to the hardware.

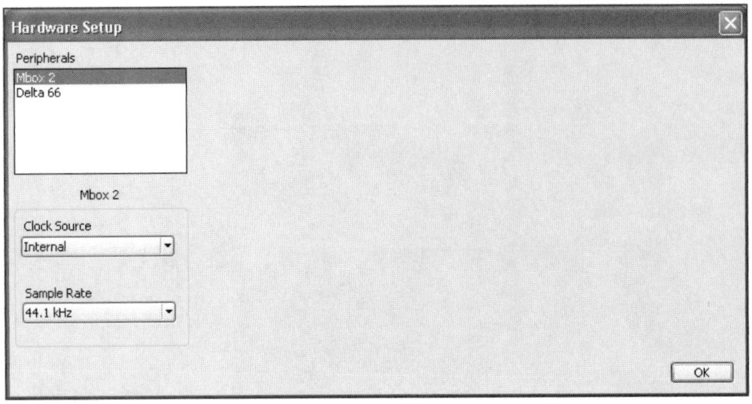

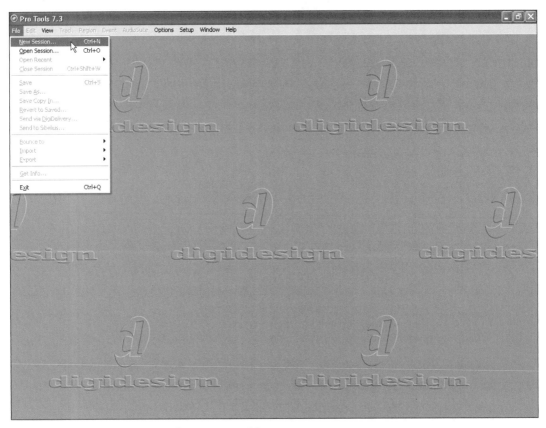

Figure 5.16 Looking good so far.

Figure 5.17 Create a new project to test with.

Figure 5.18 Choose wisely.

8. Click Create (Figure 5.20). The new track appears in the Edit window named Audio 1.

9. To see the I/O information in the Mix window, select the View>Edit Window> I/O menu (Figure 5.21). This turns on a little panel beside each track in this view so that you can see where the track is receiving its input from and where it is routing its output to. My input is coming from Input 1 in the Mbox 2, and the output is being directed to Outputs 1 and 2, which are the main outs of the Mbox 2. *Excellente.*

10. Drop out to the real world now, and connect something to the Mbox. I'm a guitar player, so I connect my guitar directly to Input 1 on the Mbox 2.

11. Select Mic or DI from the front panel of the Mbox 2, whichever is appropriate.

12. If necessary, turn on phantom power.

13. Connect your headphones or monitors to the Mbox 2. I chose headphones because it's easier to work with at this stage. If you want to arm your track now, go ahead.

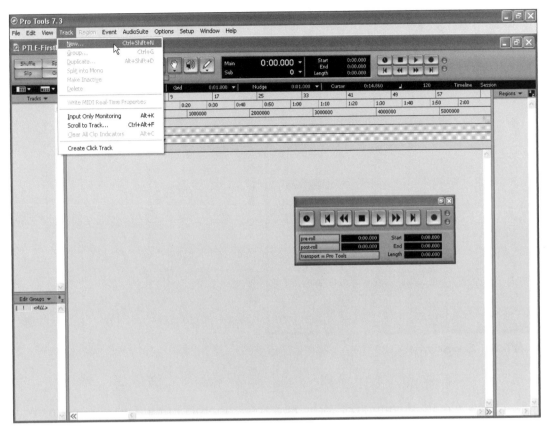

Figure 5.19 First, you need something to record on.

Figure 5.20 Creating a new track.

14. Play something to set the levels. Turn the gain up if you need to, or down if you clip (the light comes on). If your signal is so strong it clips even with the gain all the way down, engage the pad and then raise the gain. At the same time, monitor your signal through the headphones. Turn the Mix knob counter-clockwise to hear your direct signal.

15. If you haven't already, arm the track in Pro Tools by pressing the R button on the track. It turns red.

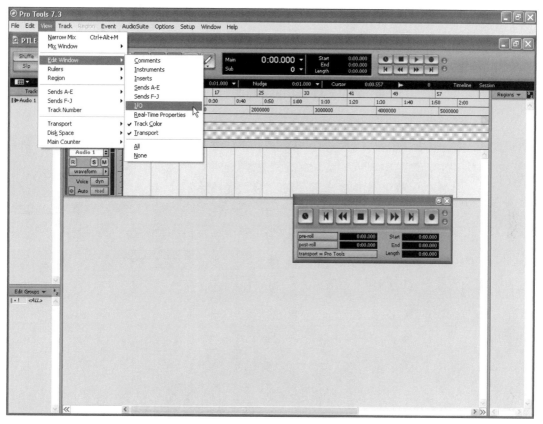

Figure 5.21   Double-checking the I/O for this track.

16.   Continue playing to double-check your levels. You should not see a clip light either on the Mbox 2 or in Pro Tools. If you do, lower your preamp gain on the Mbox 2. At this point you can play around with the Mix knob and see what it does. Turned clockwise, you hear the signal coming back out of Pro Tools and into the Mbox. You might find a noticeable lag (called latency) between when you play and what you hear, and if the Mix knob is blending the two signals together, it might sound like a chorus filter.

Confused?   There's a lot to this, and you will get a chance to get into the nitty-gritty, including faster ways to do things, in later chapters. For example, you have access to a cool mode called Quick Punch and a faster way to Return to Zero than by clicking the on-screen transport. Don't worry. If you've got an 003 Factory, you should be using the transport controls on your console for this.

---

17. All right, you're ready to record. Click the red circle on the Transport window. This is Record. Now press Play. In the days of tape, those controls were necessary because there were different tape heads that needed to be involved, depending on whether or not you were playing or recording. The Record button enabled the record heads, but it was the Play button that started the transport moving. After pressing Play, you're recording (Figure 5.22), so sing or play your instrument.

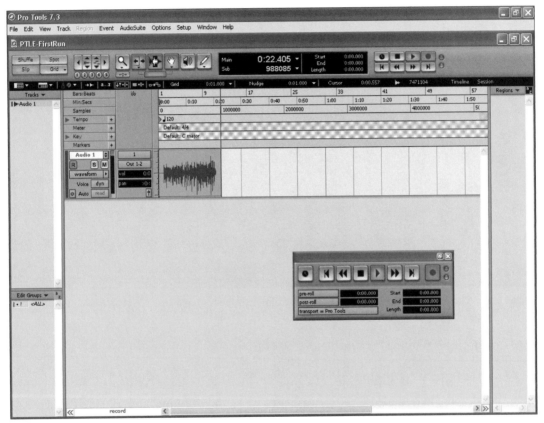

Figure 5.22 Testing the installation by actually recording something.

18. After you've recorded a bit, stop recording (hit the spacebar).

19. Hit Return to Zero (the button near the left side of the Transport window that looks like an arrow pointing to a line) and then Play to have a listen (Figure 5.23).

20. Save your file if you like, and when you're done, quit Pro Tools.

There's a lot more to it than this, obviously. You should spend a lot of time getting to know your specific hardware inside and out. That's outside of the scope of this book.

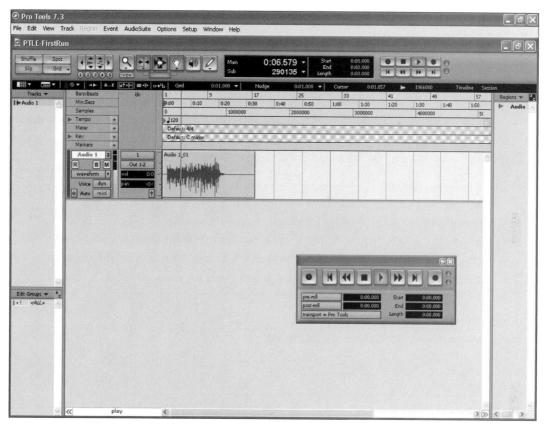

Figure 5.23   Playback is critical to test also.

I spend most of the rest of the time concentrating on the Pro Tools software, which is the part of the equation that is relatively universal (or close to it). After you get the hang of it, you will find less of a difference between all this stuff anyway. An input is an input whether it's in an 003 Rack or Mbox 2.

Installing Other Mbox 2 Hardware

Installation for the Mbox 2 Micro, Mbox 2 Mini, and Mbox 2 Pro (surprisingly) is identical to the Mbox 2. Follow the same procedure as for the Mbox 2 in the same order. The only differences are that for the Micro you plug the unit itself in rather than a USB cable and that the Mbox 2 Pro is a FireWire device rather than USB. You also won't be able to perform a recording test with the Micro. Instead, import an audio file (File>Import>Audio) into the test session as a new track and play it. For more information on importing files, check out Chapter 8, "Using Pro Tools."

I've said this ten times, but I'll say it again. Mac users should note that your install order is swapped compared to Windows. You install the software first, restart the computer, and then connect the hardware. *Capiche?*

Installing 003 and 003 Rack

Installing the 003 and 003 Rack is pretty easy, despite the fact that they are both larger and more capable than the other systems. For the Rack, you obviously need a rack space to mount the unit in. The 003 Factory just needs a large, clear space on your desktop.

Mac Users   The Mac installation is the same but different. Instead of connecting the hardware and then installing Pro Tools LE, you must install Pro Tools LE before connecting the 003. You install the software, then shut the computer off, and make the 003 connections. You can launch Pro Tools LE for the first time after you restart. Make sure to check out the proper steps for that coming up shortly.

Windows users, follow these steps. Please refer back to the screenshots for installing the Mbox 2, as many of the screens are identical.

1.   Turn your computer off.

   Take Heed   Your computer must be off the first time you connect the 003.

   ---

2.   Set the 003 on your desk or mount the 003 Rack in its rack. I refer to both as 003 from here on for the purposes of installation.

3.   Connect the 003 to AC power with the supplied cable.

   AC Power   The 003 and 003 Rack are not bus-powered. They require that the AC power cable be plugged into the wall (or wherever) to supply power to the unit.

   ---

4.   Connect the 003 to your computer with the supplied FireWire cable.

5.   Turn your computer on.

6.   Ignore the Found New Hardware messages and insert the Pro Tools LE DVD into your computer. These steps are the same as for the Mbox 2.

7.   Launch the Pro Tools LE installer setup program.

8.   Follow the steps, and shut down when finished.

At this point I would make minimal audio connections and get ready to test the hardware and software. After you're sure everything works, consider updating Pro Tools LE. Then you can make all of your audio connections and start working.

That should about cover it, but Digidesign is pretty adamant in their documentation about the steps you need to follow when you launch Pro Tools LE and turn on a 003 system. Here goes:

1. Turn the faders down on everything that is an output.

2. If you've got them, turn on any external hard disk drives. Wait ten seconds for them to get going.

3. Turn on anything that has to do with MIDI or synchronization.

4. Turn on your 003.

5. If you have any iLoks, make sure they are connected.

6. Turn on your computer.

7. Launch Pro Tools LE and any third-party applications. If this is the first time, have your authorization number ready.

You should also follow these steps when you turn things off:

1. Quit Pro Tools LE and any other relevant applications.

2. Turn down all your output volumes.

3. Shut down the computer.

4. Turn off the 003.

5. Turn off anything that has to do with MIDI or synchronization.

6. Turn off external hard disk drives.

7. Go grab a 12-ounce can or bottle of refreshment.

Updating Pro Tools LE

Please refer to Chapter 6, "Installing Pro Tools M-Powered," for information on how to update Pro Tools LE. The section titled "Updating Pro Tools" is near the end of the chapter and covers how to update Pro Tools M-Powered. Want to know what the difference is between updating the Pro Tools LE and Pro Tools M-Powered software? Nothing. Go online and register at the Digidesign website to create a profile or log in if you already have one, find the right update, download, and install it. No problem.

Make sure to check out the next chapter because I provide screenshots and a bit more explanation than I have here.

Extra Stuff

Take some time and investigate the extra stuff on the DVD. You bought some of it, so enjoy it. Digidesign has also conveniently placed things you might not have bought yet in the Paid Software Options folder on the DVD, like the Music Production Toolkit.

Look through the Readme file and What's New. The LE Getting Started guides are interesting, too. Look in the Additional Files folder for the Answerbase FAQ for information on older systems. The Additional Files folder also has the DigiDelivery installer, which is a service that allows you to transfer and exchange files, large or small, with anyone in the world (who is using DigiDelivery, that is). I've used it several times, in fact, during the writing of this book.

6 Installing Pro Tools M-Powered

I'm a big fan of M-Audio products, and I've bought and use two of the three systems I'm going to discuss in this chapter. Aside from being pretty cool, M-Audio's gear runs Pro Tools M-Powered, a member of the family that makes up my all-time favorite digital audio workstation (DAW). M-Audio is accessible and has a lot of different hardware options for different users, and I've not run into any trouble with them. The stuff works, and if it doesn't, the company does a great job supporting me as a consumer. And no, they didn't pay me to say that.

Now, I can't possibly cover all the M-Audio installation options in this chapter, or even in a book. What I can do is walk you through a detailed example of what you might run into and tell you where to really pay close attention to things that might go wrong. Even if you don't have the exact same setup, you will notice a large amount of overlap, especially if you are installing something with the same interface (FireWire, USB, or PCI).

One word of caution—I consider myself an expert at this. I've installed many different audio interfaces, and I am a longtime computer professional. I still routinely have to uninstall things and try it again. Don't fret. This is complicated stuff. It's not like buying a toaster where all you have to do is take it out of the box and plug it into the wall. Sometimes you've got to work for it. You be the master!

Installation Workflow Review

I want to quickly review the process I undertake to install M-Audio hardware and Pro Tools M-Powered.

1. **Prepare:** Get your work area ready, the computer, hardware, and so forth. Please refer to Chapter 4, "Preparing to Install," for more information.

2. **Install hardware drivers:** The audio interface has to talk to the computer. This is a pretty big deal.

3. **Make audio connections**: The lifelines. You can make this minimal for now and connect the rest of your cables after you know everything works.

4. **Initial test**: Because M-Audio gear works with other DAWs, I like to make sure the hardware works at this stage before going on. I use another DAW on my system and record with it. If you decide on an M-Audio audio interface and install it before purchasing Pro Tools M-Powered, this is your final step for now.

5. **Install Pro Tools M-Powered**: Bring out the big dog.

6. **Test again**: Make sure Pro Tools M-Powered is installed correctly, your iLok has the correct authorization, and the software interfaces with the hardware correctly.

7. **Configure Pro Tools**: I cover this in more detail in Chapter 7, "Configuring Pro Tools."

8. **Integrate Pro Tools M-Powered fully into your studio**: This is when you know it works. You can make all your connections and get down to making music.

For the rest of the chapter I'm going to delve into specifics. I'll install three M-Audio products (one from start to finish) and Pro Tools M-Powered. Keep the workflow in mind as you read along, and think of how you're going to do it yourself.

M-Audio FireWire 410

The kind folks at M-Audio were gracious enough to loan me a FireWire 410 to use for this book. When it arrived, my kids were excited and proudly announced that another "gadget" had arrived for Daddy. I was excited to get my hands on a FireWire interface to see how well it worked compared to PCI cards and USB. I also wanted to use those ten outputs to route audio out to my small console and mix with faders.

I'm going to run through this installation from start to finish with all the gory details, just the way it happened. Well, scratch that. I went through the installation the first time, took all my notes and screenshots, and when I got to the end, Pro Tools M-Powered couldn't see the FireWire 410. I make mistakes so that you can learn from them, and the mistake I made was not downloading the latest driver off the Internet.

Unpacking

The first thing I did was clean around the desk in my studio and get all the clutter put away. This cleared my mind and gave me a nice spot to put the FireWire 410.

The FireWire 410 package has a nice heft to it, more than you would think from looking at a photo of it.

Off with the shrink-wrap—one of my favorite activities. I feel like I'm opening a birthday present when I tear through the wrapping. If it's thicker than you want to dig a finger through, grab a pair of scissors and gently make an incision in the plastic, being careful of the box.

Boxes   I always try to save my boxes. The space you have for long-term storage might dictate how much you save and for how long, but if you ever sell your older, used gear to offset the price of the shiny new gizmo that you're dying to get, the box comes in handy.

Pop the lid of the box. This is a little tricky. You have to find a tab underneath the front that you have to wiggle out first; then the narrow top opens up nicely, followed by the larger front of the box.

Now you've got a layer of protective material, then the documentation and software, and that's followed by the interface itself, nicely snuggled in its place. Pay attention to how things are packed, so if you need to ship it back or return it, you can retrace your steps.

You'll find a big red sheet that looks important. It is a warning to make sure the unit is off before plugging it in. Better pay attention to that. Put all the extra material aside and clean a space where you're going to put the unit. Gently lift the unit out of the box and take the plastic covering off. Behind it are two FireWire cables and to the left is the power supply. Leave those alone for the moment.

Now is the best time to fondle your unit. Yeah, that was a cheap one. Seriously, it's not plugged in, turned on, or dusty. It's brand-spanking new and looks awesome. Turn it over in your hands and get a close look at it. Feel it. Turn the knobs to get their feel. Inspect for damage, scratches, any evidence that you might have a problem on your hands. Are the knobs wiggly? After you get things installed, you won't have this opportunity to look at it easily from every angle. Get to know it. Look at the back panel and take some time to acquaint yourself with the I/O setup. It's also a great time to look at the "fine print" on the front and back of the unit closely. Read all the labels. The FireWire 410 has nice helper labels on the top of the unit that tell you what you'll find on the back.

A warning label affixed to the rear of the FireWire 410 tells you to install the drivers before you plug the thing into your computer and power it up. That's important. Drivers are little pieces of software that communicate between your hardware and your computer. They run the hardware.

For now, don't even connect the FireWire 410. Don't power it on. Just leave it be, so you're not tempted to turn it on. Don't even get the cords out.

Downloading the Hardware Driver

The next step in the process is to download the latest hardware drivers off the Internet. Yes, this seems odd, because you have what looks like a perfectly good CD just sitting in the box begging for you to use it. Don't. I did, and then had to redo everything because it was an older driver that wasn't compatible with Pro Tools M-Powered 7.3. I got to the very end of the entire process, having installed the driver, made the connections, tested the FireWire 410 with another DAW, installed Pro Tools M-Powered, and activated my iLok. I then ran Pro Tools M-Powered for my final test, and it didn't see the unit. Follow these steps unless you want to go through what I went through:

1. Point your web browser to the M-Audio website (www.m-audio.com) to get the drivers. Click the Support link from the top menu on the main page and then click the Drivers and Updates icon, which is somewhat towards the middle (see Figure 6.1).

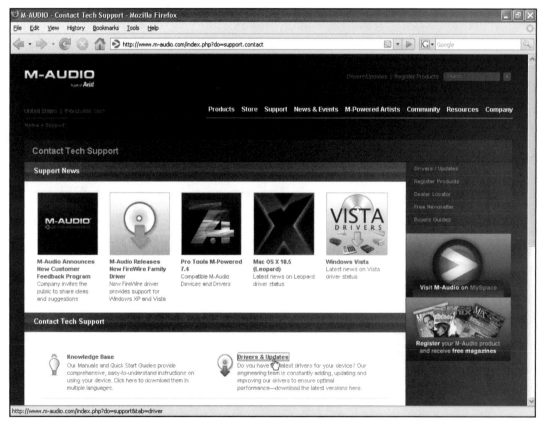

Figure 6.1 Finding the current driver.

2. Select the hardware series, specific interface, and your operating system, as shown in Figure 6.2, to gain access to the file. It's nice to be able to see the date and version of the driver. Click the driver to download it to your system.

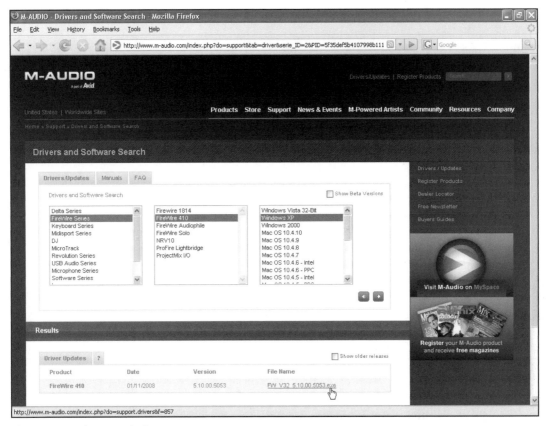

Figure 6.2 Choose wisely.

3. When it's done downloading, you're ready to install it.

Installing the Hardware Driver

With the latest version downloaded off the Internet, it's time to install the M-Audio FireWire 410 hardware driver. The process doesn't take very long. Be patient and trust that it knows what it's doing. Do not, I repeat, do not connect the hardware yet. Wait until your computer shuts down to do this. I'm serious!

Mac Installation Mac installation is remarkably similar to the Windows install, but you face a few differences. For one, you won't be getting any Windows

Logo warnings. Installation is also shorter. After your machine shuts down, connect the FireWire 410, restart, and then go to your System Preferences. Select the Sound panel, click the Output tab, and select the M-Audio FireWire 410 as the default device.

1. Select the driver from where you saved it and run it. You now see the FireWire Family installation screen, as shown in Figure 6.3. Click Next.

Figure 6.3   Welcome to the show.

2. You must agree to the license to continue (see Figure 6.4). Accept the terms and click Next.

3. This is your last chance to quit. Thus far, nothing has actually happened. Click Install (see Figure 6.5) to begin the installation.

4. You're warned that the drivers have not passed Windows Certification (for Windows users only, obviously, see Figure 6.6). You don't really have a choice here. You must press Continue.

Windows Certification   It's nice to have the drivers and software certified by the Windows Logo program, but this is a case where it really doesn't matter. It works.

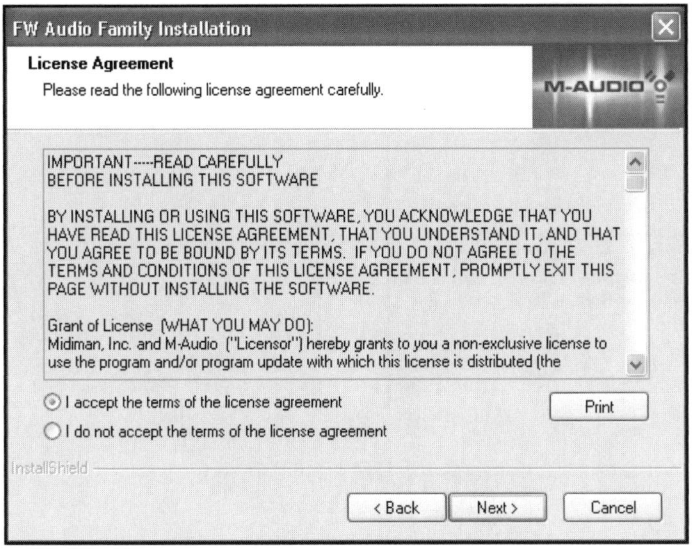

Figure 6.4 Admit one.

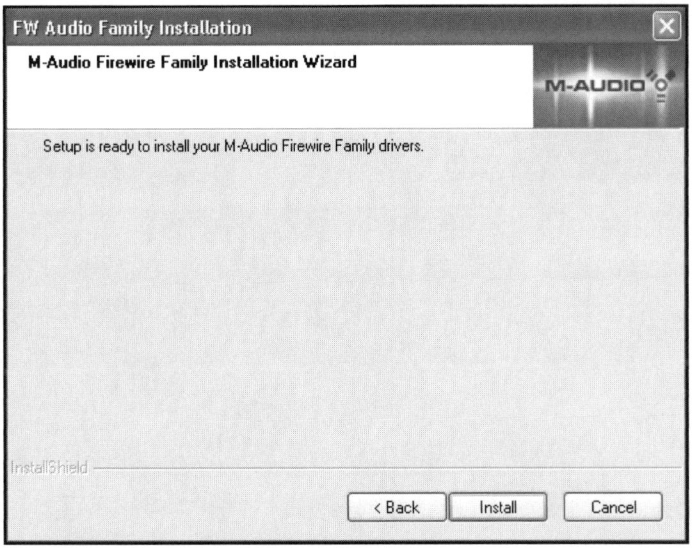

Figure 6.5 One last chance to quit.

5. After an almost imperceptible moment, you are prompted to shut down your computer now or wait until later. I'm not sure why you would want to wait, so select Yes (see Figure 6.7) and click Finish.

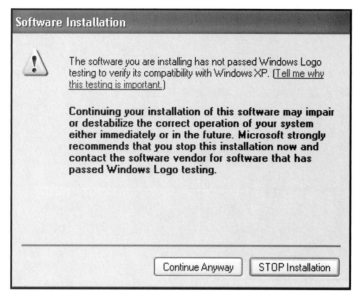

Figure 6.6 Ignore this and keep going.

Figure 6.7 Shutting down the computer.

6.   Now, let your computer shut down. Don't turn it back on yet.

7.   Get the FireWire 410 and remove the warning sticker from the FireWire port area. Grab the correct FireWire cable (you have two; one with a larger and one with a smaller end) that is compatible with your computer and make the

connection. The FireWire 410 can be powered by the FireWire bus if you insert the 6-pin FireWire connector (the larger one) into the computer (you have no choice as to the connector on the FireWire 410; it has to be the 6-pin end). Otherwise, connect the power supply and plug it into the wall now. Turn the unit on.

8. With the FireWire 410 connected to your computer and powered on, turn your computer back on.

9. When the computer boots up, it automatically detects the new hardware and continues the installation (see Figure 6.8). Choose the option to install the software automatically and then click Next.

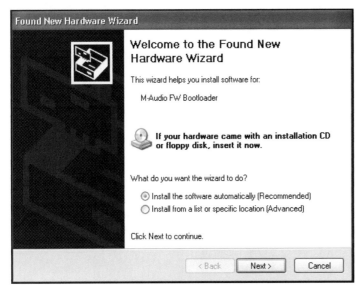

Figure 6.8 New hardware found.

10. Windows users must click away another "Windows Logo" warning (Figure 6.9). Press Continue.

11. The software continues to install (see Figure 6.10).

12. I had a "happy little accident" happen during my installation. The installer detected that the firmware (code inside the hardware) was out of date and automatically updated it (see Figure 6.11).

13. When it's all over, press Finish (Figure 6.12).

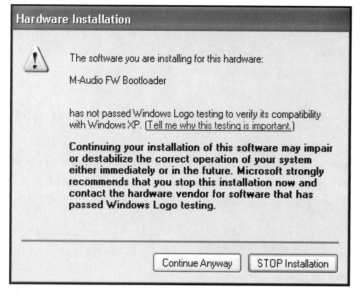

Figure 6.9 Ignore this one, too.

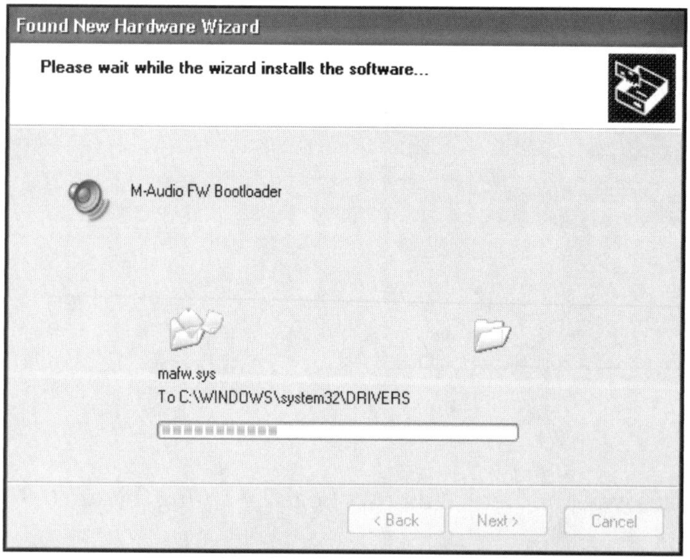

Figure 6.10 Copying files.

14. You're not done yet. It feels like you should be, but you're not. That was the M-Audio FW Bootloader. Next, Windows is able to detect the FireWire 410 for what it is and starts another round of installation (see Figure 6.13). Choose to install the software automatically and press Next.

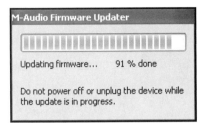

Figure 6.11   Bonus: my firmware needed updating.

Figure 6.12   Finishing the first part of the installation.

15.   Another Windows Logo warning (Figure 6.14). Click Continue.

16.   More files to transfer (see Figure 6.15).

17.   And you're done. Click Finish (Figure 6.16).

18.   To verify something was installed, right-click the M-Audio icon in your System Tray and choose Open M-Audio FireWire Control Panel (Figure 6.17).

19.   I normally explore a bit, and make my way to the About tab to check the driver version and date (see Figure 6.18). Looks great! I think I'm ready to rock.

20.   To conduct the initial test, continue on to the next section.

Figure 6.13   More hardware detected.

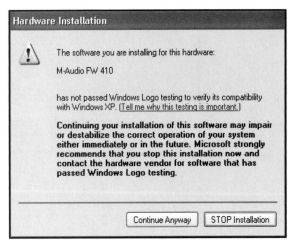

Figure 6.14   Last ignore.

Performing the Initial Test

I realize you don't need to perform this test, but I think it's a good idea to get the hardware running and tested quickly. After all, you're supposed to be able to use the M-Audio gear with other DAWs, so why not play to that strength? Aside from that, it helps limit troubleshooting options. If it doesn't work at this point, you know the problem has *nothing to do* with Pro Tools. It's a hardware fault, a driver issue, or

Figure 6.15 Copying more files.

Figure 6.16 Finally done.

a connection problem (assuming the other DAW works). So to perform the test you do the following:

1. Make sure to turn the FireWire 410 on and that the blue light is steady on the front of the unit. Make at least one audio connection to the FireWire 410.

Figure 6.17   Accessing the Control Panel.

Figure 6.18   Checking the driver version.

I play the electric guitar and have a Palmer direct box, so I route a 1/4-inch unbalanced cable from the Palmer (which gets its signal from a tap on my amp's speaker) to input channel 1 on the front of the FireWire 410.

2.   Launch a suitable DAW. I've chosen Sony ACID Pro for this test.

3.   Make the proper audio device selection within your software. I am choosing the FireWire ASIO driver to run the FireWire 410, as shown in Figure 6.19. If in doubt (Windows users), always use ASIO. They are the fastest Windows drivers.

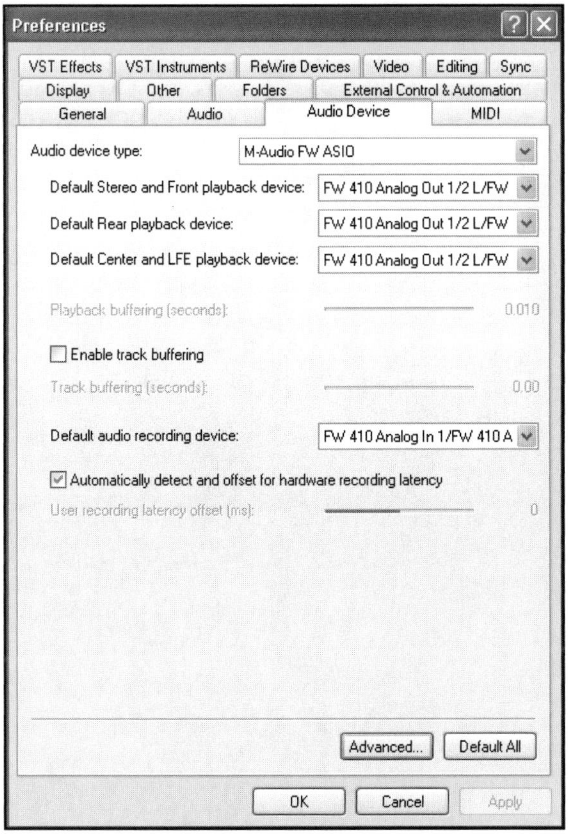

Figure 6.19   Choosing the new hardware in ACID Pro.

Levels   Make sure to set your recording levels on your audio interface before recording. If they are too hot, you clip. If they are too weak, your signal suffers from noise because of a low signal-to-noise ratio, and generally sucks. The

FireWire 410 has a clip light you can rely on to tell you if you need to turn the gain down. Play (or sing) some louder passages to make sure you don't light the light. You have to check the strength in your DAW to make sure it's not too weak, but if you can hear yourself in headphones connected to the FireWire 410 well enough, it's probably okay.

4.   Each DAW is different in the particulars, but in general, start a new project and then set a suitable sample rate and bit depth. I choose to record at a sample rate of 48 kHz with a depth of 24 bits. I have armed my track, turned on monitoring, and am merrily playing away in Figure 6.20.

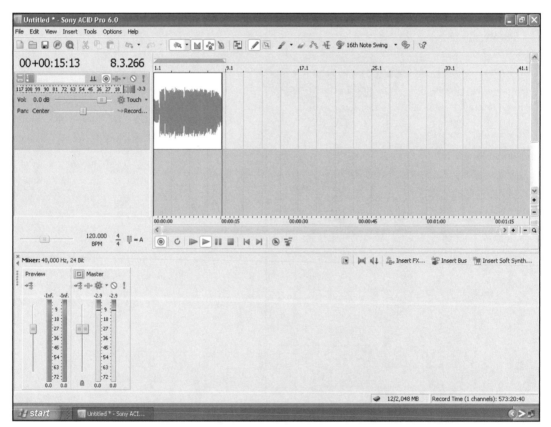

Figure 6.20 Testing the unit in another application.

5.   Stop the take and have a listen. If everything sounds good, you're ready to move on to installing Pro Tools M-Powered.

Installing Pro Tools M-Powered

This is actually not a time-consuming or stressful part of the process. It's no harder than installing a web browser.

Mac Installation   I'm using a Windows machine as I write this, as these instructions obviously reveal. Mac installation is remarkably similar and, in fact, very easy. The Pro Tools M-Powered manual essentially tells you to stick the DVD in your drive, locate Install Pro Tools on the disk, double-click it, and follow the instructions.

---

1. Insert the DVD into your computer and open it up (see Figure 6.21).

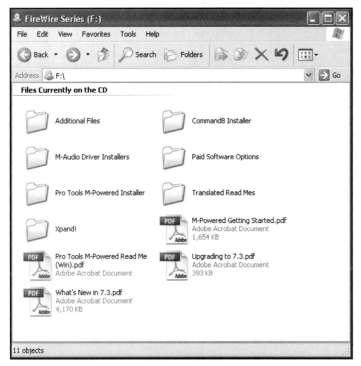

Figure 6.21   The Pro Tools M-Powered distribution DVD.

2. Read any or all of the documentation you want, then go to the Pro Tools M-Powered Installer folder (see Figure 6.22) and launch the Setup program.

3. You then see this splash screen, welcoming you (see Figure 6.23). Click Next.

Figure 6.22   Find the right folder to run the installer.

Figure 6.23   Welcome.

4. Accept the license agreement (see Figure 6.24).

5. Accept the default installation folder or choose another (Figure 6.25).

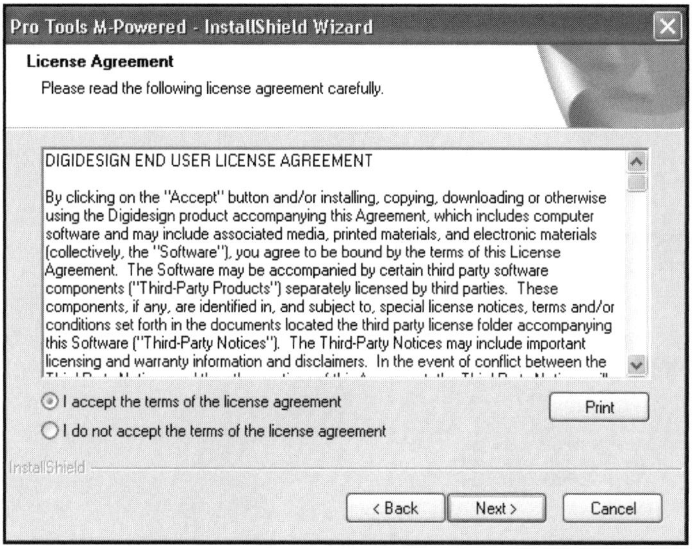

Figure 6.24   Admit one.

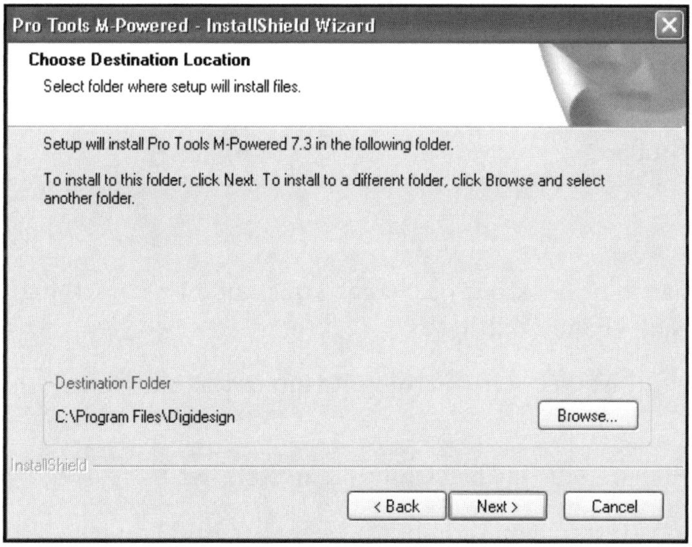

Figure 6.25   Deciding where to install.

6. Take a look at what is to be installed (Figure 6.26). The checked options are installed by default and require no additional authorization than having bought Pro Tools M-Powered. The MP3 Export Option requires you to purchase the license to do so, and the Command 8 option is useful only if you have a Command 8. It's wise to accept the defaults here unless you really know what you're doing and don't want a default option. Click Next to continue.

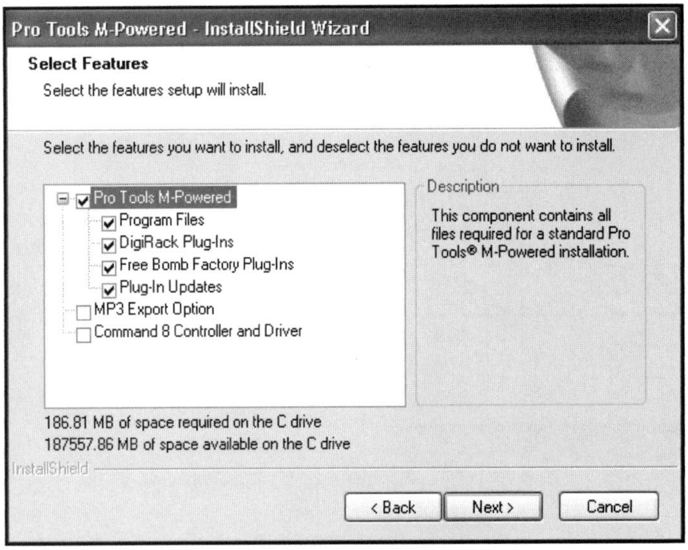

Figure 6.26   These are the standard options.

7. You're given one last chance to back out or change your mind on something. If you're ready, click Install (Figure 6.27).

8. The Pro Tools M-Powered installer starts earning its money, as shown in Figure 6.28.

9. And that's about it (see Figure 6.29). That really wasn't too hard.

10. The only thing left to do is restart your computer (Figure 6.30). You test the installation in the next section.

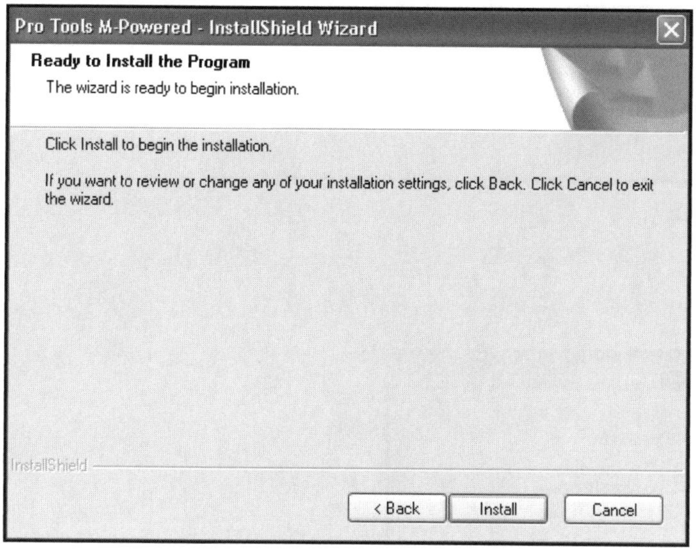

Figure 6.27   Make it so, Number One.

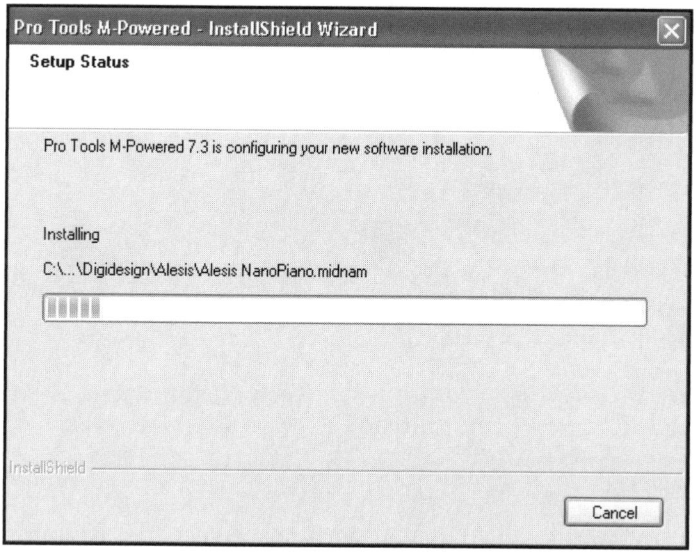

Figure 6.28   Copying files is always a good sign.

Figure 6.29 That was remarkably easy.

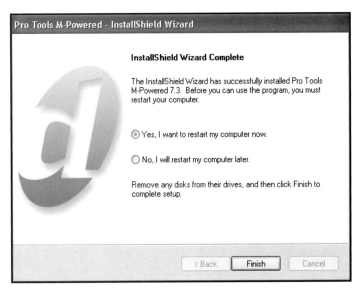

Figure 6.30 One more reboot.

Testing Again

Now it's time for the final test. This is more of a Pro Tools test than a hardware test, assuming you downloaded the correct drivers (I didn't the first time).

1. Turn your FireWire 410 on.

2. Insert your pre-authorized iLok key (if not already).

3. Launch Pro Tools M-Powered.

4. Pro Tools should "boot up" and open to a shell with no project file. If your iLok is not authorized or you forgot to connect it, you see the screen shown in Figure 6.31. If that's the case, make sure the key is inserted. If it is, go to the

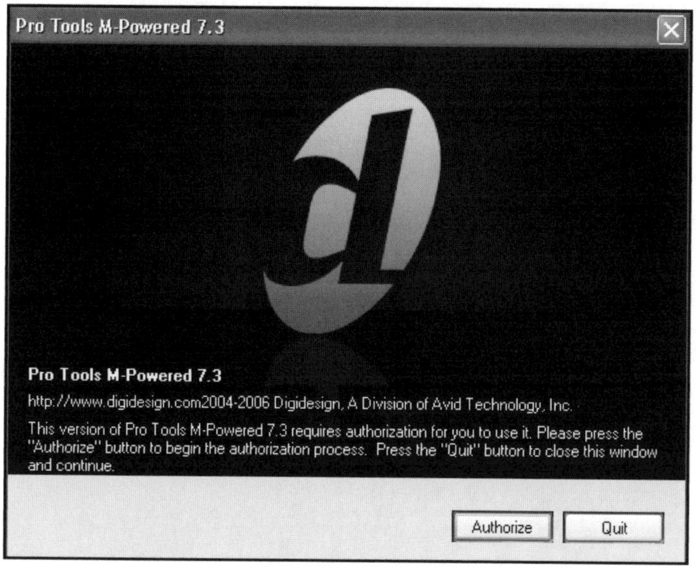

Figure 6.31 If you see this, you forgot to connect your iLok.

iLok website and make sure you have a valid Pro Tools M-Powered license on the key.

5. Before you do anything, go to the Setup>Playback Engine menu and make sure your FireWire 410 is visible (see Figure 6.32). If you don't see the FireWire 410, make sure it is plugged into the computer and on. No other audio connections are necessary for Pro Tools M-Powered to communicate with the unit.

6. I'm going to jump right into this and create a new project file (see Figure 6.33).

7. I am creating an audio track in Figure 6.34.

8. In Figure 6.35 I'm assigning an input to the new track.

9. Finally, I've armed the track, set the appropriate levels on the FireWire 410, and I am recording in Figure 6.36.

Finis

Exactly. I hope you've read through this section, regardless of what hardware you're going to install. If your gear is FireWire, it's going to be pretty close to this. If it's USB or a PCI card, keep reading, as I have a few notes to pass on regarding those general interfaces.

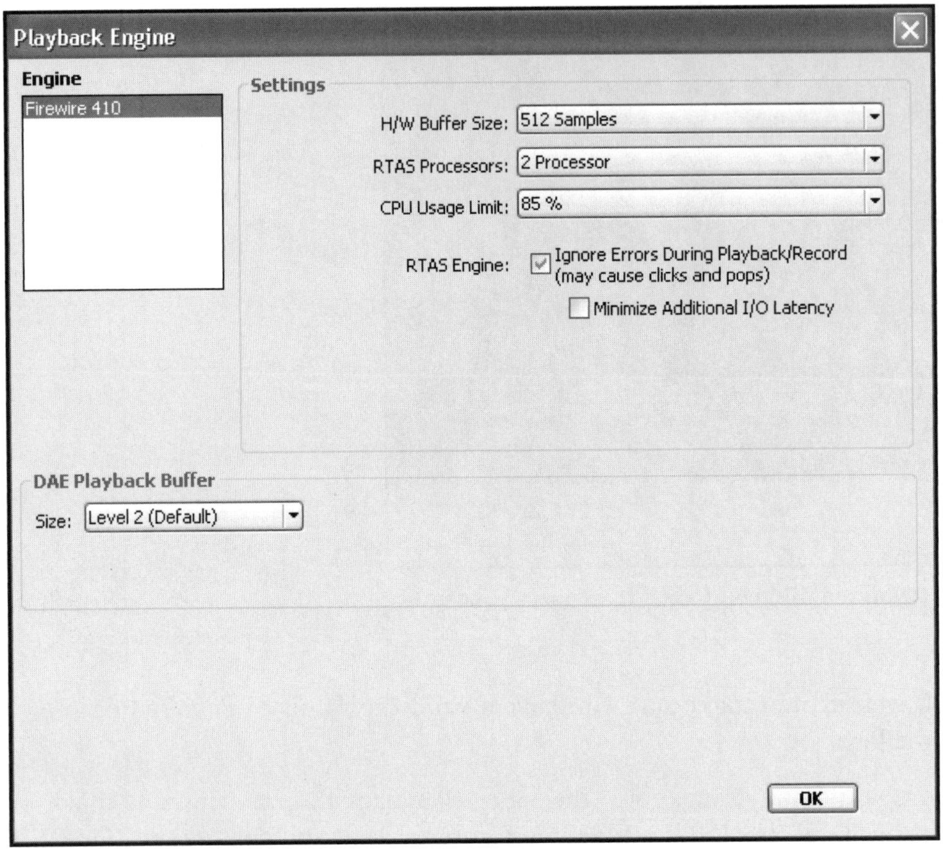

Figure 6.32 Verify the hardware.

M-Audio MobilePre USB

The M-Audio MobilePre USB is a great little box that has the distinction of being my first pro audio interface purchase. I needed something to record voiceovers with as I narrated computer tutorials. I tried using a standard computer microphone at first, but it quickly proved to be totally unsatisfactory. I shopped around and discovered (sadly and frustratingly) that you can't just buy a microphone and plug it into your computer.

Now You Can My story is not ancient, but it still happened before USB microphones with onboard A/D conversion and podcasting ushered in more computer-friendly solutions. Also, I've learned a lot in the intervening time.

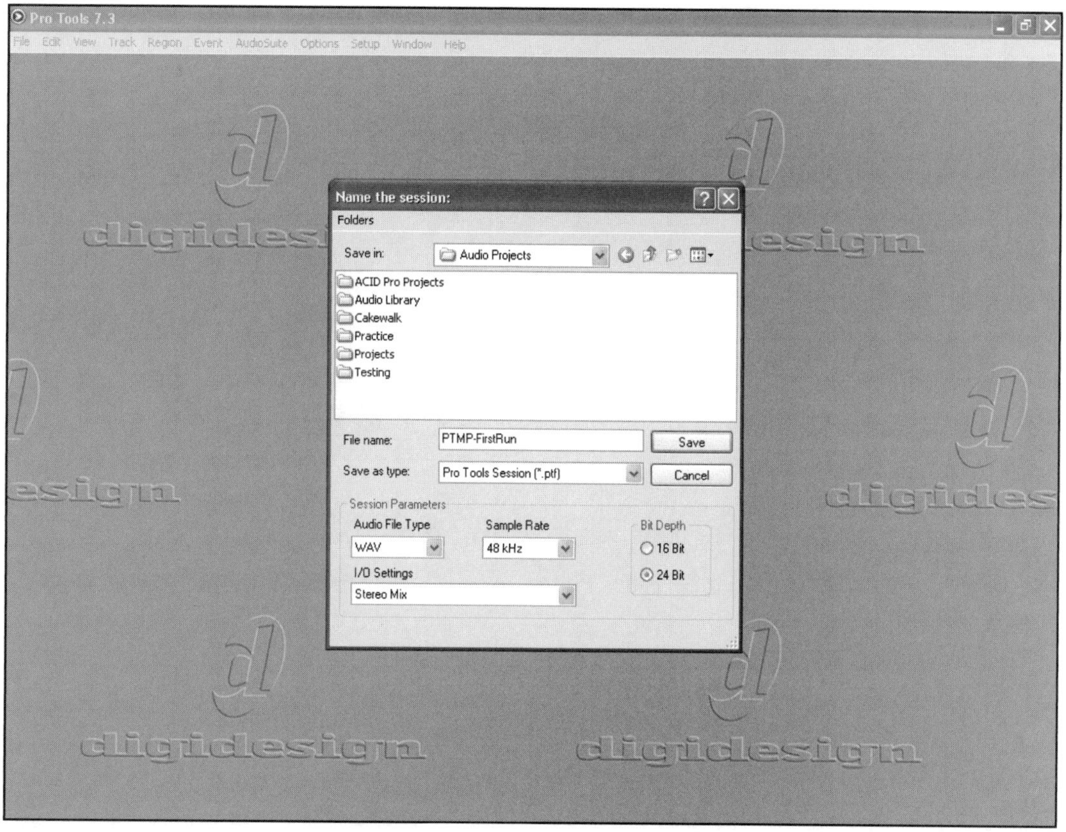

Figure 6.33 Creating a new project.

In the end, I found that I needed a preamp to connect the microphone to, which brought forth another set of difficulties. All the preamps I was shown were from the audio world. How was I supposed to connect it to my computer? USB. I discovered the MobilePre USB and that solved all my troubles. I ended up using it for far more than the voiceovers, and it still has a place in my studio. And guess what? The little MobilePre runs Pro Tools M-Powered. It's time to install it!

1. Download the latest drivers off the Internet. It's foot-stompin' time!

2. Install the hardware drivers *before* the M-Audio MobilePre USB has been connected to your computer. If you've accidentally plugged the Mobile Pre into your computer before this, you have to unplug the unit and plug it back in after the driver has been installed.

3. The computer does *not* shut down in this case.

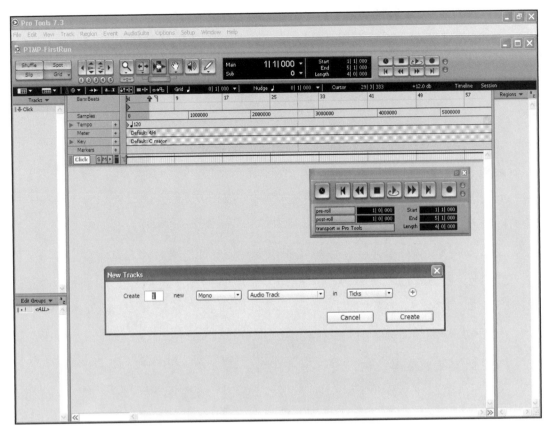

Figure 6.34 Creating a new audio track.

4. Plug the MobilePre into the computer using the supplied USB cable.

5. The computer recognizes the MobilePre and finishes the installation.

6. Now you're ready to install Pro Tools.

Figure 6.37 shows the MobilePre USB Control Panel.

M-Audio Delta 66

I really like my Delta 66. A word of warning, however—it has no preamps. This doesn't concern me, as I use my Yamaha mixing console for that purpose, but if you get something like this without having the means to amplify your signal, you have to go spend more money.

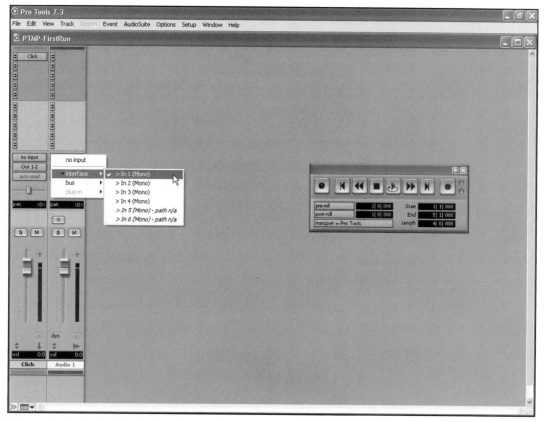

Figure 6.35   Assigning the correct input from the Mix window.

The Delta 66 is an internal card that you have to install in your computer. That makes it more intimidating for the casual computer user who isn't used to taking the case off their computer and working inside. I will not go through the entire installation process for the Delta 66 with the same level of detail as the FireWire 410. Suffice it to say that it follows the same general installation flow that I described in Chapter 4, which is as follows:

1.   Download the latest drivers off the Internet. This is pretty important. Always do this!

2.   Install the hardware drivers *before* the Delta 66 is installed within your computer.

3.   Shut down the computer.

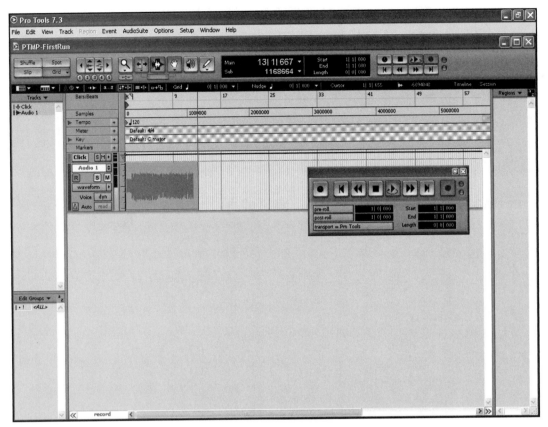

Figure 6.36 Recording looks great.

4. Open up the case of your computer and install the Delta 66 card. Don't be afraid, but clearly this installation is more involved than plugging in a USB or FireWire cable. It's not hard, but it helps to have some experience installing other cards in your computer. Don't do it unless you're comfortable. Ask a friend or contract an expert if you have sufficient doubts.

5. Turn the computer on.

6. The computer recognizes the Delta 66 and finishes the installation.

7. Now you're ready to install Pro Tools.

Test the Delta 66 just as I described in the FireWire 410 section. Open up another DAW and record with it before installing Pro Tools. Then install Pro Tools.

Figure 6.37   M-Audio MobilePre USB Control Panel.

Figure 6.38 shows the Delta 66 Control Panel. I always check the About tab to see the driver version. For some reason it gives me a warm fuzzy.

Figure 6.38   M-Audio Delta 66 Control Panel.

I have one last point relating to the Delta 66, but not exclusively so. I've got three M-Audio interfaces currently installed and working on my computer: the FireWire 410, the MobilePre USB, and the Delta 66. I can use any one of these to work with Pro Tools M-Powered. You cannot use more than one interface at a time in Pro Tools M-Powered, even if they are the same type, or, like the Delta 66, more than one can be linked together to work with other DAWs. Select the interface you want Pro Tools to use in the Setup > Playback Engine dialog box (see Figure 6.39). If you don't have a session open, you'll use the selected interface the next time you open or create one. If you make the change with a session open, Pro Tools will tell you it needs to save the current session and reopen it.

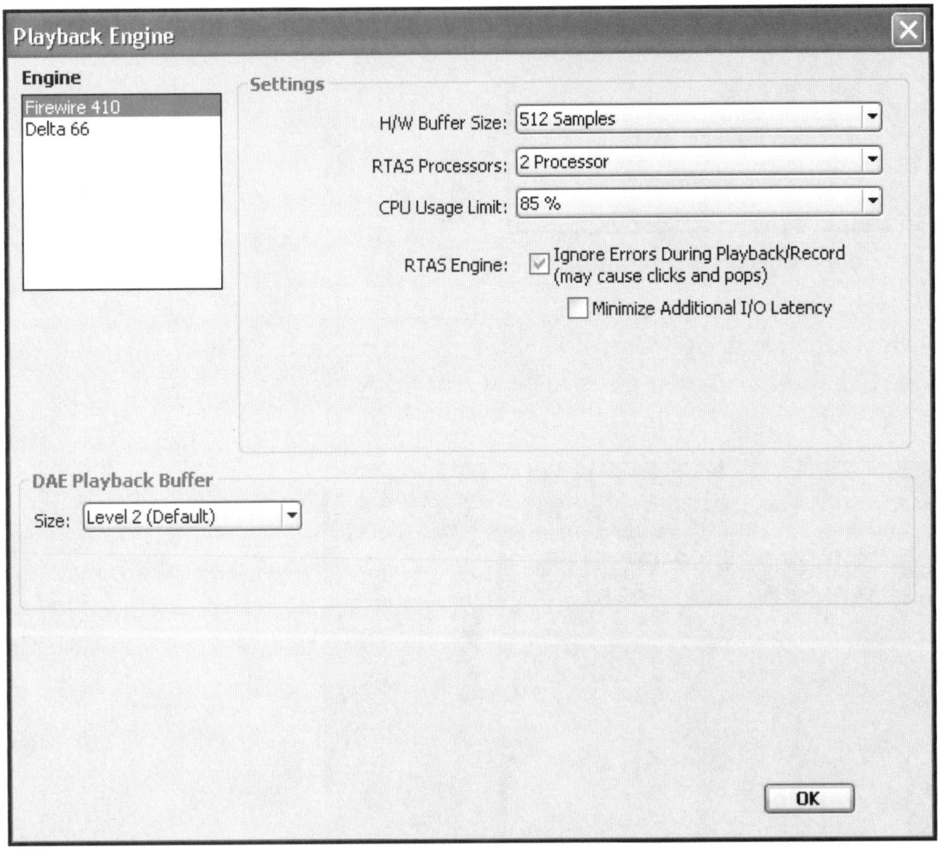

Figure 6.39 I like having lots of options.

That's what I call versatility. It's nice if you're an M-Audio lover and have several interfaces for different purposes (mobile, internal, and so on). You buy Pro Tools once but can use any of your interfaces (within the stated specifications of the units).

Updating Pro Tools

Updating Pro Tools M-Powered should be done with care. This isn't like updating a web browser, and a working, stable system, even if outdated, is preferable to a new, buggy one. Go to the Digidesign website (www.digidesign.com) and visit the Support and Downloads section to periodically check for software updates. Read the documentation and see if the update solves any problems you've been having. If so, I would strongly consider downloading and installing it. If you're running smoothly, see if the update adds any new functionality that you need.

The software I installed was Pro Tools M-Powered 7.3. Take a look now at how to update that.

1.   Go to the Digidesign site and enter the Support and Downloads area (see Figure 6.40).

Figure 6.40   Visit Support and Downloads for updates.

2.   Select your software version from the appropriate area, as shown in Figure 6.41.

Figure 6.41   Choose your version.

3.   Select Downloads (Figure 6.42).

4.   Select a point release (Figure 6.43). If you are feeling adventurous (I am today), explore the cs releases.

---

cs Release? *cs* stands for *Customer Support,* and this is Digidesign's way of releasing fixes that help solve known issues, but let you know they haven't completely finished testing the release to make sure it doesn't cause other problems. When a release is "fully qualified," it becomes a new point release or another version. In other words, use cs releases at your own risk. If you explore

Figure 6.42 Go to the Downloads tab.

Figure 6.43 Select an update.

the dates, Pro Tools version 7.3.1 was released in January 2007, whereas 7.3.1cs6 was released in January 2008. You get a lot of fixes in that newer version, but you're taking a greater chance that the fixes themselves can cause problems. Fun, isn't it?

5. Read about it. Explore this thoroughly.

6. When ready, download the file at the bottom of the information (Figure 6.44). When you click the file, you are prompted to create an account with Digidesign or log in to an existing one.

Figure 6.44   Click to download the file.

7. Save the file to disk, as seen in Figure 6.45. This is a good time to make sure Pro Tools is not running. If it is, quit it.

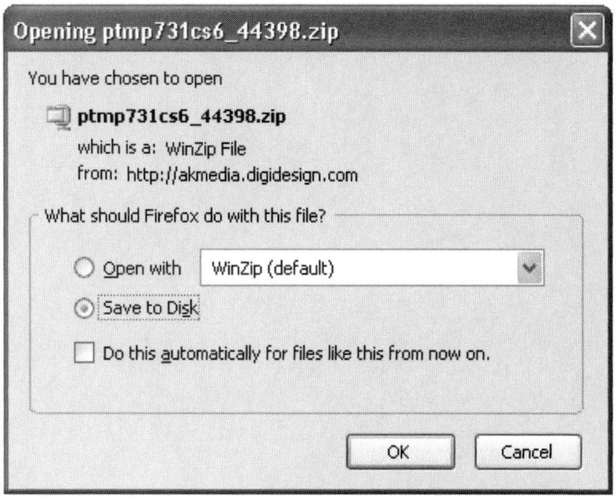

Figure 6.45   Save it to your computer.

8. Uncompress the archive and run the installer.

9. When the installer is finished, you are prompted to reboot. Do so, and then run Pro Tools and make sure it works and was updated.

7 Configuring Pro Tools

In this chapter, I walk through the major options that help you set up and allow you to configure Pro Tools. Specifically, I spend time on most of the menus under the main Setup menu. I show you some hardware setup options, fine-tune the Digidesign Audio Engine, tweak it to the task at hand, and work with Disk Allocation, I/O Setup, and more. I finish up with some tips that have a little bit of everything, including troubleshooting.

This is Pro Tools' bread and butter. Know this stuff. It can be the difference between success and failure.

Setup Menu

The Setup Menu is a pretty important area in Pro Tools LE and M-Powered. Don't rush by it on your way to record, edit, and mix your music. That's fun stuff, but this is what makes that possible, and profitable.

Hardware Setup

You are able to make certain hardware changes from the Hardware Setup dialog box, shown in Figure 7.1. Access it by selecting the Setup>Hardware menu. Much of this has to do with digital I/O. You might see some or all of the following:

Recording Digital Inputs If you want to record input from an external digital device, you may have to set the clock source either to that device or a system-wide master clock (like Apogee's BIG BEN). Do that here (the most obvious place) or in the Setup>Session dialog box.

Clock Source: This determines who's running the clock. The default is Internal, which tells your Pro Tools LE interface to be its own master clock. If you're routing signal from an external digital source (Sony/Philips Digital Interconnect Format [S/PDIF], for example), you may have to change this to the External option in order to receive

Figure 7.1 Set up Clock Source and other digital I/O features here.

signal from the external digital device. I've got an old DigiTech RP14D pedalboard that has S/PDIF out. When I record myself playing guitar through the pedalboard and use S/PDIF rather than a standard 1/4-inch analog connection, I connect the RP14D to the Mbox 2 (for example) with a S/PDIF RCA cable and then come here and switch the Clock Source to S/PDIF. Until I make that change, the Mbox 2 does not recognize any signal coming through the S/PDIF inputs. It's just trash. If you have something that can send data over S/PDIF, create a new track, select a S/PDIF (Left or Right) input, arm the track, and try it out for yourself. Depending on your gear, you might have Internal, plain old S/PDIF, S/PDIF (RCA), Optical, Word Clock, or possibly other combinations that should be easily recognized and chosen as options.

Match Sample Rates!   Make sure your session sample rate and the rate that your external digital device is set to match. If they don't, you still get the input, but it is all pitch-shifted from the original. In the case of my RP14D, it operates only at 44.1 kHz. I like working with the Mbox 2 at 48 kHz and the M-Audio FireWire 410 at 96 kHz. When I create new projects, I use those as my defaults. If I know I want to use my RP14D, and having a super-high sampling rate isn't important, I create a new session at 44.1 kHz and run with that. If I decide later on that I want a track from the RP14D but am working in a session with a higher sample rate, I can bounce what I have in my "working" session to a stereo mix, create a new "temporary" session at the proper sample rate for the RP14D, import the just-bounced stereo mix to play along with, track what I need to track in the temp session, close that out, and then open up the working session and import the audio I just recorded into it, making sure to convert it at a high quality. Whew. Yeah, that's a mouthful. If you decide to change the sample rate of the session, you can choose Edit>Save Copy In to save the session as a copy in a new location with a compatible sample rate. Of course, if your external digital gear is flexible and has different sample rates, just change the sample rate on the device to match your Pro Tools session.

Sample Rate: This is the default sample rate automatically preselected when you create a new session. You can always change it from the New Session dialog box, but if you always create sessions at 48 kHz, come here, select your hardware, and change the default sample rate. Clearly, the options you have are dependent on the hardware. Don't get tripped up by the fact that you can only change this when no session is open.

Optical Format: This is applicable only to the 003. Select S/PDIF or ADAT. The 002 has different options, but they are clearly marked.

M-Audio Gear   Gear without digital I/O won't have this at all, and M-Audio gear requires that you make these changes from the hardware control panel outside of Pro Tools.

Playback Engine

The Playback Engine dialog box (Figure 7.2) is one of the more important locations in Pro Tools. This is where you make the changes that can aggressively push your system to its limits or scale things back to keep it running smoothly. If you're running Pro Tools M-Powered and have multiple M-Audio interfaces that can all run Pro Tools, choose which one you want to use here.

Notice that the top of the Playback Engine dialog box has settings that apply to your interface. The bottom is concerned with your computer.

Buffer? What's a Buffer?   A buffer is a holding tank where data goes and waits to be used. The larger the buffer, the more data is "staged" and ready to go. The problem with computers, especially computers processing audio, is that they need a steady, unbroken stream of data to operate smoothly. If that data stream starts and stops, the resulting audio is severely degraded. Imagine working at a T-shirt booth at a concert, and every moment when you're not selling a shirt is a moment you're not getting paid. It would be nice to see a line of about ten people always waiting. That's your buffer. As long as you have people in your buffer, you won't suffer from a work stoppage. As soon as you service one customer, another is ready to take her place.

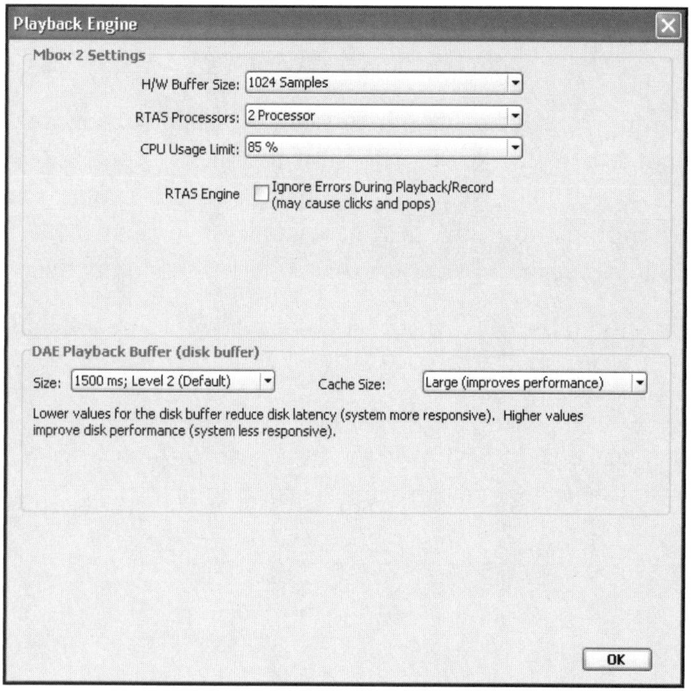

Figure 7.2 You must master the Playback Engine dialog box.

H/W Buffer Size: This is the size of the hardware buffer (this hardware is not to be confused with your computer—it is the audio interface you're running) devoted to processing Real Time AudioSuite (RTAS) plug-ins and monitoring. Values range from 128 to 2048. The larger the number of samples, the larger the buffer. The larger the buffer, the more latency you introduce between the time an event occurs and the time you hear it. The actual time difference depends on your sample rate. It's always good to have as low a buffer as possible, especially while tracking, because you want the lowest monitoring latency possible while recording. The advantage of setting a large buffer while you mix is that you can run more plug-ins and place more stress on your system without losing audio. The buffer gives you more capability, primarily at the expense of being "real time." Remember: tracking is a real-time task whereas mixing is not. Track with as low a buffer as possible. This is the number-one setting that affects recording latency.

RTAS Processors: This is the number of processors you want to devote to RTAS processing. If you have two, like I do, the options are 1 or 2. If you have a smokin' quad-core rig, you have four from which to choose. The most important thing to remember about this setting is that it has to do with RTAS processing, which is entirely dependent on how many (and what type of) RTAS plug-ins you have active on your tracks. If you don't have any, then setting RTAS Processors to 2 is a waste. You don't need that, and you are taking horsepower away from other tasks, in addition to the system in general. In conjunction with the next setting (CPU Usage Limit), you can tune where your processing power needs to go. More RTAS plug-ins? Make sure to increase the number of RTAS Processors here. Don't have many plug-ins? Then come by and lower this setting.

CPU Usage Limit: Here you have the maximum amount of CPU usage, given as a percentage, devoted to RTAS processing *and other host tasks*. Right, the "other host tasks" part is important. This usage limit is not specific to RTAS processing, but includes other Pro Tools tasks like redrawing the screen. Basically, this boils down to how much of your computer you want to turn over to Pro Tools.

Host Processing You see the term *host processing* or *host tasks* in Digidesign material a lot, because Pro Tools LE (and the underlying architecture of RTAS plug-ins) relies on the host processor, which is the CPU in your computer, to do the work. In other words, when you assign an electronic equalization (EQ) plug-in to a track, your CPU is performing the calculations that change the audio. Pro Tools HD, on the other hand, has dedicated Digital Signal Processing (DSP) cards that take the burden off the CPU and handle the work themselves (like a graphics card handles the graphics processing in your computer). It wasn't too long ago that DSP cards were the only viable way to produce professional audio on PCs. Today, the power of multicore processors gives you more computing power than ever. In ten years you will laugh at this and think it's quaint.

RTAS Engine: This enables (unchecked, the default) or disables (checked) RTAS error reporting. This is also called "enabling RTAS Error Suppression," which seems like a double-negative. It's waiting to trip you up, and I have to read the thing five times to make sure I'm doing what I want to be doing. Here's the deal. You can turn RTAS Error Suppression on or off. When you turn error suppression off, you're telling Pro Tools to *not suppress error reporting*. In other words, you want it to tell you the errors. When you turn error suppression on, you're telling Pro Tools to *suppress error reporting*. In other words, you don't want it to tell you when things are going wrong. Why would you want Pro Tools to ignore errors and keep chugging away without telling you? When you're getting so many errors that it keeps you from making music, this loosens the rules a bit, at the expense of audio quality, to let you at least finish what you're doing. Digidesign recommends unchecking this box (the simplest way of saying it) to get the highest quality audio, but be warned that you might be interrupted because of the fact that Pro Tools will report RTAS engine errors. Check the box if you're getting so many errors it's driving you crazy. Clear? You might also have the option of Minimizing Additional I/O Latency if error reporting has been disabled (box checked). This seems supremely overcomplicated, but essentially what happens is that when you are suppressing errors, you incur some additional latency. This option tries to minimize that by reducing the additional buffer required to suppress errors to 128 samples.

RTAS Engine Summary   Unchecked—Enables error reporting, resulting in high-quality audio but possible work-stoppage if the engine runs into errors.

Checked—Disables error reporting, allowing you to keep running despite errors, but might lower the quality of the audio. You might hear pops and clicks that would ordinarily cause Pro Tools to stop playback/recording and tell you, "Hey, something's wrong!"

Minimize Additional I/O Latency—Check if you need to reduce latency when error reporting is turned off.

DAE Playback Buffer: This is the buffer that Pro Tools creates out of your system's memory to handle hard disk drive read operations (playback). This does not apply to recording, although it can have an effect on recording. You have several options and levels to choose from, but Digidesign recommends you leave this at Level 2. At this level, you are buffering 1500 msec of audio being read from your computer's hard drive. Lower levels decrease the speed at which playback and recording start, but at the expense of reliability when the system is under stress (lots of tracks, edits, and plug-ins). Higher levels have the opposite effect.

DAE?   DAE stands for Digidesign Audio Engine.

Cache Size (Pro Tools 7.4 only): Careful now, this is a setting that only applies when you're using Elastic Audio, which is new in Pro Tools 7.4. That's critical. If you don't have tracks that take advantage of Elastic Audio, set this to Minimal and forget it. This cache might not be enabled by the inner workings of Pro Tools unless you have Elastic

Audio–enabled tracks, in which case this setting would do something, but I would set it to Minimum to be safe. If you do use Elastic Audio, this is for you. The Cache Size sets the amount of your computer's memory that the DAE uses to prebuffer audio when you are using Elastic Audio for playback and looping. Got that? Now you are dealing with prebuffers to the buffer. Think of the cache as a stash of audio that can be repeatedly played back. It makes sense to store this in a temporary place and then feed it into the buffer when needed. After playback, that audio is not in the buffer anymore, but it's still in the cache. That way, and this is truly important when looping, the system doesn't have to read it off the hard disk drive every time you play it. The DAE retrieves it out of the memory (RAM) cache, making the operation much more efficient. Larger settings are obviously better, but the tradeoff is less system memory for other tasks. The compromise is to set it to Normal.

Elastic Audio?   Elastic Audio is Digidesign's entry into the world of real-time track-based audio time-compressing and expansion. Individual beats within audio regions can be warped to follow a chosen tempo and beat by using Event and Warp markers. Many use Elastic Audio for loop creation or as a real-time replacement for the TCE tool and AudioSuite TCE.

Disk Allocation

I used to think Disk Allocation had something to do with all the audio in a session, whether you recorded it or imported it. It doesn't. Disk Allocation applies only to where Pro Tools saves newly recorded material. By default, Pro Tools saves each session's recordings in a folder called Audio Files, which is located within the session folder (Figure 7.3).

Workspace   Open up the Pro Tools Workspace (Window>Workspace) to find out which hard disk drives Pro Tools sees in your system and their volume designation. Possible designations are as follows: *Record* and *Playback*, *Playback* only, or data *Transfer*. You can change the designation of internal and external hard drives.

At times you will want to double-check the disk allocation of a session, especially if you're opening one that someone else created on a different computer. If you see this dialog box (see Figure 7.4) when you open a session, it means the original disk allocation can't be used and you should check the settings.

Figure 7.3   Normal allocation in session subfolders.

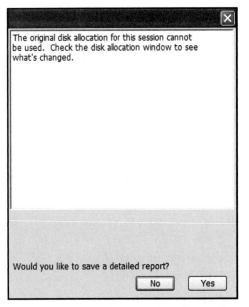

Figure 7.4   Disk Allocation has changed warning.

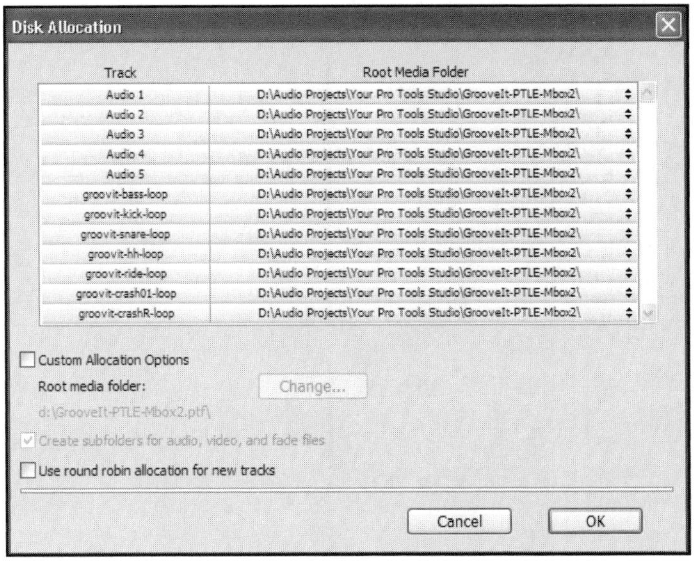

Figure 7.5   Where new recordings are saved.

Access the Disk Allocation dialog box (Figure 7.5) from the Options>Disk Allocation menu.

If you take a look at the dialog box, it is divided into a window and then some options. The window lists the tracks (not regions or clips) in the current session in the Track column and the tracks' storage assignment in the Root Media Folder area. Each track has a folder assigned to it. If you record once or 50 times on that same track, all the clips are stored in the same location.

New Recordings Only   Remember, Disk Allocation refers only to where Pro Tools saves newly recorded material. It has nothing to do with anything else.

You can make a few changes from this window. Most practically, you can change the root media folder by following these simple steps:

1.   Select the Custom Allocation Options checkbox from within the Disk Allocation dialog box. This enables the Change . . . button, as seen in Figure 7.6. You can also choose whether or not Pro Tools creates subfolders (as is the case by default, but not when you choose to customize) to store separate types of data.

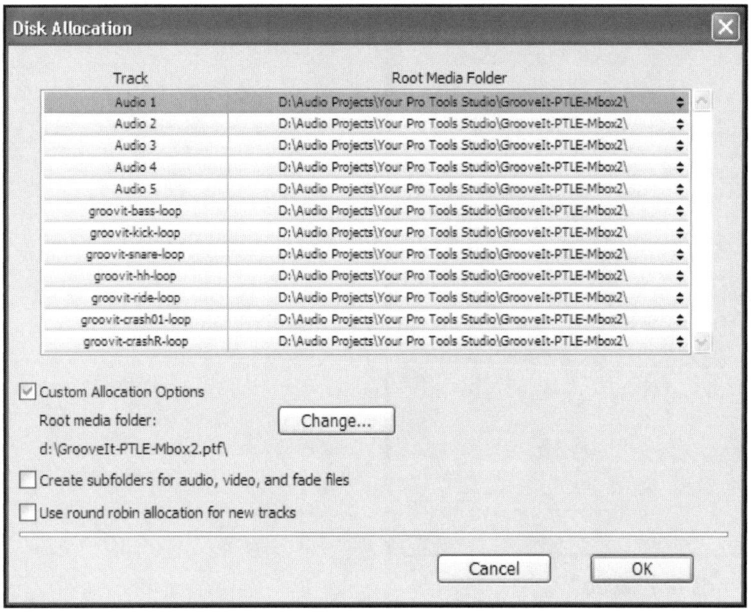

Figure 7.6 Selecting Custom Allocation Options.

2. Click Change. . . . This opens up a dialog box (Figure 7.7) that allows you to navigate to the new root media folder.

3. When you get there, select Use Current Folder.

4. Figure 7.8 shows the new allocation.

You can do more from this dialog box, such as changing the hard drive assigned to each track (click and hold the double-arrows beside a track) and enabling Round Robin Allocation.

Round Robin Allocation is an option that directs Pro Tools to assign a different drive (up to the number in your system, and possibly including your system drive) to each track that is recorded, in round-robin fashion. The rationale behind this is that it's faster to have each track on a separate hard disk drive for recording and playback. That makes sense when you think about it because hard drives can't read or write from more than one location at a time.

Revenge of the Tape   How many tracks can be played (I'm talking literally here) simultaneously from a 24-track system running 2-inch tape? Why 24, of course. Each track has individual play and record heads that operate at the exact same time and do not interfere in any way with the operation of the other heads.

Because of the heads and the way the tape is set up, each track on the tape can be accessed at the exact same moment in time. Hard drives, although pretty nifty, can't do the same thing. If you're running 24 tracks in Pro Tools LE and they are all stored on the same hard drive (there's the tie-in to Disk Allocation), and you're recording to and/or playing back from all 24 at the same time, you're really not. You just think you are because of the way Pro Tools reads/writes and buffers data. No matter how fast or powerful, a hard drive can read from or write to only one place at a time, not 24. Sessions with a large number of tracks clearly benefit from having as many different hard drives defined as possible, up to the number of the tracks. This is why you shouldn't always look down your nose at the old-school way of doing things. In many ways it was pretty awesome.

Figure 7.7 Find the new location.

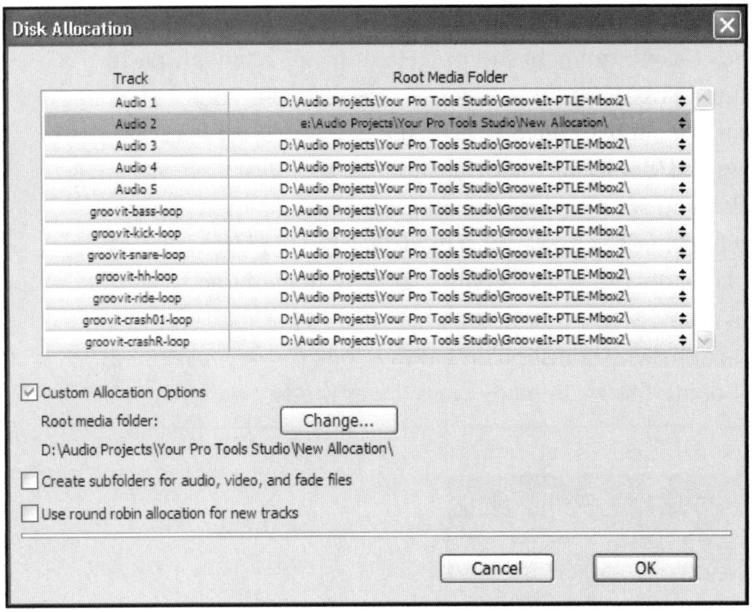

Figure 7.8 New allocation for Audio 2 track is shown.

Peripherals

Peripherals are external devices that can connect to, and be synchronized with, Pro Tools. Most often the connection is through MIDI, but wireless, USB/FireWire, and Ethernet connections are also possible. Most often these devices are add-on control surfaces like Digidesign's own Command|8, M-Audio's Project Mix I/O, or Frontier Design Group's AlphaTrack (one fader with several controls) or TranzPort (transport controller). These control surfaces take some of the engineering out of the computer and put it into your hands via different knobs, buttons, and faders that you interact with directly and physically, rather than clicking your mouse to move a knob on your computer screen.

Set up all of these devices from the Peripherals dialog box (Setup>Peripherals).

Synchronization

Synchronization lets you assign MIDI Time Code (MTC) Reader and Generator Ports. You need this if your system has to sync multiple MIDI-generating or MIDI-receiving devices. MTC is different from Word Clock. Word Clock is a timing scheme that keeps digital I/O from multiple devices in sync with each other. Here, you use MTC to sync up gear with MIDI messages. The performance is being timed (and hence synchronized with MTC), not the data flow (which is Word Clock). Most people think of a MIDI keyboard controller when they think of MIDI, but many other devices, such as sequencers, drum machines, and audio- or videotape machines, use MIDI. MTC keeps them on the same page.

Machine Control

Machine control allows you to control (as the master) an external device's transport via MIDI machine code (MMC) sent from Pro Tools. For example, say (for some wild reason) you have an Alesis HD24 digital recorder. The HD24 accepts MMC to control its transport controls like Play and Record (not track arming, unfortunately). Hook that puppy up to your audio interface with a MIDI cable and then come here to configure Pro Tools as the master. Alternatively, you can control the transport within Pro Tools externally if you designate Pro Tools as the slave.

MIDI Controllers

MIDI controllers is the example I used at the beginning of this section and most likely what you're going to need to configure. Here is where you identify and set up the controller. Under Type, you might see the name of the unit (such as the Command|8) or a protocol. Non-Digidesign control protocols (also known as modes) are HUI (Human User Interface protocol, created by Mackie and Digidesign) and MotorMix (an older control protocol that supports CM Lab's MotorMix control surface, but which appears to be unsupported).

Ethernet Controllers

Ethernet controllers, like the Control|24, use Ethernet to communicate with and control Pro Tools. To use them, enable and designate an Ethernet port and then select the correct unit. For those of you who don't know, Ethernet is a networking protocol used most often to hook computers together in a network. The cable looks like a larger version of a telephone cord with bigger jacks on the end.

I/O Setup

When you're selecting inputs, outputs, inserts, and busses in the Mix and Edit windows, Pro Tools has default names for each signal path. If you want to know what Out 2 corresponds to, open I/O Setup from the Setup>I/O Setup menu and look at the Output tab (see Figure 7.9). It tells you what each path name refers to in relation to your hardware.

But wait, that's not all. You can also rename each of the paths and import and export your settings. This is really convenient in a couple of ways. First, if you're tired of seeing "In 1" when you always have your guitar plugged into Input 1, change the name to "Guitar In 1" or any other convenient name. That's fun, but not all that much to write home about. The real power comes when you're labeling inserts and busses. For example, if you always use Bus 1-2 as your main reverb send, rename it!

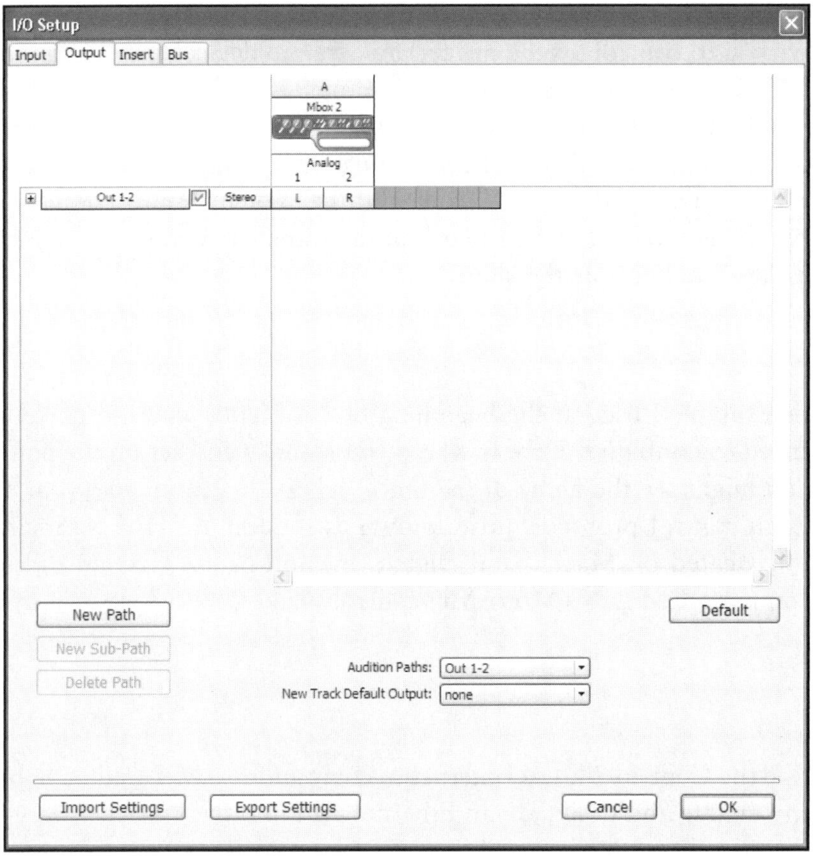

Figure 7.9 Standard Output for Mbox 2.

Hardware Inserts   You have to have enough parallel ins and outs (for example, Input 4 and Output 4) on your hardware to make viable use of hardware (H/W) inserts. For example, the Mbox 2 has only two analog outs. If you need those to monitor with, you have no analog H/W insert capability. If your outboard gear uses S/PDIF, you should be able to configure that as a viable insert. The original Mbox had inserts, but these were removed in all versions of the Mbox 2.

The dialog box as a whole shows you a graphic of your hardware (if you have Digidesign hardware). If you are running Pro Tools M-Powered you'll see the name of your interface. Each tab works the same way. You have an expandable list of named signal paths on the left, beside which is a checkbox that indicates if it is active (hint: you can deactivate a path by unchecking the box). Italicized names indicate the path is unavailable.

Beside the checkbox, you have a Stereo or Mono label and then the Grid, which takes up most of the window. The Grid cross-references the names to the left with the actual hardware I/O (or software capability I/O in the case of Pro Tools LE and M-Powered's 32 internal mix busses). Functionally speaking, you click on something to change it.

Now it's time to take a look at each of the four tabs:

- **Input:** What your inputs are called and what hardware inputs (not counting MIDI) they receive signal from.

- **Output:** What your outputs are called and (not surprisingly) where they are routed.

- **Insert:** Hardware inserts, which, for most Pro Tools LE users, are not going to be much of an option. Depending on your system, you might have enough ins and outs to do it, but it's not really that convenient. Sadly, although not surprisingly, hardware inserts are far less practical at this level (I'm assuming, like me, you're not running a million-dollar studio with Pro Tools HD and a penchant for outboard gear). In general, they have been replaced by software inserts (plug-ins) at most levels of digital recording and mixing.

- **Bus:** This is where signals go to be grouped into submixes, which can serve various purposes. Don't confuse a bus with an Aux Input track. For example, to create a reverb send and return, I create a stereo Aux Input track and assign a reverb plug-in on one of the inserts and then assign a bus (say Bus 1-2) as the input of the Aux Input track. I can then create a stereo send on each track in the session and route them all to Bus 1-2 to "send" signals to the reverb plug-in (whose "return" is the track's fader). Assigning the input of the Aux Input track to Bus 1-2 "collects" the signal from the bus, but doesn't alter the signal on the bus in any way. You can have more Aux Input tracks (or Audio tracks for that matter) and assign them all to receive input from Bus 1-2 and not disturb the reverb. The fun part here is to name busses according to how you work. If you always want Bus 1-2 as reverb, rename it "Main Reverb" or something. I've done just that, and I am naming a Guitar Bus in Figure 7.10.

My Bus Structure   I differentiate between effects busses and my submix groups by using lower-numbered busses for Aux Input tracks that receive my sends and the mid-level busses for submixes.

Notice on the Output tab two additional options: Audition Paths and New Track Default Output. The latter is pretty self-explanatory—that option assigns a standard output that is applied to any new track you create. The former allows you to send

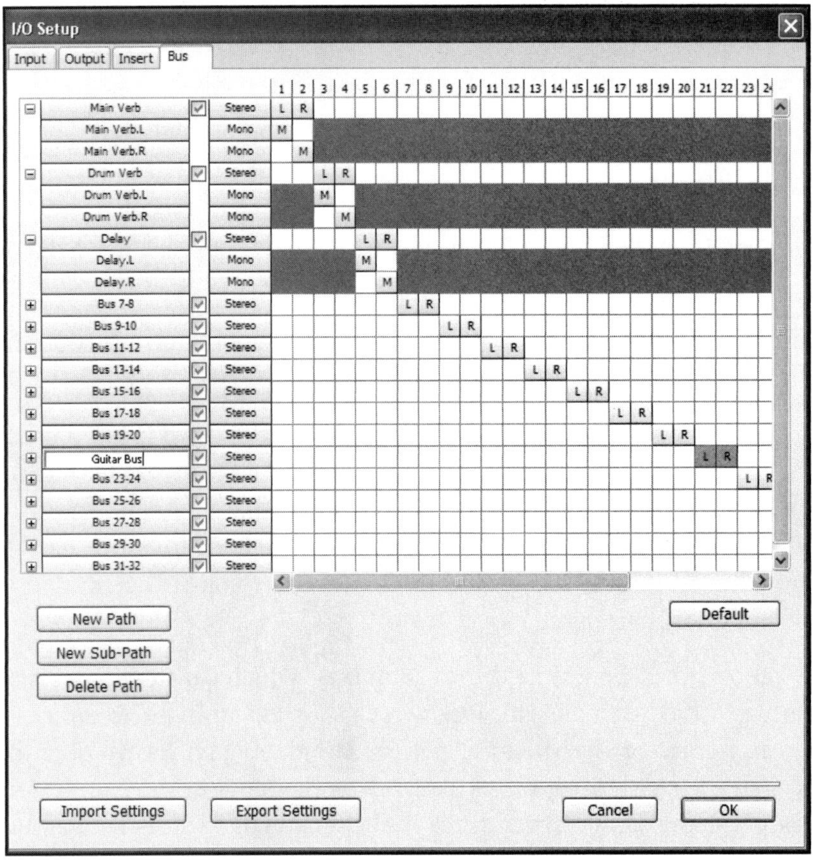

Figure 7.10 Renamed busses.

auditions such as previewing a region in the Region List to any valid Output path on your system.

To rename a path (or subpath), double-click on the name. Type the new name and press Enter or Return. To delete paths, just click on the path name and press the Delete Path button.

I'm not going to get into creating paths very deeply, as you should be able to hit the defaults and get going. Simply put, to create paths, press the New Path button, make it mono or stereo, assign inputs (or output), and then create sub-paths under it if necessary.

If you get lost and want to load the default I/O values for your hardware, go to each tab, select and delete all the existing paths, and then click Default. It's important that you clean out the old paths first.

To export settings, make whatever changes you want, and then click the Export Settings button. Name the file and decide where to save it (the default location is always a great place).

To import previously saved settings, open up the I/O Settings dialog box and click Import Settings. Find the setting file and double-click it.

Click and Countoff Options

The Click/Countoff Options dialog box (Figure 7.11) enables you to alter the click and countoff behavior. A click helps establish the beat by playing a note (from the DigiRack Click plug-in or MIDI source) on each beat of a measure. The difference between the two sources is what they sound like.

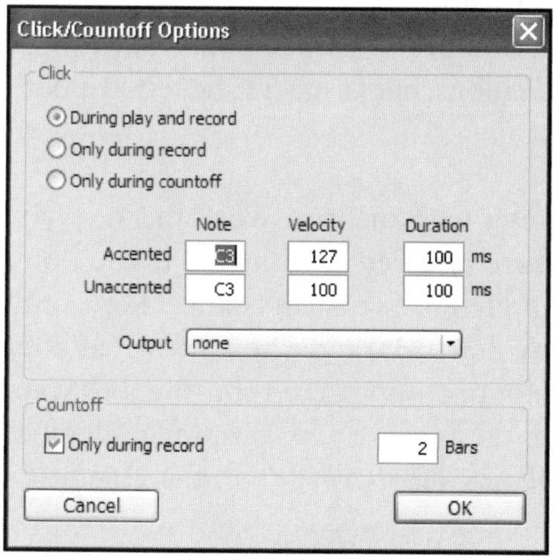

Figure 7.11   Click/Countoff options.

These are pretty useful options. I want to take a look at the Click options first. You can enable the click (assuming you have created a click track) to be heard during the following modes of operation:

- **Play and Record:** Useful for practicing and clearly recording.

- **Record only:** When you don't want to hear it while you're mixing.

- **Countoff only:** Plays the click during the play or record countoff. A countoff is what "counts you off" before the transport actually starts going.

Countoff? What Stinking Countoff?   Enabling the Countoff is one of the all-time most confusing things about Pro Tools. Set the preferences in the Click/Countoff dialog box and enable it on the Transport controls. The problem is, by default (Windows only), the section of the Transport where you click to enable the Countoff is hidden. Turn it on by selecting View>Transport>MIDI Controls and then click the button that tells you how many bars of Countoff you have. Click is easier, as it has a menu option to turn it on or off.

In the next section of the dialog box, enter different MIDI notes, velocities (how hard they are struck), and durations for Accented and Unaccented beats. Below that is the Output list box where you choose the MIDI instrument, should you be using that instead of the DigiRack Click plug-in to generate the sound of the click.

Finally, you can have the Countoff count off only during record (the default option) or, if you uncheck that, during playback as well. Enter a number of bars to count off, from 1 (I tried 0 and it didn't work) to 99 (which is pretty ridiculous, but I sat here and tested it out).

Preferences

The more you use Pro Tools, the more you're going to want it to work the way you work, instead of the other way around. This is where preferences come in. If you don't like how something works, check to see if it has a preference you can change. For example, Pro Tools' default behavior is to reset the Play Start Marker where it started after playback, like an instant rewind. If you're doing a lot of stopping and starting, but want to keep going forward without having to continually rest where you start, the preference is called *Timeline Insertion/Play Start Marker Follows Playback*. It's in the Operation tab of the Preferences dialog box.

The next sections delve into the tabs found in the Preferences dialog box.

Short Titles   I'm going to shorten some titles in this section to try and keep it brief. In other words, I abridge *Play Start Marker Follows Timeline Selection* to *Play Start Marker. . . .* The italics let you know it's a preference title and the ellipses show you it's been shortened. Thank you, and make sure to tip the wait staff.

Display

The Display tab (Figure 7.12) has display-oriented preferences, divided into three functional areas: Basics, Meters, and Color Coding. Most things here are self-explanatory. If you use Track Position Numbers and have hidden tracks, beware that the default behavior is for Pro Tools to renumber every track (via the position number) when you hide or show tracks. In other words, Track 23 becomes Track 22 if you hide something from 1–22. To keep the numbering despite having hidden tracks, click the *Track Position Numbers . . .* option.

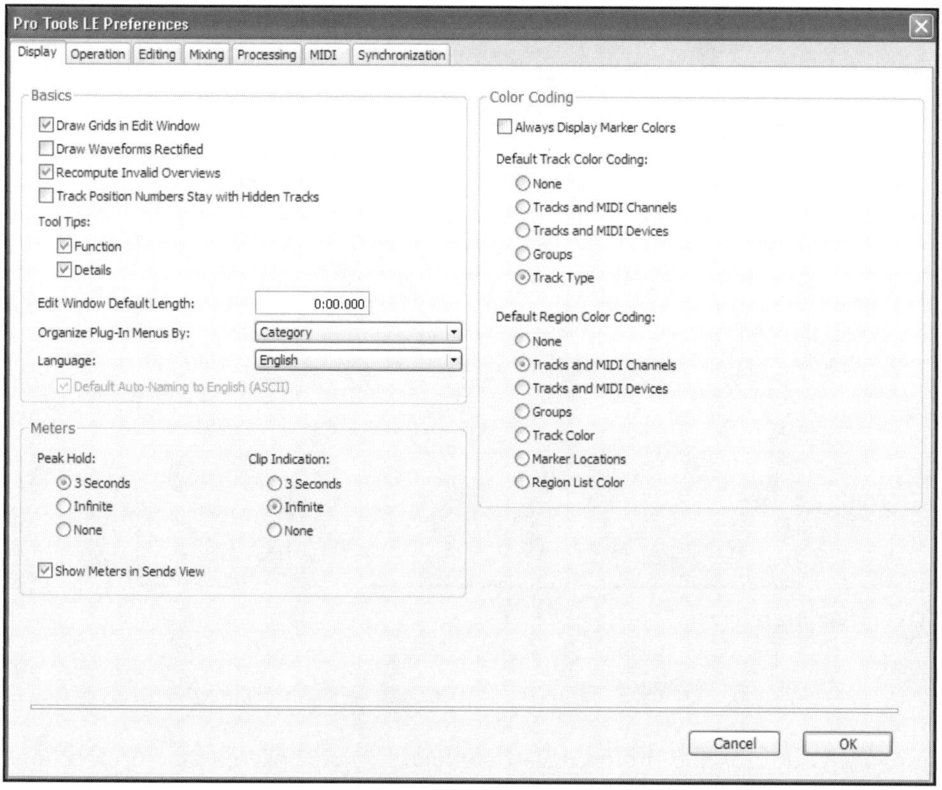

Figure 7.12   Display-oriented preferences.

Operation

Operation (Figure 7.13) contains preferences that are grouped into Transport, Video, Auto Backup, and Record areas. The *Timeline Insertion . . . Follows Playback* option is handy when you want the "tape" to stop and start where you stop it. This is handy in certain playback and review situations. The *Play Start Marker . . .* option is available only when Dynamic Transport is active and enables you to make selections independently of where the transport is set up to play. Auto backup is a life-saver but, on the other hand, can glitch if you're in a heavy session and Pro Tools decides to save your session at the precisely wrong moment in time. I turn that off when the system is under a heavy load and I'm recording.

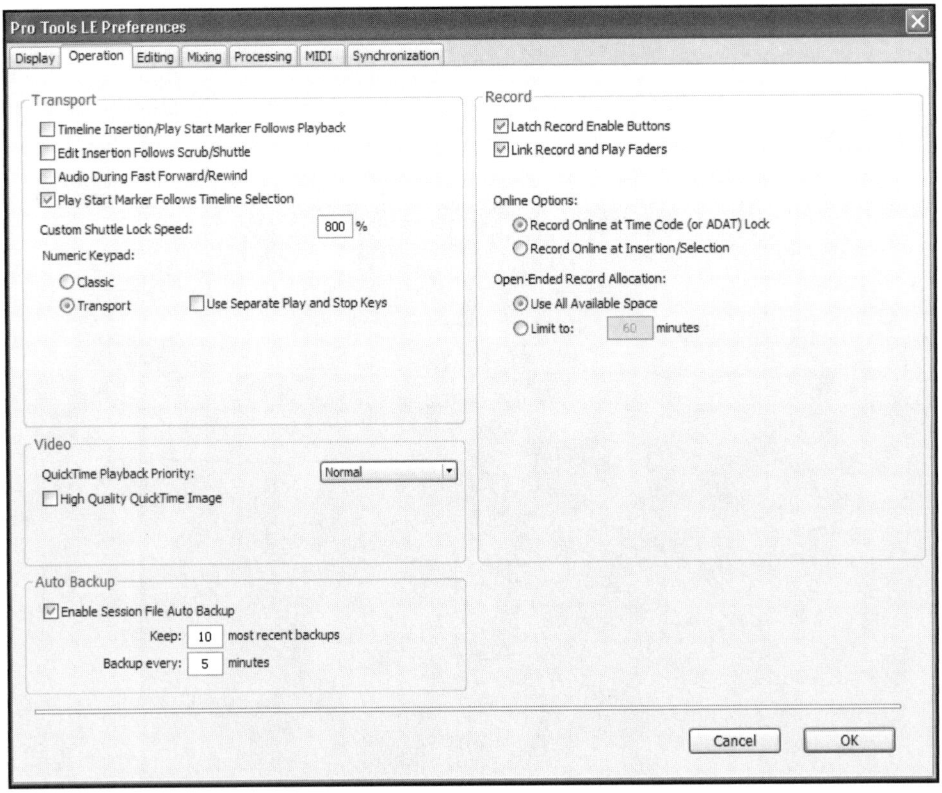

Figure 7.13   Operation preferences.

Editing

Editing (Figure 7.14) houses the preferences that relate to editing operations, grouped into these areas: Regions, Memory Locations, Tracks, Fades, Zoom Toggle, and Undo. The Tracks area is helpful if you want to set all your tracks to samples or ticks. Uncheck to make new track timebases Sample, or check to make new tracks Tick. The Default Fade Settings are also useful if you find yourself always changing fades to a different type than in the current default. Finally, if you're trying to squeeze out all the memory you can, lower the Undo levels. The initial value of 32 is the maximum.

Mixing

Mixing (Figure 7.15) contains mixing preferences, organized into Setup, Automation, and Controller areas. You find lots of good stuff here. If you're like me and you always set your Sends to unity gain (0 dB), uncheck *Sends Default to "-INF."* Likewise, another timesaver is to identify the EQ and Dynamics plug-ins that you use all the time. They then appear in the Insert menu in a more convenient location.

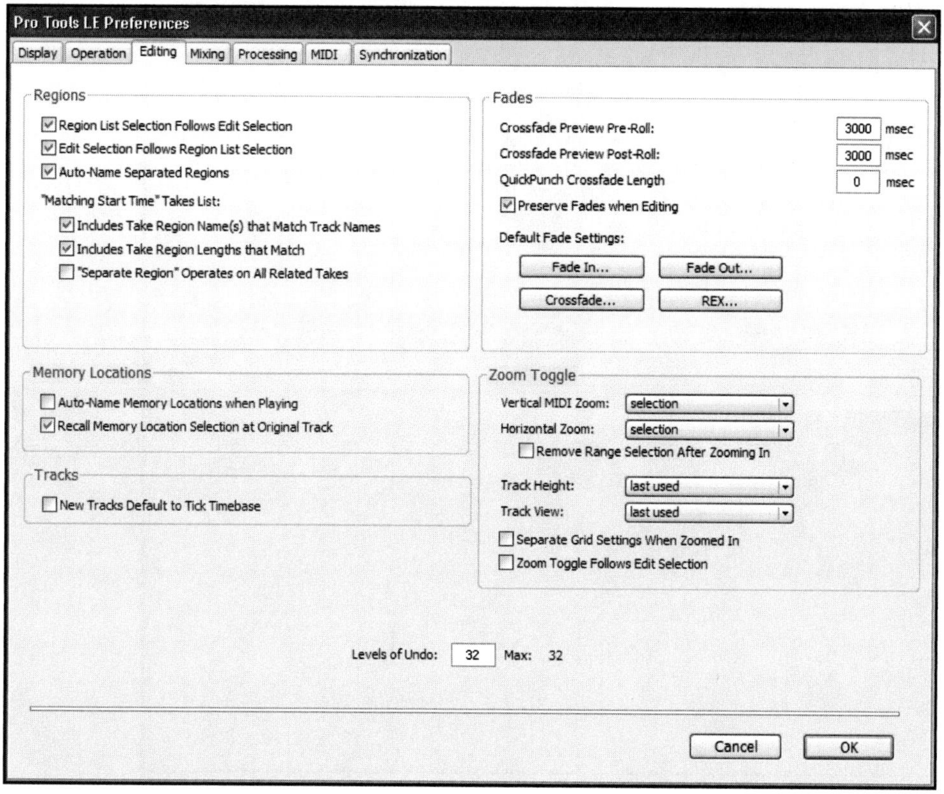

Figure 7.14   Editing preferences.

Processing

Processing (Figure 7.16) groups processing preferences into AudioSuite, Import, TC/E, and Elastic Audio functional areas. AudioSuite plug-ins are disk-based processes. In other words, standard AudioSuite plug-ins (as opposed to RTAS) are not real time, do not process audio files during playback, and either replace the original files or save copies back to your disk. Therefore, the AudioSuite preferences are not RTAS preferences. Change these preferences if you use standard AudioSuite plug-ins and need to tweak them. If you are always changing the import conversion quality when you import files that don't match the sample rate of your session (like I am), change the *Sample Rate Conversion Quality* to match your preference. Of the rest, the Elastic Audio area is most useful when you are making sure Elastic Audio is not enabled on new tracks. If you are into beats and loops and use Elastic Audio all the time, you might benefit from the *Enable Elastic Audio . . .* option.

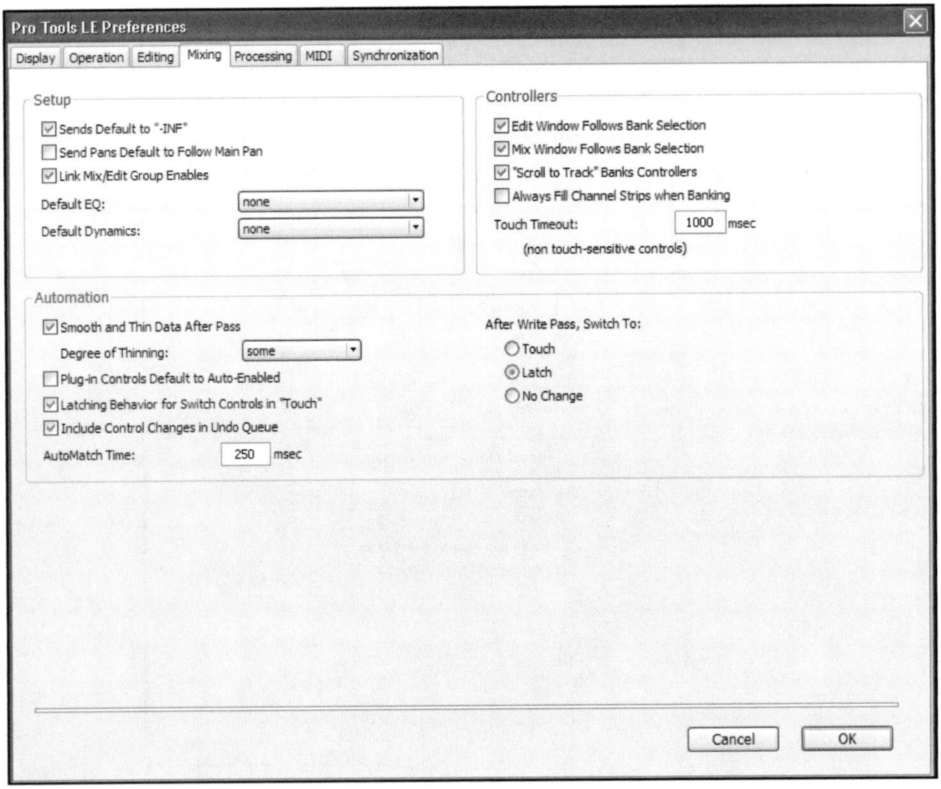

Figure 7.15   Mixing preferences.

The Rest

This MIDI tab (not shown) has the MIDI preferences, organized into Basics and Note Display areas. I cover MIDI in Chapter 11, "Using MIDI."

The Synchronization tab (not shown) contains preferences you might need to set if you have connected an external transport to Pro Tools.

Other Configuration Options

You have other configuration options available that you might want to get into, depending on your specific task. These are pretty specialized (many have to do with video), so I am just going to list them and tell you what they do.

- **Video Sync Offset:** Compensates for the delay in processing or displaying video.

- **Session:** Displays information about your current session and allows you to change the clock source and alter time code and frames-per-second settings.

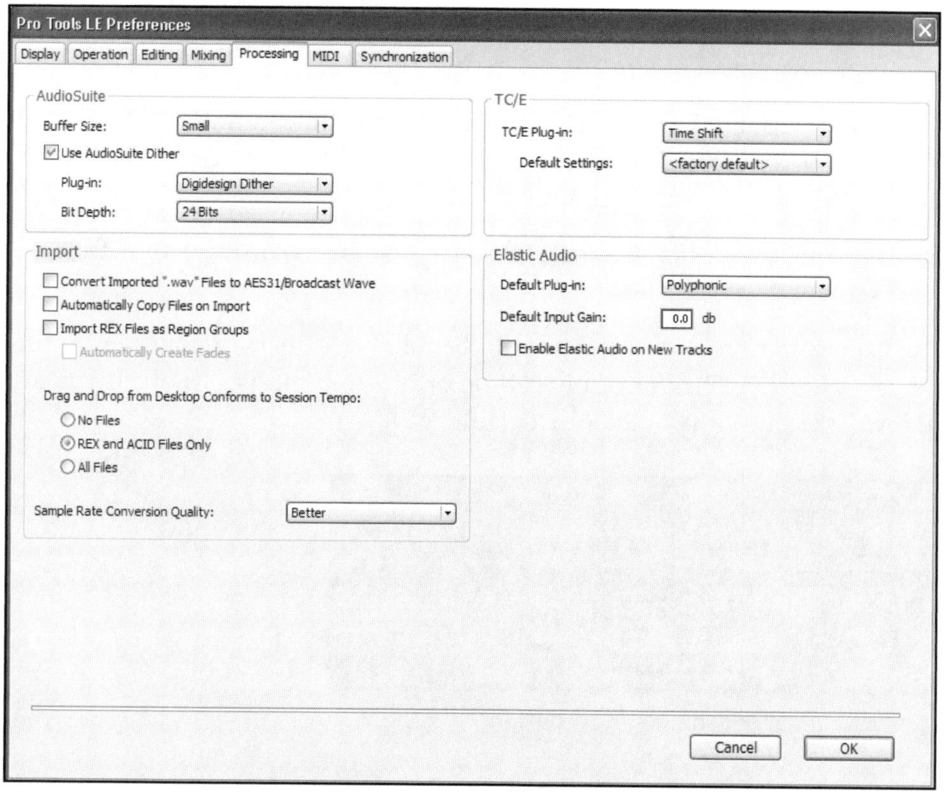

Figure 7.16   Processing preferences.

- **Current Timecode Position:** This is available only if you have the DV Toolkit 2 installed in Pro Tools LE. Use this option to redefine the session's starting time code position.

- **MIDI:** This provides lots of MIDI options, which I cover in Chapter 11.

Helpful Tips

I wanted to end with a section of helpful tips and hints, to review some things to help you, point out some things that might trip you up, and talk a little about troubleshooting. This is that section.

RTMs: That's right. Read the manuals. The purpose of this book is not to replace or supercede the manuals or any other documentation Digidesign or M-Audio gives you. Read it all. You can learn and benefit from it. My goal here is to provide value-added information that comes from my experience, wisdom, talent, and general coolness. I hope to provide insight and perspective, but can't go into the same depth as

Digidesign's 981-page *Pro Tools Reference Guide*. Nor can I compete with the hardware-specific detail of the 181-page *Getting Started 003 & 003 Rack*.

There's More than One Manual: Digidesign separates the documentation into hardware-specific *Basics* and *Getting Started* guides, Pro Tools (LE or M-Powered) reference docs, plug-in guides, keyboard shortcuts, and more.

Digital I/O: Make sure to specify a master clock if you are recording input from an external digital source.

Countoff: The Countoff button itself shows you the number of bars of countoff, in this case, two bars (see Figure 7.17). Turn Countoff on or off from the Transport. If you are running Windows, the button is hidden by default.

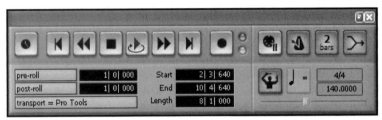

Figure 7.17 Don't forget about the Countoff button.

Mac/Win: Absolutely no difference exists between Windows and Macintosh platforms in terms of working with specific audio hardware. An Mbox 2 is still an Mbox 2.

Trashing Preferences: A pretty good place to start troubleshooting. Also, delete the Digidesign Databases folders on all hard disk drives. Mac users can visit http://web.mac .com/jcdeshaies/DeleteProToolsPrefs/Bienvenue.html and download a great little OS X utility for trashing preferences.

Wide Fader Meters: This is cool, but relatively obscure and hidden. Windows users press and hold Ctrl+Start+Alt and click on a track's fader(s) in the Mix or Edit windows to make them wider and easier to see. Mac users press Command+Option+Ctrl and click. If you're in "Narrow Mix" mode, the effect is only observable on mono tracks.

Room Acoustics: The ideal control room controls reflections to produce the best listening environment. Generally speaking, you should have a dead end behind and beside the monitors that absorbs sound and a live end behind you with tightly controlled reverberation. You should hear the direct sound from the monitors most clearly, augmented by limited room reverberation. That's why controlling reflections is so important and why room acoustics are such a part of this gig. Rooms that reverberate too much (because of their surface properties and to some degree shape and dimensions) can fool you into making changes to account for that "false data" and ruin what otherwise might have been a fine mix. Mix position is important relative to the walls in the room because the walls (and floor, ceiling, plus all the corners) are the main reflectors. No room is perfect, but you will find a range of good spots and bad spots in every room. In a rectangular room, try sitting facing a shorter wall, with the monitors along that wall, but spaced out from it if possible. You can be near the center of the room length-wise (it depends), but definitely in the middle side-to-side. In other words, you should have the same space on your left and right, but not necessarily front to back. You should be closer to the wall with the monitors and farther away from the wall behind you, but the exact distance depends on the actual size of the room. Orient the monitors so they point directly at your head. You can find a lot of formulas and calculations for determining the exact sweet spot, but they vary from one degree to another, so I won't publish them here. If you're interested, you can find a lot of information in books on acoustics or online.

Isolation versus Reverberation: Isolate your studio to prevent outside sounds from coming inside and affecting your recording or mixing and to protect your neighbors from your loud and obnoxious music. Bass frequencies are the hardest to stop, and in general require construction techniques to reduce or eliminate. Stopping reverberation has to do with keeping the sound that you generate in your studio from bouncing around on all the walls and creating a false "sonic picture" of what you're doing. Use bass traps, absorption panels, foam, diffusers, finishing materials, curtains, carpet, and other material to control reflections, targeted broadly or at very specific frequencies. Use gobos and isolation booths to channel or block direct sound paths.

Troubleshooting: You're going to have trouble. No matter how good you are or how good the gear is, you're going to run into situations that test you and your troubleshooting skills. It helps to have some.

Practice: This stuff takes practice.

Dig Deep: Treat Pro Tools like an instrument you are learning to play. Don't avoid the harder parts. Push yourself and dig deep. Overcome!

Join the Community: Knowing and being friends with other people who are going through what you're going through can help you over the hump. You might be the source of knowledge or inspiration for someone else. A great place to start is the Digidesign User Conference at duc.digidesign.com.

System Usage and Elastic Audio: If you are looking at how much work your system is doing in the System Usage window, see activity in the CPU (Elastic) bar, but know you don't have any Elastic tracks and are confused, join the club. This is a known issue in Pro Tools 7.4.

Isolate the Problem: This is a pillar of troubleshooting. If you can't isolate the problem, it might be anything. Check cables, instruments, gear, the computer, settings, preferences, and ask around. Try to work from one end of the signal chain to the other.

Nudging Problems: When nudging, if you're pressing your keys and nothing is happening, check the track to make sure you are looking at the waveform, blocks, or another view that is not an automation or controller view (which will have an automation line on it). If you're looking at volume automation, for example, nudging will not move the selected region.

Windows XP Prefs: These are located in the C:\Documents and Settings\[user name] \Application Data\Digidesign folder.

Windows Vista Prefs: These are located in the C:\Users\[user name]\AppData\Roaming \Digidesign folder. I think.

Mac Prefs: These are located in MacHD:User:[user name]:Library:Preferences.

8 Using Pro Tools

I do a lot of describing in this chapter. It's unavoidable. I'm a firm believer that if you know your way around the Pro Tools interface you can concentrate on making music, not working the program. Use this aspect of the chapter to familiarize yourself with the Pro Tools interface now and to serve as a quick reference later. I have taken great pains to try and keep this practical as well. I've included lots of little tips and techniques as I describe things, and I have created additional tip sections to quickly (and succinctly) spell out how to do many things.

The Interface

First, I want to take a good look at the entire Pro Tools interface (Figure 8.1). This is your office, your Pro Tools control room. You must be able to find your way around. If you have a good handle on what everything is and where things are, you can concentrate on recording, editing, mixing, and producing your music instead of constantly looking for things. You find a lot of duplication in Pro Tools. So, you can have your favorite way of working with things that might be different than someone else's.

Work, Don't Look I'm being serious when I tell you how important it is to know the Pro Tools interface. It's what connects you to your music. It enables you to pursue your dreams and accomplish your goals. It's like having the most tricked-out garage and best tools in town. Time for some "rah-rahs." You are going to get the most out of your garage and know where every tool is and what it does. You'll learn to spend your time working and not looking for things. You're going to be able to do it without thinking about it.

Pro Tools Interface Elements

Broadly speaking, you need to grasp several important elements in the program:

- **Edit window:** The Edit window is one of two main windows in Pro Tools. The window's paradigm revolves around the timeline, which displays each track from

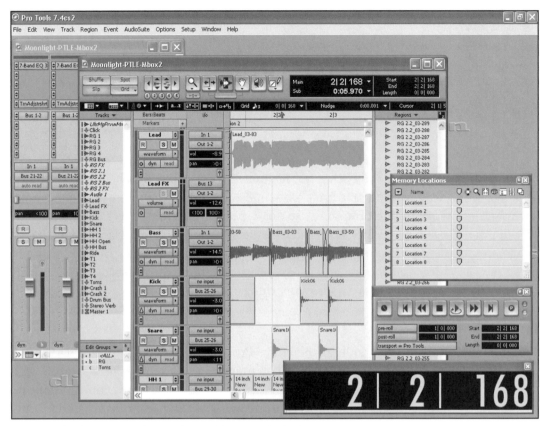

Figure 8.1 The Pro Tools interface with several windows open.

left to right and shows you the audio or automation. Don't let the name keep you from using this window for other tasks (tracking, mixing, and so on) as you can control just about everything you need to from here. Many people use this window as their main "control center."

- **Mix window:** The Mix window looks and functions a lot like a traditional mixing console or control surface. The tracks are arranged vertically, and you have no timeline. This is my favorite place to work. I love it because it makes you listen to what you're doing. Some things, however, you cannot do in the Mix window, such as dragging and dropping regions, changing tempo, and other Edit window specialties.

- **Menus:** The menus are a very important part of Pro Tools. Don't neglect them. They serve as your entry into controlling the application, as opposed to working with your audio. I'm not going to specifically cover menus. Look through them and get to know them.

- **Floating windows:** Floating windows are task-specific windows and range in type from the Transport to the Color Palette.

- **Lists (Track, Group, Region):** Lists hang out on both sides of the Edit window and on one side of the Mix window. They show all the tracks in your session, whether visible or hidden, your groups, and audio or MIDI regions.

- **Browsers:** Browsers access the DigiBase database and allow you to perform many file (and disk) management functions.

- **Tools:** Six tools are at the heart of editing in Pro Tools. Learn them. Love them. Know them. Take them out to lunch and woo them. Send them flowers on Valentine's Day. Seriously. They are located to the left of the Edit window Counters and are square buttons with rounded corners. They are the Zoomer tool, Trim tool, Selector tool, Grabber tool, Scrubber tool, and Pencil tool.

- **Buttons and controls:** Buttons and controls are literally all over the place. Grab a fader. It's a control. Turn a pan pot (potentiometer). It's a control. Click Solo. Gotcha. That's a button.

- **Displays:** Displays show you important information, like a track's volume level or where you are along the timeline. Most of the time, displays are green text on a black background. You can click on many displays and change or enter new data. Try it.

I cover the main features of the Edit and Mix window as well as some of the more important other interface elements shortly.

I also want you to think of the Pro Tools interface along the following lines (which are closely tied to analog recording tools and techniques, with the uniquely digital elements that are an inseparable part of Pro Tools):

- **Program:** In other words, the Pro Tools interface elements that enable you to control or work in Pro Tools. These quite often have nothing to do with any particular project. Often, the challenge of using Pro Tools comes down to finding a way you like to work and how to view things, creating your own workspace, and managing how Pro Tools works.

- **Timeline:** The timeline is one of the most significant advances that digital music production gives you. You can look backwards and forwards in time as you edit, arrange, automate, compose MIDI (there is a built-in sequencer in the timeline), and so forth, and all the while know exactly where you are *to the sample*. One word of warning: With this tremendous power comes great danger. The more you look at something instead of listen to it, the more likely you are to settle for what your eyes can do with audio instead of your ears.

- **Tracks:** Tracks are the meat and potatoes of your sessions. It's all about the tracks. Everything is meant to serve them. The Edit window, timeline, Mix window—they all revolve around displaying and giving you the tools to control the tracks. As such, things like volume faders are consistently available in both main windows and in other ways. If you're thinking of tracks, no matter where you are, you should be able to control them.

- **Transport:** The Transport allows you to play; record; rewind; fast forward; loop playback; loop record; enable countoff, pre-roll, and post-roll; and so forth. This is your tape machine. Everything that has to do with the above is associated with the Transport.

- **"Outboard gear":** By that I mean plug-ins, essentially. Traditional studios have a plethora of outboard gear (leaving aside built-in console electronic equalization [EQ] and dynamics processing) to process or affect a track's audio. Pro Tools gives you AudioSuite and Real-Time AudioSuite (RTAS) plug-ins to perform the same tasks. RTAS plug-ins are your inserts. So, instead of grabbing a patch cord and inserting a compressor into the signal flow of track 3 on an analog console, you would insert compressor (or dynamics) plug-in into one of the five inserts available to track 3 in Pro Tools. Sends and returns are set up differently, with the point being to send signal to an insert from many tracks and return it.

Mac versus Win I need to point out the minor differences here between the Mac and Windows interfaces. Most differences come down to how each operating system does things. For example, the window controls on Windows machines are in the top-right corner of a window and the name that is in the Title bar is left-aligned. Macs have the controls at the top-left corner of the window (those cute colored buttons) and center the text in the Title bar. The window controls in the lower-right appear to be the same. None of this makes a huge difference, aside from irking an author who is trying to be as inclusive as possible.

Interface Tips

Switch between Edit and Mix windows: Use the Window menu or, my favorite, press Ctrl+Equal (Windows) or Command+Equal (Mac).

Save or recall specific windows layouts: Select the Window>Configurations menu and look for the appropriate submenu.

Nothing Visible?   Did you know that after you open (or create) a session you can close all its windows and be looking at an empty Pro Tools workspace, and the project is still open? It doesn't close unless you select the File>Close Session menu or try to open a different session.

The Edit Window

The Edit window is where you do a lot of work in Pro Tools. That work centers around the timeline, which takes up most of the window's space. What's the big deal about the timeline? It lets you manage and manipulate audio regions on all tracks anywhere in the song (or piece, if it's not music). As much as I love the Mix window, it is more limited than the Edit window. You can put fades on regions; crossfade between regions; draw automation; mute regions as opposed to tracks; nudge; compose MIDI; change tempo, meter, key, and so forth from the Edit window. Get the picture?

Edit Window Layout

Broadly speaking, here is how the Edit window (Figure 8.2) is organized and a brief description of each element.

- **Window controls:** The Edit window can be resized and dragged around the Pro Tools workspace. You can even close it without closing the session. The Edit window has the session name in its Title bar (top left for Windows, centered for Macs), and window controls on the top (top-left for Macs) and lower-right. If the session's contents (number of tracks and the length of the session) can't fit into the window, you see scrollbars. Most people work with this window maximized, and if you have dual monitors, you can put this and the Mix window on separate screens.

- **Tools:** The top of the Edit window contains several critically important buttons and tools. They are (from left to right) the four edit mode buttons (Shuffle, Spot, Slip, and Grid); the zoom buttons; the six main editing tools (Zoomer, Trim, Selector, Grabber, Scrubber, and Pencil); the Counter display; and the Transport controls.

- **Edit window bar:** This black bar, just below the top tool area, has several selectors and indicators whose functionality ranges from changing the view to modifying nudge values.

- **Tracks list:** This area (if it's not visible, click the right-facing double arrows in the bottom-left corner of the Edit window) lists all the tracks in the current session and allows you to show, hide, and sort tracks, show certain tracks, and activate or

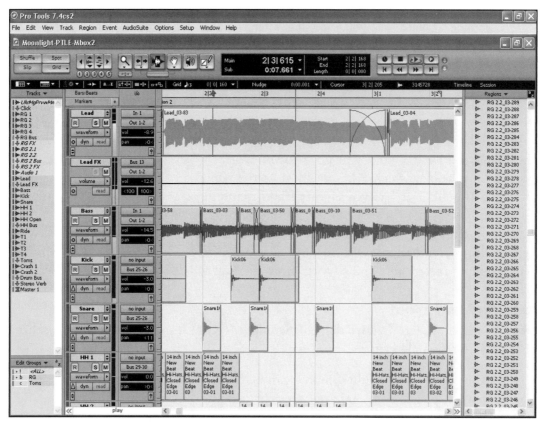

Figure 8.2 The Edit window.

deactivate any track. You can increase the width of this entire area by dragging the vertical bar that separates it from the main part of the Edit window.

- **Edit Groups list:** This area is below the Tracks list and contains information about your groups. If you haven't created any, you still have the <ALL> group. Here's where you can enable, disable, and manage all your groups. The Edit Groups list is shown or hidden with the Tracks list by the same double-arrow.

- **Regions list:** The Regions list is much like the Tracks and Edit Groups lists in that you can show or hide it using double arrows on the bottom-right side of the Edit window. Manage regions in your session from this list: you can do a lot of things, ranging from dragging regions to a track to deleting them from your hard disk.

- **Timebase and Rulers:** These are just below the Edit window bar. This area contains rulers that show you where you are in the timeline of a session based on beats, samples, time, and so forth, as well as Conductor rulers, which show the tempo, meter, key, and markers. This isn't just pretty to look at. You can change settings (and selections or loop points) here. You can turn individual rulers on and off.

- **Tracks**: Finally, the main portion of the Edit window is devoted to displaying the tracks (those that aren't hidden) in your session. From left to right, you see the track's color, its name (which is editable), and several readouts and controls. This area can have quite a bit of information, which you can customize by showing or hiding things you do or don't want to see (I/O and comments, for example). Turn off things to reclaim space. Next to the track information and controls, the track itself is shown along the timeline. You see regions of audio, MIDI, and automation all along the timeline. You can move tracks up or down in your session, resize them vertically, zoom in, change the title color, hide or deactivate them, and a whole host of other things.

Edit Window Tips

View or turn off specific Edit window elements: Use the View menu. Some of these items apply to the Mix window, but many (especially those in the View>Edit menu) apply to the Edit window.

Save space: Turn off the lists and various track components (I/O, inserts, sends, and so on) and turn off one or all of the rulers.

Modes and Tools

Modes and tools are the bread and butter (you would think I eat a lot of bread and butter as many times as I say that, but I don't) of editing audio within Pro Tools. Modes control how the timeline works, and tools are some of the specific actions you take (or they define the cursor that allows you to take a certain action). You are always in one mode or another and have a tool selected.

- **Shuffle mode (F1)**: This mode squishes audio regions next to each other, not allowing any empty space between them. The first region always snaps to the beginning of the session. Use Ctrl+click (Win) or Command+click (Mac) when not in Shuffle mode to lock yourself out of it. Yes, that seems odd, but if you're working away and don't realize you accidentally switched over to Shuffle mode, it can ruin a session. This also affects regions you trim with the Trim tool.

- **Slip mode (F2)**: This is the freeform placement mode. You have no restrictions here.

- **Spot mode (F3)**: When you select a region with the Grabber tool in Spot mode, you place the region by entering new values in the Spot dialog (Figure 8.3). Spot also works when selecting MIDI notes with the Grabber. Spot also affects the use of the Trim tool.

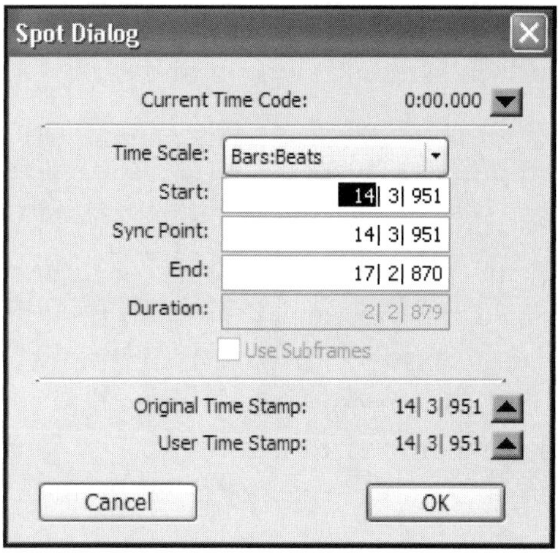

Spot Dialog

Current Time Code:	0:00.000 ▼
Time Scale:	Bars:Beats ▾
Start:	**14**| 3| 951
Sync Point:	14| 3| 951
End:	17| 2| 870
Duration:	2| 2| 879
☐ Use Subframes	
Original Time Stamp:	14| 3| 951 ▲
User Time Stamp:	14| 3| 951 ▲

Cancel   OK

Figure 8.3   Enter specific values in the Spot dialog box.

■ **Grid mode (F4):** This mode comes in two flavors: Absolute and Relative. Click the Grid button and hold your mouse button down for a second to access the submenu and choose between them (or hit the keyboard shortcut again to cycle the submodes). Absolute Grid mode establishes a grid and shows it onscreen. You can't select an area of the timeline or place or nudge any region, MIDI note, or automation point outside of this (configurable) grid. Locate and change grid settings with the Grid Value Indicator and Grid Pop-up on the Edit window bar. This is exceptionally helpful when you're trying to keep things arranged according to measures and beats or in a certain timing. Relative Grid mode is the same in terms of making selections with the Selector tool (it happens on the grid), but you can grab a region that isn't on a grid line and nudge or move it by the relative grid amount. In other words, if you have a grid of one bar, you're in Relative Grid mode, and if you select a region (or MIDI note) that begins in between bars, you can move it one bar in either direction, ignoring the fact that it won't snap to a grid line. That's the point. Absolute Grid mode snaps everything to a grid line, whether it starts on one or not. If you click on a ruler name (Min:Secs, for example), the box with the ruler name becomes highlighted, and you switch to that grid. If that's what you're on, it turns the grid lines on or off.

■ **Zoom section:** The Zoom section has four zoom buttons and five preset buttons underneath. The left- and right-facing arrows on the ends zoom the Edit window out (left arrow) and in (right arrow) horizontally. The middle buttons affect audio and MIDI tracks, respectively, only they zoom in vertically. This has nothing to do with track height, so be careful here. Zooming vertically makes the waveform (if audio)

or note size (if MIDI) larger, given the same track height. The default behavior
here is to zoom all tracks of the appropriate type in and out at the same time. You
can selectively zoom vertically if you have the Zoomer tool selected, hold the Start
(Windows) or Control (Mac) key down, and drag your mouse up or down over the
track you want to affect. Finally, you can quickly get to five preset zoom levels from
the numbered buttons on the bottom part of the Zoom section. You can even save
your own zoom presets. Get your zoom on; then press and hold the number you
want to save it as and select Save Zoom Preset.

Zooming   You seem to have a million and one ways to zoom in and out, save
presets, toggle back and forth between different zoom levels, and so on and so
on. I'm covering as many as I can without making this a chapter on Zooming.

- **Zoomer tool (F5):** This is a tool that zooms horizontally in. Select it and drag a box
  around the area you want to zoom in on. Easy. Zoom out by selecting the Zoomer
  and holding Alt (Windows) or Option (Mac) down while clicking. Selecting the
  Single Zoom tool returns you to the tool you were just using. Double-clicking the
  Zoomer zooms all the way out and views your entire session (horizontally). You can
  toggle zooms by pressing the Zoom Toggle button underneath the Zoomer. This
  toggles between a predefined zoom state and the current zoom, depending on the
  preferences you have set in the Setup>Preferences menu under the Editing tab.

- **Trim tool (F6):** This tool trims regions, either by shortening them or, oddly enough,
  if they have been trimmed already, by expanding them up to their original size.
  Underneath the normal Trim tool, you have the Time Compression/Expander (TCE)
  and Loop Trimmer tool. The TCE tool expands or contracts a region to where you
  drag it, and the Loop Trimmer tool creates and trims loops.

- **Selection tool (F7):** This selects an area of the timeline or an area within one or
  more tracks. Click and drag to make the selection. If you drag up or down, you can
  select audio from any number of tracks. Double-click a region to select it. This is
  also how you place the cursor in the timeline at a certain point. This is about
  the only "safe" tool. You can't change anything with it. All you can do is select time
  or regions.

- **Grabber tool (F8):** The Grabber tool selects regions and inputs automation points
  (like the Pencil tool, but different). Grab regions with a single-click and drag them
  around. You can even drag them to different tracks. You can select additional
  regions by holding down Shift and clicking on regions in the same or adjacent tracks.

You have a couple different types of Grab tools underneath the default (which is called the Time Grabber): the Separation Grabber and the Object Grabber. The Separation Grabber is cool. Normally, you can move only entire regions. With the Separation Grabber, you can select a portion of a region with the Selection tool, then switch to the Separation Grabber, and move just what you've selected. The Object Grabber allows you to select multiple regions that aren't connected to each other. You have to hold Shift down, but it works.

■ **Smart tool (F6+F7 or F7+F8):** The Smart tool is three-in-one. Click the bar underneath the Trim, Selection, and Grabber tools, and you have the Smart tool. Depending on what part of a track or region you are hovering the cursor over, you see the cursor change to reflect what tool you can use. Some people swear by the Smart tool, but I've never really gotten into it, with the exception of the fade/cross-fading capability.

■ **Scrubber tool (F9):** Use the Scrubber tool to listen to two tracks of audio (not MIDI) play back as you move your mouse back and forth (or just back, or just forth). Click and hold the mouse button down as you move the cursor. You hear the track (or tracks if you click on the border between them) played back at a slow speed, which is a great way to see if sound effects match video. If you want to hear faster-than-normal playback, press Alt (Windows) or Option (Mac) as you click (you can let the key go after it starts). This is called Scrub/Shuttle, or just Shuttle, mode.

■ **Pencil tool (F10):** The Pencil tool does a lot. Normally, you use it to draw tempo changes, MIDI notes and other data, and automation. However, you can also use it to alter the waveforms of your audio if you are zoomed in to the sample level (you see the audio as a line, not a waveform).

Modes and Tools Tips

Switch between tools and mode: Use the handy keyboard shortcut or click the button.

Cycle through sub-buttons or modes (in the case of Grid): Press the same keyboard shortcut again or press and hold any tool or mode button that has an arrow to access the tools "beneath" it.

Make a selection of time or audio: Use the Selection tool.

Select a region: Use the Grabber or double-click a region with the Selection tool.

Zoom in or out: You have many ways to do this. Use the Zoom buttons or the Zoomer. Configure presets and save zoom toggle states. Go crazy!

Select a precise region start time: Use Spot mode.

Quickly set the cursor in the timeline: Use the Selection tool and click where you want to start.

Counters and Indicators

The counters and indicators (Figure 8.4) are both informational and useful. Their primary purpose is to show you where you are in your session and give you an indication of what you have selected.

Figure 8.4   Edit window counters and indicators.

- **Main counter:** This is where the Insertion point is on the timeline. It can be measured in a variety of ways. Click the down arrow to change between them. Click in the counter to enter new values to move the Insertion point.

- **Sub counter:** This is the same thing, only smaller. So, you can look at your position in a couple of different ways.

- **Start selection:** This is the beginning of a selection, according to the scale of the Main counter. If nothing is selected, this displays the location of the Insertion point. Click to enter new values.

Dragging   Click+hold and drag your mouse up or down in any of the selection or MIDI counters/indicators to change its value. This is an interesting way of "scrubbing" your way to where you want to go.

- **End selection:** This is the end of a selection, according to the scale of the Main counter. If nothing is selected, this displays the location of the Insertion point. Click to enter new values.

- **Selection length:** This is the computed length of your selection, according to the scale of the Main counter.

- **MIDI note pitch:** This is the pitch of the currently selected MIDI note. This area is hidden unless you have a MIDI note selected.

- **MIDI note attack:** This is the attack velocity of the currently selected MIDI note. This area is hidden unless you have a MIDI note selected.

- **MIDI note release:** This is the release velocity of the currently selected MIDI note. This area is hidden unless you have a MIDI note selected.

Edit Window Transport Controls

The Edit window has its own small group of Transport controls (Figure 8.5), which you can turn off from the View>Edit Window>Transport menu. These are handy if for no other reasons than that they show you what play or record mode you're in and are out of the way. Even if you don't click on them, I think they're useful.

Figure 8.5 Edit window Transport controls.

- **Online:** This control gets Pro Tools online and ready if playback and recording are being triggered externally.

- **Stop:** This stops playback or recording. I use the spacebar.

- **Play:** This starts playback. I use the spacebar. Here's a weird twist for you. When dealing with tape, the Play button (on whatever tape transport you're dealing with) starts the transport moving, so you still have to hit Play when you want to record. That holds over to the world of Pro Tools. Right-click the Play button for more options.

- **Record:** This puts the transport in Record mode. This does not start "tape rolling." All it does is get things ready. You still have to press Play to begin recording. You don't have to press the buttons at the same time. Hit Record and then wait to hit Play when you're ready. I bypass all the finger-fumbling and use the number 3 on my numeric keypad. Right-click for more options.

- **Return to Zero:** This returns the Transport to the very beginning. I use the keyboard Enter button (not the one on the numeric keypad) for this (Macs should use Return).

- **Rewind:** This rewinds a small amount. The increment is determined by the main time scale format, so you could rewind by the second, frame, bar, or foot.

- **Fast Forward:** This control works the same way as Rewind only in a forward direction.

- **Go to End:** This goes to the end of the session, which is the end of your last region or a brief time past your last automation point.

- **Record Enable Monitor indicator:** This lights up red if you have an armed track.

- **Input Monitor indicator:** This lights up green if Input Only monitoring is enabled and is grayed out if you are in Auto Input monitoring mode. If you've used Pro Tools HD before, you should know that you cannot switch monitoring modes on a track-by-track basis. One size fits all in LE.

Monitoring Modes   If you're wondering what Input Only and Auto Input mean, here's the answer. Pro Tools (indeed, any digital audio workstation [DAW] or analog recording setup) can "play" audio from one of two sources: the Transport (what's already been recorded) and/or the active inputs (armed tracks).

These modes determine where Pro Tools pulls the signal from with regards to armed tracks.

Input Only directs the Transport to play only what it is receiving from the active inputs and ignore (for armed tracks only) anything already recorded, regardless of whether the Transport is stopped or in Play or Record. Tracks that are not armed play normally.

Auto Input, on the other hand, makes it situation-dependent. If the Transport is stopped, you hear input because hearing playback is impossible. If it's in Play, you hear existing material (if any) but no external input from the armed track(s). If it's in Record, you hear input. This mode is very useful, especially for punch-ins, which are situations where you are playing back material and quickly "punch in" and re-record material (sometimes just one note). This way you hear what exists up to the point where you punch in, then hear the input as you record it.

No matter what mode you're in, if you have armed tracks and record, you hear input, not playback.

Edit Window Transport Tips

Show more buttons: You can't see all the Transport controls on this handy "mini" transport. You have to open the Transport window separately.

Turn the handy transport off: Select View>Edit Window>Transport.

Access more play or record options: Right-click the Play and Record buttons for more options.

Edit Window Bar

Don't let its size fool you; this tiny little guy (Figure 8.6) is chock full of goodness. It has handy buttons that change views, and grid and nudge values, to mention a few. I use it all the time.

Figure 8.6 The Edit window bar.

- **View Selector:** You configure the Edit window view with this selector. Turn things on or off. It's very handy to be able to customize the view and reclaim screen space.

- **Ruler View Selector:** With this you customize which rulers are visible.

- **Linearity Display Mode:** I'm tempted to say there's a rip in the fabric of the space-time continuum and you have to run a Level 3 diagnostic and implement Attack Plan Delta. But I think *Star Trek: The Next Generation* has been over long enough that many of you won't get that. Simply put, you can change the timeline display scale between samples and ticks here. And you find a big difference between the two. If you're working with sample-based material (normal audio), keep it on Sample. If you're using Elastic Audio, lots of MIDI, and in general, tick-based material, switch to ticks. Try this on for size. Open a session and note the tempo at measure 1. It doesn't matter what it is. Go to measure 3 and set a new tempo (use the counter to set the new measure or click in the timeline with the Selection tool and then click the plus symbol beside the Temp ruler and enter the new value). If you are in Linear Sample Display, the measures should look different. Now, switch to Linear Tick Display. They change to the same size.

Samples and Ticks   Samples are beat-independent. They are time-based in that at a given sample rate (say 48 kHz), it takes a certain amount of time to play a sample. Put another way, you can play 48,000 samples in one second at that rate, regardless of the song's tempo. Changing the tempo does nothing to sample-based audio other than change the timeline around it.

Tick-based material is entirely beat-dependent and has nothing to do with time. If a note is scheduled to be played on the 320th beat (this can be MIDI, most obviously, or beatmapped audio), it matters not whether the tempo of a song is 120 bpm or 90 bpm. When you change the tempo, tick-based material moves to the correct beat in the song, no matter what the time is.

- **Tab to Transients:** Click this to turn the Tab key into a transient-finding wonder. When activated, choose the Selector tool and click in an audio track (make sure you're viewing waveforms). When you press Tab, the Insertion point jumps to just before the next transient peak. The default behavior of the Tab key is to go to the next region boundary and any Warp markers. When you're working with Elastic Audio and are in Warp view, this mode tabs you to all event and Warp markers in a region.

- **Commands Keyboard Focus:** This toggle activates keyboard focus to the Edit window. Which window has focus determines what happens when you use certain keyboard shortcuts (the Groups and Region Lists have a small a...z button/indicator in the top-right corner of their windows that tells you whether they have focus or not).

- **Link Timeline and Edit Selection:** When timelines and edit selection are linked (click to do that), whether you make a selection in the timeline (the rulers) or within a track (the edit selection), the corresponding selection is made in both. When unlinked, you can make a selection along the timeline that is independent of what you select in the main window.

- **Link Track and Edit Selection:** This is the same concept as linking the timeline to the edit selection, but in this case you are dealing with tracks. When the track and edit selection are linked, you can't select anything without also selecting the track. When they are unlinked, you can make a selection in the Edit window and then independently select another track.

- **Mirrored MIDI Editing:** This applies all MIDI edits to regions of the same name— or not, should you turn this off.

- **Grid Value indicator and pop-up:** This lets you know at a glance what the grid is set at, and if you click the pop-up, you can change it.

- **Nudge Value indicator and pop-up:** This lets you know at a glance what the current nudge value is, and if you click the pop-up, you can change it.

- **Cursor Location indicator:** This is the current location of the cursor in the Edit window, measured using the same scale as the Main counter. This is where you're moving your mouse, not where the playback or edit cursor is.

- **Cursor Location Value indicator:** This is the value pertaining to whatever your mouse (cursor) is hovering over which depends on what the track is displaying (waveforms, automation, and so on). Audio tracks in waveform and block display indicate volume as a product of bit depth, whereas other displays display different things. If you're editing MIDI, you might see the MIDI note, attack velocity, or other MIDI parameters.

8388608?   A bit depth of 24 equates to 16,777,215 possible values to measure signal strength, which must be divided by 2 (rounded up) because waveforms have positive and negative amplitudes, which means each side of the waveform display measures from 0–8,388,608 levels. Recording at 16 bits changes this to 32,768 levels on each side (65,535 divided by 2, rounded up). Anyone want to argue whether 16 bits is just as good as 24 bits? Not counting noise floor considerations, I'll take the precision of 16,777,215 levels of volume control over 65,535 any day. Even if you can't access these levels with faders, plug-ins do far less rounding and fudging to calculate their true effects.

- **Timeline Data Online Status indicator:** This gives you an indication (by its green color) that all the files in your track's playlists are available. If it's red, something is offline, being processed, or otherwise unavailable.

- **Session Data Online Status indicator:** This lets you know if all the audio and fade files in your session are locked and loaded. If this indicator is red, something is offline, being processed, or can't be found.

Rulers

The ruler area (Figure 8.7) can be a confusing mess of different parameters. Don't let that keep you from using it. You can customize the rulers to show the ones you want or hide the ones you don't want to use, and the ruler area also contains very important tempo information. This is critical when using a click track.

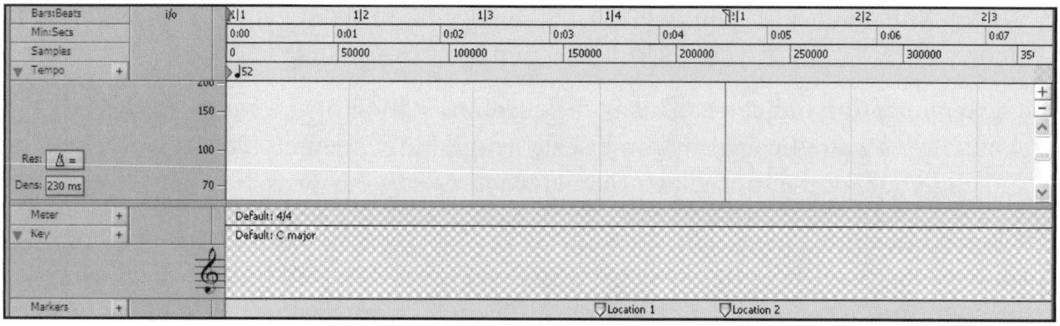

Figure 8.7 All the Pro Tools rulers.

- **Bars:Beats:** This shows a ruler that displays the timeline in bars and beats.

- **Min:Secs:** This shows a ruler that displays the timeline in minutes and seconds.

- **Samples:** This shows a ruler that displays the timeline in samples.

- **Tempo:** This shows a tempo ruler, which displays the session's opening tempo in beats per minute and any changes. Click the plus symbol to add a new tempo or change one at a given location. Double-click a tempo marker (with any tool) to change it.

- **Tempo Editor:** Use the Pencil tool to draw very detailed and intricate tempo changes. You can change the resolution and density of tempo changes. Use the Grabber to click and move points. Double-click with the Grabber to edit.

- **Meter:** This shows the current time meter, which defaults to 4/4. Add or change meter as you would tempo.

- **Key:** This shows the current key signature.

- **Key Signature Staff:** This shows the key signature using musical staff notation.

- **Markers:** This shows markers along the timeline. You can edit, rename, delete, and reposition markers along the timeline as well.

Ruler Tips

Turn rulers on or off: Use any of the Views menus.

Reorder rulers: Click and drag them up or down.

Switch the Main counter scale: Click on the ruler title that has the scale you want to load into the Main counter. This applies only to the Bars:Beats, Min:Sec, or Samples rulers.

Create new data points on a ruler: Click the plus sign.

Change or edit existing data points on a ruler: Double-click the symbol (different rulers display different symbols so you can tell them apart). If you don't see any symbols on a ruler, that means you haven't changed or added anything.

Track Controls

Track controls (Figure 8.8) are where you manage your tracks in Pro Tools. Each track has its own control, and the specific controls might vary slightly, depending on whether the track is audio, MIDI, an Instrument, Aux Input, or Master Fader.

Some of the controls (those towards the end) might not be visible. Turn them on or off from the View>Edit Window menu. From left to right, each track has several control areas.

Figure 8.8   Edit window track controls.

- **Track Controls:** This section has a lot of important track controls that identify and control the way a track is displayed and heard. This is also where you arm a track for recording.

- **Comments (not shown):** Click to enter comments, such as the preamp level, artist, or anything else that might be important to remember.

- **Instrument (not shown):** This has instrument controls for Instrument tracks.

- **Inserts:** This shows the plug-ins inserted into the track's signal flow. It works like the Mix window.

- **Sends (A–E):** Shows the A–E sends. This works like the Mix window.

- **Sends (F–J)(not shown):** Shows the F–J sends. This works like the Mix window.

- **I/O:** This shows (and allows you to choose and change) signal input and output, as well as volume and panning.

- **Real-Time Properties (not shown):** This shows real-time properties on MIDI and Instrument tracks that you can change on the fly. These settings apply to tracks, not individual regions.

More specifically, the controls in the basic control area are as follows:

- **Color Bar:** This enables you to color-code tracks for whatever purpose you design. You can set color by function, type, instrument, or mood. Double-click to set. Select multiple tracks and double-click to set them all at once.

- **Name and Number:** This is the track name and, if shown, number.

- **Playlist:** This allows you to select (or create) different playlists for each track. This is a great way to store multiple takes and choose which one (or parts) you like later (a process called "comping").

- **Record Enable:** This arms a track for recording. It has to have a valid input.

- **Solo:** This solos a track so that all the other tracks (except any other tracks that are soloed) are muted.

- **Mute:** This mutes a track, which is not the same thing as making the track inactive. If you want to free up system resources, inactivate a track.

Solo, Mute, and Group By default, when you solo or mute a track, all other tracks that are a part of that active group are soloed or muted at the same time.

- **Track View:** This switches between different ways of viewing the track, such as block or waveform. This is also where you access specific automation views, such as volume and panning.

- **Track Height:** This changes the track height to one of several preset heights.

- **Timebase:** This control changes between sample and tick-based.

- **Voice:** This allows you to turn dynamic voice allocation off for audio tracks (this frees up voices if you have a lot of tracks).

- **Automation Mode:** This changes automation modes. The options are off (self-explanatory), read (reads automation off the track), touch (writes automation if you touch a control; otherwise reads it), latch (similar to touch, only after you start writing, you must stop playback to stop writing automation), and write (write only, a good way to erase existing automation).

- **Elastic Audio plug-in:** This allows you to select from one of several Elastic Audio plug-ins.

- **Level Meter:** This shows the playback level of the current track, or input if record enabled.

The following I/O controls warrant more discussion:

- **Input path:** Click to select an input path that has a signal you want to record. If you are mixing, you are not choosing input paths from your hardware, but you are probably using busses (hence, you need to choose them as an input).

- **Output path:** Click to choose an output path (interface or bus) for the track's signal.

- **Volume:** This is pretty self-explanatory. Click to drag to a new position. Ctrl+Click (Windows), Command+Click (Mac) to change the readout from volume to peak level or delay.

- **Pan:** This is also self-explanatory. However, mono tracks pan from left to right whereas stereo tracks have two pan controls that set each channel's (left and right) pan independently.

- **Output window:** Click to open a larger (and more console-like) window where you can push a fader, turn pan knobs, and do a few other things.

Edit Window Track Controls Tips

Changing track height: Click the Track Height selector, which is just under the Mute button. Select a new height. Alternatively, you can move your mouse to the bottom edge of the track (in the controls area). The cursor changes to the shape of arrows pointing up and down with a bar in the middle. Click and drag the track border down to enlarge or up to shrink.

Check for automation: Automation can "hide" from you if you don't check for it. If you think something weird is happening (the fader jumps back when you try and set it), look for automation by changing the Track View and cycle through different automation parameters.

Color-coding regions: Color-code regions within tracks by selecting a region, double-clicking the color bar for that track, and applying a new color to the region by using the Apply to Selected list.

Nudging trouble: If you're trying to nudge and it doesn't seem to be working, check the increment, because it might be too small for you to see at your current zoom level. Also, check to see if you are looking at a different Track View than waveform or block (or warp if in Elastic Audio). If you're looking at automation, for example, nudging won't work.

Global I/O changes: You can set all tracks (except MIDI tracks) to the same I/O values at once (very helpful for clearing things out). Alt+click (Windows) or Option+click (Mac) the I/O path button on one track and choose what you want applied to all. This also works for choosing, bypassing, deactivating, activating, or muting inserts and sends.

The Timeline

This is where you see the audio regions, MIDI data, and automation displayed on the timeline. All the work you do with the tools occurs here, and the modes you select appear here. I've pretty much described this area in terms of how your other choices affect it.

The Mix Window

The Mix window is my favorite place in Pro Tools because I have a passion for mixing consoles and control surfaces. I love faders, inserts, sends, watching the level meters, and more. The whole feel of the Mix window is designed to be like an actual mixing console or control surface, whether an old-school analog board like a Sony MCI JH-600 series or a new fangled ICON D-Control.

Large or small, new or old, mixing consoles look, feel, and act remarkably the same. That's because the design works. Arranging tracks into channel strips from left to right, with individual track controls grouped vertically, is a powerful paradigm. It looks impressive. Part of the secret of mastering a board is learning one channel strip and then applying that knowledge to the rest of the board.

Mix Window Layout

The Mix window (Figure 8.9) is pure console or control surface. It's functional, clean, and classic.

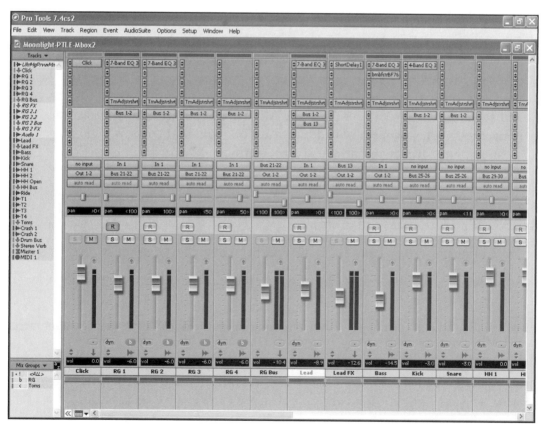

Figure 8.9   The Pro Tools Mix window.

Although you can do everything from the Edit window, I encourage you to mix here. The Mix window gives you the power to mix without distracting you with all the waveforms and MIDI. It also, by virtue of not having to draw all the waveforms, is less stressful on your system. If you're close to maxing out your capability, you can edit in the Edit window with playback stopped and then play from the Mix window to listen.

- **Window controls:** Just as it is with the Edit window, you can resize and position the Mix window within the Pro Tools workspace or close it entirely. You control it exactly the same way.

- **Tracks list:** This area is exactly the same and in the same position as in the Edit window.

- **Edit Groups list:** This area is exactly the same and in the same position as in the Edit window.

- **View Selector:** This is that little thing at the bottom of the window that looks like a calendar. It's a shortcut to view controls that turn things on and off in the channel strips, and it duplicates the View>Mix window menu.

- **Channel Strips:** Oh yeah, here's where it's at. Each channel strip represents one track in your session. These can be mono or stereo Audio, MIDI, Instrument, Aux Input, or Master Fader tracks. Just as with the Edit window, you can turn certain views on or off, move tracks around, hide them, recolor them, group them together, and so forth. What you can't do in the Mix window is arbitrarily resize tracks horizontally (you change mix width instead) or zoom in. I cover what each portion of the channel strip is and how it works shortly.

Mix Window Tips

Move tracks: Select, drag, and drop.

See the Regions List: You can't see that from here. Switch to the Edit window.

Narrow the mix: Select the View>Narrow mix menu. This allows you to squeeze more tracks onto the screen.

Show a hidden track: Turn on the Tracks List and select the track name so it is highlighted.

Channel Strip Controls

These controls (Figure 8.10) are essentially the same as the track controls in the Edit window. They are simplified, however, in that you can't change track height, choose an Elastic Audio mode, or switch from sample-based to tick-based and back.

Figure 8.10   A channel strip in the Mix window.

From top to bottom, the controls on each channel strip are as follows:

- **Color Bar:** Same functionality as in the Edit window.

- **Instrument (not shown):** Same functionality as in the Edit window.

- **Inserts:** Same functionality as in the Edit window.

- **Sends (A–E):** Same functionality as in the Edit window.

- **Sends (F–J)(not shown):** Same functionality as in the Edit window.

- **Input path:** Same functionality as in the Edit window.

- **Output path:** Same functionality as in the Edit window.

- **Automation Mode:** Same functionality as in the Edit window, only the word "Auto" is shown as part of the mode name (unless in Narrow Mix).

- **Pan Sliders:** Work these to change the pan.

- **Pan Indicators:** These have no functionality aside from telling you the pan position.

- **Solo, Mute, Record Enable:** Same functionality as in the Edit window.

- **Output Window button:** Same functionality as in the Edit window.

- **Volume Fader:** Same functionality as in the Edit window only it's bigger and nicer.

- **Level Meter:** Same functionality as in the Edit window only it's bigger and nicer.

- **Voice or Patch Select:** Allows you to turn dynamic voice allocation off for audio tracks (this frees up voices if you have a lot of tracks) or to select a different patch if a MIDI or Instrument track.

- **Mix Group:** Shows you a track that is a part of an active mix group and which one it belongs to. A lowercase letter tells you a track is part of one active group. If it is a capital letter, that tells you it's a member of more than one group, and the letter is the lowest group letter is belongs to. In other words, if a track is a member of the "p" and "t" groups and both are active, you see "P" displayed. You find no corresponding Mix Group indicator in the Edit window. Click the letter to access more functions.

- **Track Type:** Shows you the track type with a little graphic: Audio (waveform), Aux Input (down arrow), MIDI (5-pin MIDI cable), Instrument (keys), and Master Fader (the Greek letter sigma, which is the summation operator in mathematics that is used to represent signals being summed together).

- **Volume (Peak and Delay):** Unlike in the Edit window, you don't control the volume from here; you just look at it. Ctrl+click (Windows) or Command+click (Mac) to show peak level or channel delay.

- **Name and Number:** This is just a readout in the Mix window. You can't access playlists from here.

- **Color Bar:** Same as up top.

- **Comments:** Same functionality as in the Edit window.

Channel Strip Tips

Selecting tracks: Click the name or color bar.

Selecting multiple tracks: Shift+click to grab adjacent tracks or Ctrl+click (Windows)/ Command+click (Mac) to select multiple nonadjacent tracks.

Color Bar defaults: You can change the way Pro Tools assigns colors to new tracks from the Display tab in Preferences.

Solo safe returns: Solo safe (also known as solo isolate) returns (the Aux Input track they are on) so they aren't muted when you solo a different track that is sending its signal. Do this by Ctrl+clicking (Windows) or Command+clicking (Mac) the Solo button on the track. It is grayed out as a result. For example, I always solo safe the Aux Input track I put my reverb on so I can solo whatever track I want to and hear the reverb without having to mess with soloing it, too.

Set to 0: Alt+click (Windows) or Option+click (Mac) pan or volume controls to set them to 0. This works on any pan or volume control that you can find.

Clearing meters: Alt+click (Windows) or Option+click (Mac) a meter to clear it.

Wide meters: Windows users, press and hold Ctrl+Start+Alt and click on a track's fader(s) in the Mix or Edit windows to make them wider and easier to see. Mac users, press Command+Option+Control and click. If you're in "Narrow Mix" mode, the effect is observable only on mono tracks.

Fine-tuning: To move a control in finer increments, press and hold Ctrl (Windows) or Command (Mac) while you click the control (or automation point) and move it.

Other Interface Elements

A good number of other interface elements are still left to describe. I cover most of the remaining ones here with a short description and screenshot.

Track List

This lists all the tracks in a session, whether they are hidden in the Mix and Edit windows or not. If the track list is not visible, turn it on by clicking the left-facing double-arrows at the bottom left of the Mix or Edit window. Turn it off the same way. Click the arrow beside the word Tracks to view the Tracks list menu, or right-click over any track to see the track-specific menu. You can resize this window by clicking and dragging the bar separating it from the Mix Groups list. Click to hide or show tracks in the Mix and Edit windows. Highlighted tracks are visible. Tracks in italics are inactive.

Group List

This lists all the groups in the current session. To turn a group on, click its name to highlight it. You always have an <ALL> group. Be careful when the <ALL> group is selected because every edit, every fader touch, and many other changes are applied to every track! Access the Groups list menu by clicking the arrow beside the name. Access group-specific menus by right-clicking a group name. You can have a lot of fun with groups.

Regions List

This lists all the regions in the current session. The Regions list is available only from the Edit window. Many projects won't require much use of this list, but it's convenient to have. The Regions list shows every region in your session, whether it is active and on a track or not. Click and drag regions from the list to tracks in your session to add them. You can also delete regions, used or unused, from your project. Click the arrow beside the name for the Regions menu, or right-click a region to see a context-sensitive menu. Double-click to rename a region. Stereo regions can be expanded to see both channels. MIDI regions appear in this list as well.

Transport Window

The Transport window (Window>Transport) is a floating window with the standard transport controls (Play, Record, Stop, and so forth) as well as pre- and post-roll times, selection data, counters, and MIDI controls. Figure 8.11 illustrates the Transport window.

Figure 8.11   The floating Transport window with all controls visible.

Task Manager

The Task Manager (Window>Task Manager) is a DigiBase Browser window that allows you to view and manage Pro Tools background tasks, such as finding and relinking files and fades.

Workspace Browser

The Workspace (Window>Workspace) is a DigiBase Browser window that allows you to access all the online volumes without having to switch out to the operating system.

Project Browser

The Project browser (Window>Project) is a tool that lets you manage files that are in your current session.

Memory Locations

The Memory Locations dialog box (Figure 8.12) is where you can view, select, go to, and manage memory locations.

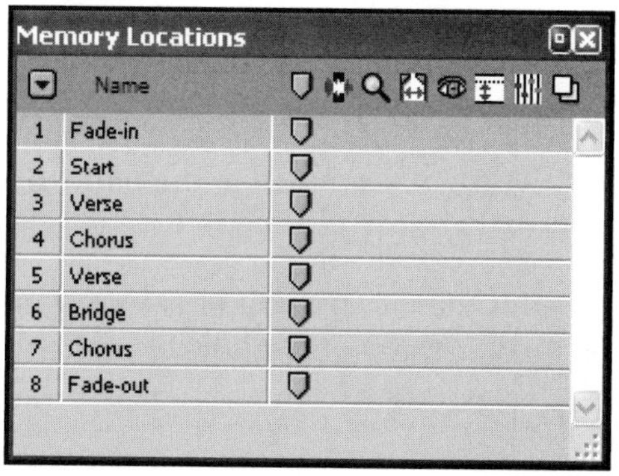

Figure 8.12   Memory locations speed navigation.

Disk Space and System Usage

These indicators show you how much disk space you have and the current drain on your system. Figure 8.13 shows the System Usage dialog box while a song is playing.

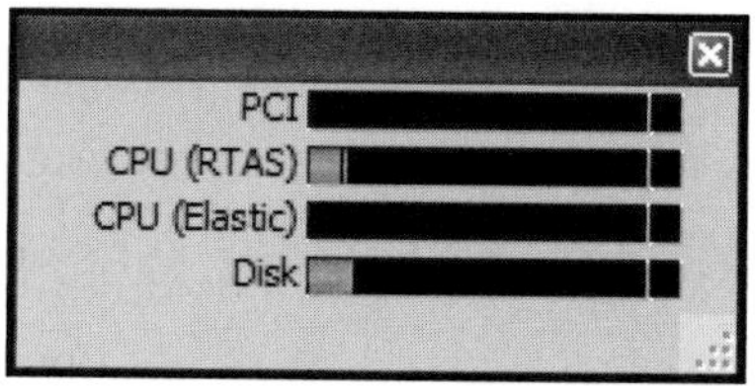

Figure 8.13   System usage warns of impending doom.

The Rest

I still haven't covered some aspects of the interface. I've tried to keep this chapter oriented to the big picture while being practical. Pro Tools is a beast of a program (in a good way), however, with different views, many different windows, and a multitude of different ways to customize it to suit your workflow and methods. Start here. Learn the basics. Become comfortable with them and then move onwards and upwards.

More Tips

Creating a new session: Select the File>New menu, choose a location to store the session, enter a name, and decide on the bit depth and sample rate.

Opening a session: You can open previously opened sessions from the File>Open Recent menu. Otherwise, select File>Open and find the session on your hard drive to open it. You can double-click any session file from your operating system or use the Workspace (Windows>Workspace) to find a session and open it.

Closing a session: Select File>Close session. Closing the Mix and Edit windows does not close a session.

Saving a session: Select File>Save, or File>Save As, if you want to change the name of the session.

Saving copies: Select File>Save Copy In to save a copy of the session in a new location. You select what items you want copied and can even change the bit depth of the session. The dialog box is shown in Figure 8.14.

Creating tracks: Select Track>New to create new tracks (see Figure 8.15). These are placed to the right of the currently selected track in your session. You can create more than one type of track at a time and more than one of each type. Click the plus button to add track types and change options from the pull-down menus.

Selecting tracks: Click the track name to select it. You can select more than one track by pressing Shift and then clicking further "down the line," or if the tracks aren't adjacent, press and hold Ctrl (Windows) or Command (Mac) then click individual tracks to add them to the selection.

Deselecting tracks: Click on a track that isn't selected. If all tracks are selected (this gets me all the time), press Ctrl (Windows) or Command (Mac) and click any track to deselect it. After you have a deselected track, select it normally, and all the others become deselected.

Deleting tracks: Select the track you want to delete, and choose the Track>Delete menu.

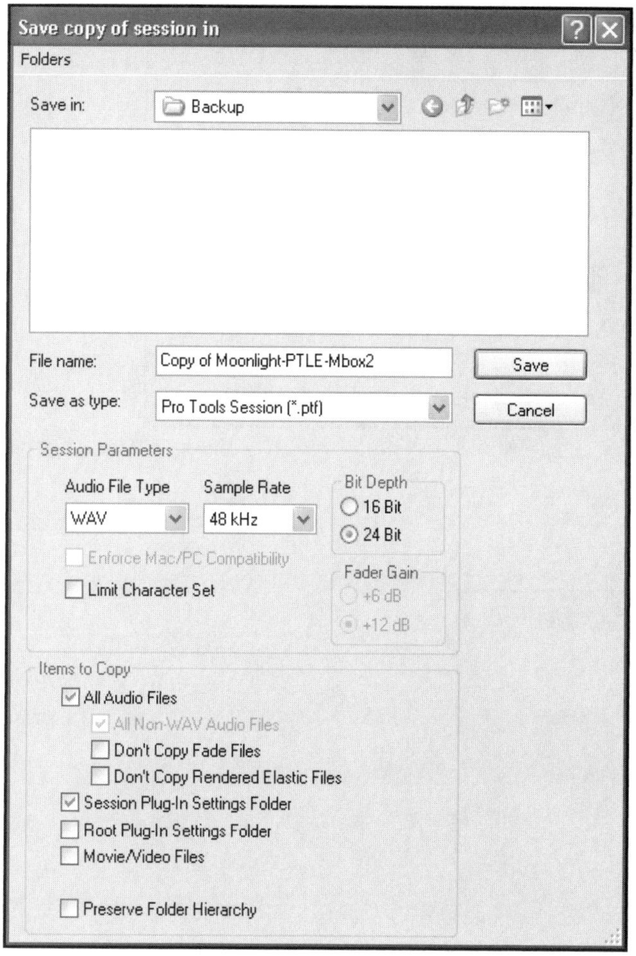

Figure 8.14 Saving a copy of a session with audio.

Moving tracks: Click the track name and drag it to a new location. You can move multiple tracks, whether they start out adjacent or not (they end up that way).

Grouping tracks: Select the tracks you want to group and then choose the Track>Group menu (see Figure 8.16).

Changing track names: Double-click the track name to change it. As soon as you are editing the name of one track, you can "scroll" to other tracks by pressing Ctrl (Windows) or Command (Mac) and the arrow keys.

Changing track colors: If you are changing one track, just double-click on its color bar. If you are changing more than one at a time, select them and then double-click on the color bar of a selected track.

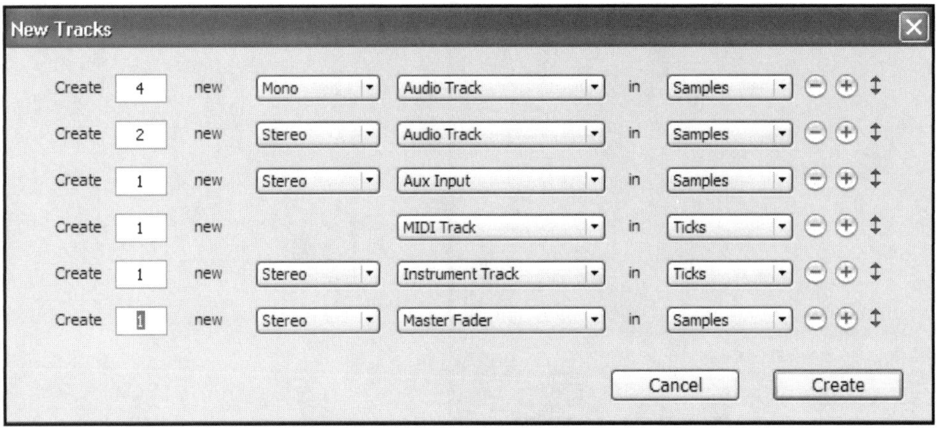

Figure 8.15 Creating several new tracks at once.

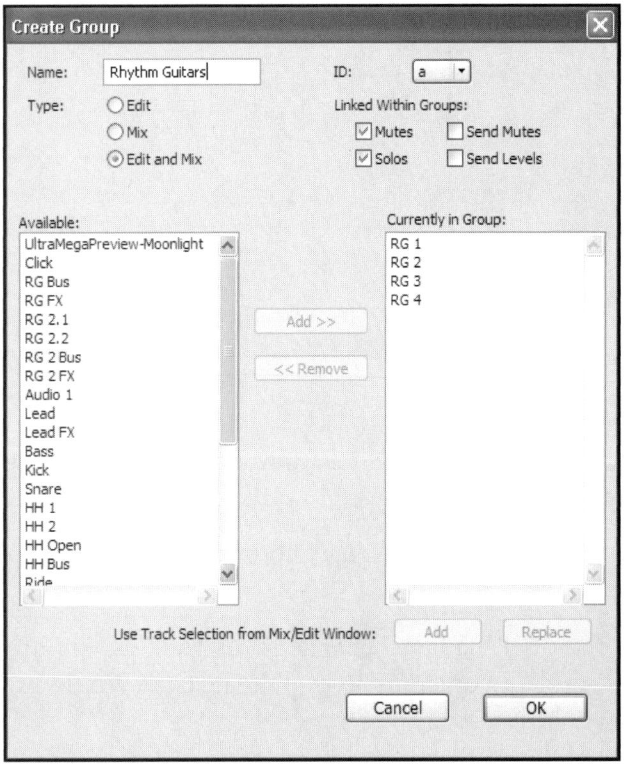

Figure 8.16 Assigning a group.

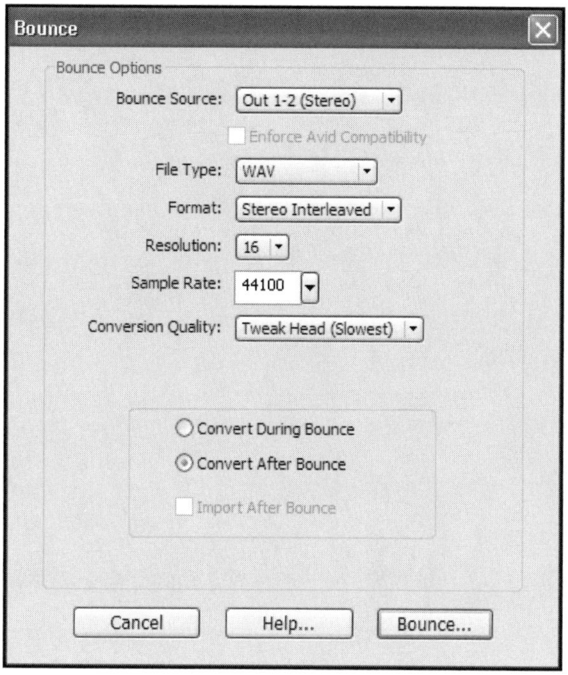

Figure 8.17   Bouncing my stereo mix.

Hiding tracks: Right-click a track name and select hide. Click a track name from within the Tracks List to show or hide it. When a track is hidden, its name becomes unhighlighted in the Tracks List.

Showing tracks: Click on a track name in the Tracks List to highlight it.

Deactivating tracks: Right-click a track name and choose Make Inactive.

Activating tracks: If the track is not hidden, right-click the track name and select Make Active.

Bouncing your mix: This is how you produce the final version of your mix (Figure 8.17). From the Edit window, select the area you want to bounce. Make sure to get everything, including any initial fade-in or fade-out. Select the File>Bounce to>Disk menu. For the most part, the options stay the same. If you have purchased the MP3 export option, you can bounce your files as MP3s. For stereo files, make sure Stereo Interleaved is chosen, and if necessary, select a bit depth (Resolution) and Sample Rate. Convert During Bounce requires more work from your processor. I always click Convert After Bounce.

9 Recording Audio

A lot of decisions must be made before you ever press Record in Pro Tools. Many of those decisions depend on your understanding of what you're doing. What is sound? What is phase? How can you capture this performance the best? Do you need to track in stereo? Should you use a cardioid, a hypercardioid, or an omnidirectional microphone? How do you set preamp levels? What bit depth do you use? What sample rate?

Engineering Primer

As you can see, you have some homework to do. Before you get into Pro Tools proper, I want to set the stage with some audio engineering fundamentals.

Sound

Simply put, sound is a disturbance in air pressure. Technically speaking, it doesn't have to be air, but you get the idea. Something disturbs the air. In many ways air acts like a fluid, and when you are talking about sound, that is especially true. You see, fluid molecules stick together, even though they move around as a group a lot and aren't locked into a solid shape. When an outside force pushes on it, each molecule that makes up the fluid pushes and pulls on the ones around it, like a line of people holding hands. Push one person and he or she will move toward the person next to them (compression) and pull away from the person who pushed them (rarefaction). Air behaves the same way when sound moves through it.

So, you have the air disturbance, a person singing or playing an instrument, for example. When I pluck a guitar string, it vibrates and disturbs the air around it. My ears pick up the disturbance in air pressure, and my brain translates that into what I perceive as sound. I find that transformation, something we take for granted, incredible. Think about it. Your eardrums detect disturbances in air pressure, an esoteric thing if I ever heard one, and your mind hears Ludwig van.

Sound waves are disturbances in the air that, as far as you need to be concerned here, have three notable properties: frequency, amplitude, and phase.

Frequency

Frequency measures the rate at which the areas of compression and rarefaction occur. One period of peak to peak, be it compression or rarefaction, is called a cycle, and you measure cycles by the second. The unit of measurement of cycles per second (which is frequency) is called Hertz. For example, a sound that has a frequency of 440 cycles per second is said to be 440 Hz. You might recognize that as the note (or pitch) A, which often serves as a reference to tune certain musical instruments. You perceive lower frequencies as lower notes, and higher frequencies as higher notes. It is generally accepted that humans have a hearing range from approximately 20 Hz to 20,000 Hz (or 20 kilohertz, which is written as 20 kHz).

Amplitude

Amplitude, which is a fancy word for "How loud is it?", is measured in decibels. The most important thing you need to know about decibels is that they are not connected directly to reality. A decibel (or dB) is nothing more than a ratio, a comparison between an agreed-upon reference point and what you're measuring. It's not like measuring the temperature on an absolute scale, for example, 22 degrees Celsius. That temperature has meaning in and of itself. It does not depend on anything else for you to interpret it.

This decibel ratio is why you can measure how loud a rock concert is and say it is 100 dB and at the same time say that the signal on the Master Fader of your Pro Tools session is 0 dB. How can that be? These two systems use different reference points.

At a rock concert, the 0 dB reference point is based on the minimum level of air pressure disturbance that you can discern. What's the threshold of human hearing? By definition, it is 0 dB. Up from there, you move (logarithmically) to whispers, talking, office noise, and on up to rock concerts and jet engines.

In music (when you're talking about signals), it gets crazy because there are many different reference points. In the digital world, the 0 dB reference point is that point where all your bits are used up and you've got no more volume to give. It's called Full Scale Digital, or 0 dBFSD. After that, digital clipping occurs. On an analog board, which uses electricity instead of bits, the dB is a ratio of voltage, not bits and not sound pressure. Despite using different reference points, both digital and analog methods symbolize the same thing. The top of the scale is 0 dB (remember, this signifies different things between the two systems and 0dBFSD is often upwards of +18 dBu as measured on an analog VU meter) and as the signal gets softer, the signal strength as measured in decibels moves down into negative values.

Consumer gear tends to send and receive signals at −10 dB, whereas professional gear sends and receives signal at +4 dB. Why the difference? It costs more to design and build gear that operates with much "hotter" signals, and consumers generally don't need the extra power. Professionals, however, do!

Phase

Phase is a description of where the wave is in its cycle from peak to peak or valley to valley. Taken in isolation, phase has little relevance. Where it matters is when you start adding waveform to waveform. Sound is cumulative in that when you add the amplitude of one wave to the amplitude of another, the waveform at all points over time sums together.

Go make some waves in a pool. Have another person make waves at various distances away from you. The waves add together, but the sum depends on whether you're adding a peak to a peak or a peak to a trough or somewhere in between. Peak-to-peak summation increases the strength of the wave, whereas peak-to-trough summation cancels it out.

Therefore, you want to (in general) avoid peak-to-trough summation when you record and mix audio. That is a phenomenon called phase cancellation. Those signals partially or entirely cancel each other out. Phase cancellation is most likely when you mic up one source (say a drum kit) with more than one microphone (such as overheads in a stereo spaced pair configuration). If you place the mics at a point where they are receiving the same signal but at the opposite phase, they cancel each other out.

Bit Depth

Bit depth is the number of bits used to encode the amplitude information of an analog signal into digital audio. Bit depth has a few important effects to consider: precision, dynamic range, and noise floor.

Bit depth directly equates to precision. A bit depth of 16 bits results in 65,535 possible values to measure amplitude. Going to 24 bits raises that to 16,777,215 possible values. To get a sense of that, consider that's the same difference between setting your computer monitor (through the display adapter) to display thousands versus millions of colors. Sure, you might be able to get by with thousands, but millions make what you see on-screen far closer to the original. In addition to that, if you were editing a photo or creating a piece of computer art and only had thousands of colors to use instead of millions, your creativity would be limited.

Bit depth also contributes to determining the noise floor of your system. It does this by defining the maximum possible dynamic range of what you can record and play back. Dynamic range is the difference between the softest and loudest you can play (or hear). Roughly speaking, each bit of bit depth gives you 6 dB of dynamic range. Therefore, a 16-bit file or session has a total possible (not necessarily actual) dynamic range of 96 dB.

Dynamic Range and Format   CDs, which play 16-bit audio, have a dynamic range (rounding) of 96 dB, which is far more than tapes, whose dynamic range is in the middle 50s, or records, which are in the middle 60s. You don't hear much of this range today, because everyone compresses their mixes so much that it's like listening to something always pegged at "11." You might hear only 10 to 20 percent of the total possible dynamic range that CDs are capable of, which is sad.

When you get to 24 bits, things get really exciting. The dynamic range of a 24-bit system is theoretically 144 dB. I say *theoretically* because that extends down so far that you're starting to hear electron noise (below −130 dB or so). In practical terms, this means that your gear becomes the limiting factor. Pro Tools LE and M-Powered compete very well, but only have between (very generally) 100 dB and 105 dB of dynamic range. This sets the noise floor for those systems. In comparison, the Pro Tools HD I/O module, the 192 I/O (whose cost far exceeds anything in the Pro Tools LE and M-Powered universe), has about 120 dB of dynamic range. The practical upshot of this is that at 24 bits, you're guaranteed to have a dynamic range that exceeds any equipment in your signal chain and gives you far more precision when manipulating gain "inside the box," where electron noise isn't a problem.

Suffice it to say that more bits increases file sizes and the processing power required. Despite being less capable, 16 bits is a viable bit depth to record a mix at. It is easier on your hardware and software, so if you're pushing the limits, consider working at 16 bits.

Bit Depth and Audio Quality   You can reap tremendous benefits in the quality of your audio by moving from 16 to 24 bits, more than the perceived gain from increasing sample rate. If you've got the capability, use 24 bits.

However, don't just take it from me. Create two sessions, one at 16 and one at 24 bits. Record something you know well and mix with the exact same plug-ins and settings. Bounce to the same format and compare.

Sample Rate

Sample rate is a hugely contested and often misunderstood setting. You might think that more is always better, but that might not be the case. But, before I get too far ahead of myself, I should explain what it is.

Sample rate is the rate at which data is sampled and measured from an analog stream for conversion into a digital format.

I'm going to use an analogy based on temperature and the weather to help illustrate this. Temperature is an analog data stream that changes throughout the day. It can go up, go down, or stay the same. Sampling rate is how often you go out and measure it. If you go out once a day to measure the temperature, then that's your sample rate: once per day. You can immediately see the problem with that. Once per day is clearly not often enough. Temperature fluctuates throughout a 24-hour cycle, and measuring it once a day misses a lot of fluctuation. So, how fast is fast enough—once an hour? Once every five minutes?

When you are measuring audio, the minimum sample rate is derived from the frequency spectrum you need to measure. Do you need to measure all frequencies? No. Humans can't hear above 20 kHz, so too far over that is overkill, unless you're making an album for dogs (although, as always, there are differences of opinion on how far beyond 20 kHz we can somehow perceive but not actually hear). The good news is that someone has already done the math for us. A man named Harry Nyquist (and, alternatively or jointly, Claude Shannon and others) came up with a sampling theory that states, when translated into less technical and audio-centric language, that a sample rate is adequate for the bandwidth of the data you are trying to measure if it is twice the frequency of the highest frequency of that bandwidth. Human bandwidth tops out at about 20 kHz, so twice that is 40 kHz. Any sample rate above 40 kHz can measure the entire frequency spectrum that you can hear. That's why when CDs were developed, a sample rate of 44.1 kHz was chosen. With a bit of leeway, 44.1 kHz is completely adequate to measure (and play back) everything humans can hear.

Returning to the temperature analogy, you reach a point somewhere along the line where you aren't going to gain anything from going out to measure the temperature faster and faster. In fact, you start to make mistakes, and it becomes too tiring. Can you go out every third of a second? Nope. By the same token, the audio community is engaging in a debate over just where the best sample rate is. Even though 44.1 kHz is adequate to measure the entire spectrum that humans can hear, some people swear that 192 kHz is better.

Sweet Spot   Dan Lavry, of Lavry Engineering, Inc., has written a paper called *Sampling Theory for Digital Audio* that I find compelling. Through his paper and contributions to several forums on the web, he concludes that the best tradeoff between sample rate speed and digital conversion accuracy is between 48 kHz and 96 kHz.

As always, it's up to you to decide which direction you go. For Pro Tools LE systems, your only choice is between 44.1 kHz and 48 or possibly 96 kHz. Some M-Audio systems offer much higher sample rates. You don't necessarily need to push your system to get the best sonic quality you expect out of it. Create some test sessions and try different sample rates out to see if you can hear the difference. If you don't have high-quality mics, preamps, room acoustics, and other supporting gear, you probably won't.

Mono versus Stereo

It's important to note the difference between a mono and stereo track.

Mono tracks record input from one microphone. You have one signal that can be panned between the left and right speakers. Most recording is done in mono. You've got one singer with one microphone going through one preamp onto one track. That's mono.

The large-format consoles that I'm familiar with have a large number of channels, from 24 to 36. Each channel is a mono track. There are no stereo tracks. Instead, you bring in mics that are set up in stereo on adjacent channels (or bus them) and then pan those channels hard left and hard right. Stereo.

My small analog mixer has four sets of stereo tracks, each taking two mono inputs. What makes them different from the purely mono tracks is that they are under the control of one fader, pan pot, and one set of other controls (like electronic equalization [EQ], sends, and returns). However, they still start out as mono sources. The reason for this is that you can't carry more than one separate channel over an analog cable at a time.

FM Radio and Multiplexing   As soon as I typed that, my mind came to rest on Stereo FM radio, which is a stereo stream contained in one broadcast. I won't get into the technical details, but you could use various multiplexing and modulation techniques to send discrete analog channels over one analog cable. The only time I've seen that, however, has been in relation to digital audio (Audio Engineering Society [AES]/European Broadcast Union [EBU], Sony/Philips Digital Interconnect Format [S/PDIF], or Alesis Digital Audio Tape [ADAT]).

It gets a little weird when you consider that a mono track can be played out of either or both monitors. Panning changes this balance to varying degrees of left to right or centered. The thing to remember here is that the same signal is being played from both monitors, just at different levels. The difference in levels is what makes the sound appear to change positions on the sound "stage."

Stereo is different in that you have two different signals being played out of the two monitors. This gives you a sense not only of left-to-right balance, but also of depth. Signals that make the most of that are of the same source, only slightly different. In other words, two identical tracks played out of the monitors are going to sound like a mono track. That's why you can't duplicate a mono track, pan the resulting two mono tracks hard left and hard right, and magically turn it into stereo. They're the same! By the same token, two vastly different mono signals (vocal on the left and guitar on the right) do not sound like stereo either, but just two mono tracks being played out of different speakers. However, two microphones set up to capture a stereo image of a drum kit will be perceived as stereo. The cues that give the perception of stereo in this case are the volume differences between the two signals that the microphone picks up.

Mono to Stereo   When you have a mono track and insert a plug-in that can turn it into stereo, you see the plug-in name followed by (mono/stereo). The plug-in takes the mono source and creates two slightly different signals, most often by applying different volume levels, delays, or modulations, which can be used to simulate a stereo track.

In the digital world, you can save two mono streams as one stereo file. This is called stereo interleaving. However, Pro Tools does not support stereo interleaved files. As a result, stereo audio tracks that you create and record are saved as two mono files. Any stereo interleaved files that you import into your session are separated into two mono files as they are imported. That's one reason you can so easily split (Track>Split Into Mono) a stereo track into two mono tracks in Pro Tools.

Pro Tools makes another distinction when it comes to plug-ins: multimono. Multimono plug-ins treat a stereo track as if it were two mono tracks. The channels do not affect each other in any way. For example, you can link channel settings and apply the same EQ to each channel, or unlink them and EQ the left and right channel differently.

To sum up, stereo tracks in Pro Tools are simply two mono files under the control of one channel strip. They are displayed and edited on one track space on the timeline. However, what you hear out of the monitors and whether or not you perceive it as stereo depends on the nature of the mono sources and plug-ins you have applied.

Levels and Meters

Given that sound has a frequency, amplitude, and phase, how do you observe that in Pro Tools?

Frequency and phase are things you listen for. There are ways to measure frequency, obviously, such as when you're pitch-correcting a vocal or are looking at the frequency spectrum of a track or mix, but broadly speaking, you listen to it. Likewise, if you want to zoom in and look at a track's waveform very closely, you can indeed see its phase as compared to other tracks. However, most often, you listen for phase in the form of phase cancellation.

Phase Experiment   Record a mono track. It doesn't matter what it is. Duplicate it. Insert an EQ plug-in (the standard 1-Band EQ 3 will suffice) on one of the two tracks, open it up, and hit the Phase Reverse button. This is the button by the Input area that is a circle with a line through it. Have a listen. Pan the two tracks hard left and right to see what happens. Center them, and the sound should all but disappear. They are canceling each other out! With the tracks centered, bypass the plug-in (or just toggle the phase button) and listen as the tracks add to each other and then cancel each other out.

This is what you listen for when investigating phase cancellation, which can happen when either stereo or multiple mono tracks are summed together.

Amplitude is indicated from the plethora of level meters in Pro Tools, as well as from the clip indicator on your hardware. The level meters in Pro Tools measure the signal strength that you are recording or playing back in dBFS, or decibels full scale. You have nothing higher than 0 dB in this scheme. Beyond that, because you have no more bits to measure amplitude, the waveform clips, or turns into a square wave. Pro Tools gives you warning of impending doom by making the meter green at a point well below clipping, turning it yellow when you get close, and hitting you with a red clip indicator when you've hit max. Notice that I say "hit max." You can't go over.

You can see level meters on tracks in the Edit and Mix windows, on Output windows, and on many plug-ins. They're very important. Watch and listen to make sure you don't clip.

You have two ways to measure signal strength: by measuring where the signal peaks and by measuring its average (called RMS, or root mean square). Peaks are an indication of what the maximum amplitude is, no matter how short a time the signal spends at that amplitude. It also tells you how much headroom you have before you clip. RMS is more like an average and is closer to the way you perceive loudness. Peak amplitude is like a flashbulb going off, whereas RMS is more like turning a room's lights up. Both of these ways of measuring amplitude are important.

I want to mention a couple other things before moving on. Set your meters to Pre-Fader mode or (the default) Post-Fader mode from the Options>Pre-Fader Metering menu. To access meter display preferences, select the Setup>Preferences menu and choose the Display tab. Adjust the Peak Hold and Clip Indication settings to your liking. The *Show Meters in Sends View* preference shows or hides meters when you are viewing sends in the Edit or Mix window by send, not assignment. Having a ton of meters on and active can slow down screen redraw time.

Faders

If levels are a way of measuring amplitude, faders (and the occasional knob) are a way to control it. Faders go from negative infinity (no signal) to +12 dB. At 0 dB, faders are neither cutting nor boosting the signal that passes through them. When you turn them down, they reduce the signal to the degree you specify. Above 0 dB, they amplify. This is a case where you should realize that 0 dB on the fader is not the same thing as 0 dB on the level meter. When you push the fader above 0 dB, you are not automatically heading into digital clipping. What you are doing is amplifying the signal by 12 dB.

When you are playing back, faders control the signal strength of the audio being retrieved from your hard disk drive. When you are recording, faders control the level that you monitor at, not what you are recording.

Play and Record Faders   Here's a cool trick. A preference in the Options>Preference menu, Operations tab, links or unlinks record and playback faders. They are linked by default, which means you've got one set of faders to work with, and they have the same values whether you're playing back or recording. If you unlink them, you get, in essence, two sets of faders for each track that you arm (record enable). In other words, you can set different fader levels when a track is armed and when it is not, and Pro Tools can toggle between them when you arm or disarm the track.

Clipping

Don't.

The most critical time and place to avoid clipping is when you're recording. If you record distorted and clipped material, it's hard to recover. Pay attention to the clip light on your interface and listen for preamp distortion, which should precede clipping. You can tell how hot a signal is after you record enable the track in Pro Tools and have the artist play something for you to set the appropriate levels. Look at the track's meter, and if it's in the yellow, back off on the preamp.

Most people track (the "in" way of saying "record") way too hot. If you're working at 24 bits, you have no need to go above -12 dB peak signal strength. Anything more pushes the hardware where it doesn't want to go. Those preamps are meant to output a line-level signal, not super-heated steam.

> **Gain Control While Tracking**   It's important to know at this stage that you con-trol gain from the preamp, not from within Pro Tools. Every fader within Pro Tools affects monitoring, not the level your interface records at.

You can also insert a level meter on the track to see greater level detail, and often switch between peak and RMS metering to see how strong a signal is. The Bomb Factory BF Essential Bridge that comes standard with Pro Tools is just such a plug-in.

Clipping while mixing is just as bad, but far easier to fix. Pay attention to those red clip lights, and if you see them go on, back off on something. If the entire mix is too hot (the red light on your Master Fader track continually goes on) back off on everything.

Team Effort

I want to briefly discuss three team members that impact your Pro Tools studio:

- Artists
- Engineers
- Producers

Artists are the musical (or performing) talent. They are the music creators, the people with the "mad skillz." They can be singers, musicians, or both. (Some are neither, but that's another story.) Artists play an incredibly important role in the process of creating professional audio. Their central contribution is in their performance. That's the magic. However, they might also be engineers and in many ways producers. Know who the artists are in your sessions. Respect them. Know their role. The artist knows the music and the instrument.

Engineers are responsible for recording and mixing, including all the preparation that goes on to make that possible. They are the technical expertise. This is most likely you, if you're the one doing the recording. Who knows Pro Tools? The engineer. Who sets up the session, handles the mics, routes the cables, and sets the levels? The engineer. Who presses the red button to record? The engineer. The engineer knows the gear and the recording process.

Producers are responsible for "running the show." They help the artists turn their vision into reality. They help the engineer keep on track and not let the session degenerate into an unproductive free-for-all. Often, the producer is the one with the creative vision, and the artists take their direction from their producer. Even megastars have producers that give them constructive criticism and invaluable perspective. The producer knows the schedule, the budget, the vision, and the audience.

Often the lines are blurred, and people play many roles in a project. That's okay. When I record myself, I'm the entire team. That makes it harder, but not unrewarding or unproductive. Having someone else record or produce me, however, enables me to focus on my performance. Likewise, if I'm recording someone else, I can concentrate on pressing the buttons. Finally, if I am producing, I can sit back and not worry about performing or pressing buttons and devote my energy to listening and orchestrating what's happening. In general, larger projects and sessions benefit from separating different people into these roles.

Microphones

Microphones convert sound energy to electrical energy, much like how your ears convert sound energy to nerve impulses. To say they are an important part of the recording process is an understatement. In large studios, the total cost of the microphones in their inventory can equal or exceed many of their other expenses. This helps separate home and project studios from larger operations. For example, miking up a four-piece rock band (lead singer, lead guitar, bass, and drums) and tracking everyone at the same time would run you on the order of 10–18 microphones, 8–10 of which could be devoted to the drum kit.

You obviously won't be having sessions that large if you are running Pro Tools LE with the Mbox 2, but if you have the 003 or some of the M-Audio systems with a large number of inputs, you could come close.

At any rate, you need to know what types of microphones are available so you can begin to choose which ones you want to invest in, given the gigs you'll be recording.

Microphone Types

All microphones produce an electrical signal that travels down the cable and into your recording interface. How they do this is dependent on their design. The main distinction between mics of different types is their capsule design. Here are the three main types:

- **Dynamic:** Sound waves induce an electrical signal by moving a diaphragm that is attached to a coil in a magnetic field. This type of microphone is often the most rugged and does not require power to operate. Because of this, dynamic mics also tend to be able to handle the greatest sound pressure levels. Excellent examples of dynamic mics are the Shure SM57, AKG D 112, Sennheiser MD 421, and Electro-Voice RE20.

- **Condenser:** Sound waves interact with a capacitor that is composed of a diaphragm and a charged magnetic plate. The distance between these two elements changes as a result of the diaphragm being hit with the sound waves, and these changes in distance generate an electrical signal. It takes power to charge the capacitor, which means condenser mics require batteries or phantom power. Condenser mics tend to be more sensitive and responsive to transients than dynamic mics, but also generate some internal noise. Condenser mics can also use vacuum tubes rather than solid-state circuitry to amplify their signal. You can find many different quality condenser mics out there. A few examples are the RØDE NT1000, Shure SM81, AKG 414, and the Neumann TLM 103.

- **Ribbon:** These are dynamic mics that have a metallic ribbon suspended in a magnetic field. Sound waves move the ribbon, which induces an electrical signal. Ribbon mics are very sensitive and require no external power to operate. Older ribbon mics can be damaged quite easily.

You will run across different diaphragm sizes when you shop for mics:

- **Large diaphragm:** The size varies, but can be up to an inch or so. Larger diaphragms are more sensitive, but some might be less able to handle high sound pressure levels. High-end, large-diaphragm condenser mics are typically among a studio's most prized possessions and can cost thousands of dollars. Thankfully, very good but more economic models exist for the rest of us.

- **Small diaphragm:** These are commonly called pencil mics and can be dynamic or condenser. Many times, small-diaphragm mics are used as stereo pairs, whether as drum overheads, on acoustic guitars, or on pianos. Small-diaphragm mics are valued for their precision.

Be Yourself   Although engineers have spent decades coming up with common "tried and true" mics for given applications, the ultimate decision of whether you should use a particular mic for a given purpose rests with you and your ears. Experiment. Try things out. Develop your own ideas. Use what you like and discard the rest. Differences in opinion are what makes music interesting, and if everyone used the same mics for the same purposes with the same hardware with the same plug-ins using the same settings…well, then it wouldn't leave much room for individuality.

Typical dynamic and condenser mics offer a couple of different diaphragm orientations as well. Make sure you are aware of the address of your mic before pointing it at something. The two common forms of address are:

- **Direct Address:** This is where the diaphragm is inline with the microphone body, like the Shure SM57. Most dynamic and small-diaphragm condensers are direct address.

- **Side Address:** This is where the diaphragm is oriented so that it faces one side of the mic, not along the longitudinal axis. Most large-diaphragm condensers, like the Neumann TLM 103, are side address.

Microphone Patterns

Whether they are dynamic, condenser, ribbon, or "other," all microphones have a pattern. A pattern indicates what type of directionality the mic has. They are as follows (see Figure 9.1 for comparison):

- **Omnidirectional:** Omni mics pick up signals from all directions. They are very well suited to situations where you want to pick up a lot of ambience or "room" sounds. They are less than stellar when you need to be able to reject sounds from other instruments and directions.

- **Cardioid:** This is a directional microphone that picks up signal well from the front of the mic and rejects signals from the rear and less so from the side. It's great for miking drum kits and other applications where you want to minimize "bleed."

- **Hypercardioid:** This is another directional mic with a narrower front pattern than the cardioid but more likely to pick up signals from the rear of the mic.

- **Supercardioid:** This is similar to hypercardioid, but with a smaller rear response area.

- **Bidirectional**: This is also called Figure-8. This pattern is responsive to the front and rear but not to the sides. One bidirectional mic is required for the M-S stereo technique.

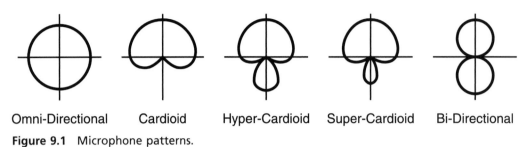

Omni-Directional   Cardioid   Hyper-Cardioid   Super-Cardioid   Bi-Directional

Figure 9.1 Microphone patterns.

Enhancing Mic Versatility   Some microphones do one thing exceedingly well. Others offer different controls that enhance the versatility of the mic. These controls typically include switchable patterns, one or more selectable pads, and bass rolloff or other low-frequency filters.

Frequency Response

Finally, be aware of the frequency response of your mics, including any presence peaks or dips. Not all microphones pick up the same frequencies. In fact, most don't!

This is especially important when recording instruments that produce very low frequencies, such as a kick drum; very high frequencies, such as a violin; or those with very broad ranges, such as organs and pianos. Presence peaks or rolloffs also affect how a mic sounds and often are the difference between choosing one mic over another.

Microphone Placement

Microphone placement is an art and science. Don't be intimidated, and don't overthink it. I'm not going to give you every possible combination. Too many exist, and it all depends on what sound you're after, what mics you have, where you're recording, and a host of other variables.

It all comes down to one question. What's making the sound?

If it's an acoustic guitar, point the mic at the sound hole. If it's a person, point the mic at their sound hole. If it's a guitar amplifier, point the mic at the sound hole (speaker). If it's a drum, point the mic at the drum head where the beater or drum stick is going to hit. You can find endless variations of this, but it all fundamentally comes down to pointing the microphone at what you want to record.

Single Mic Placement

After answering the question of what's making the sound, single microphone placement essentially comes down to controlling two variables: direction and distance.

- **Direction:** This variable applies to directional mics. Generally speaking, you get the best results if you point the mic directly at the person or instrument you want to record. For large sources, such as choirs or an entire orchestra, point the microphone at the center of the sound. Most often you want the axis of the microphone capsule directly inline with whatever is producing the sound. This can present a problem with drums, as you can't get in the way of the drummer. If you think of the drum (toms and snares, especially) as a speaker, however, you can point the microphone at the center of the "speaker cone" without being directly in front of the speaker itself. Guitar and bass amp cabinet miking is an art in and of itself, and people sometimes use an oblique mic technique. Remember to consider the polar pattern of the mic and orient "dead zones" at instruments (or other sources of noise) that you want to reject.

- **Distance:** This variable applies to all mics. The closer you are to the sound source, the more direct, and hence "dry," it sounds. Typically speaking, if you want more ambience, experiment with miking farther away. You can also set up mics for that express purpose and dual-track a performance with one close and one far mic. Distance affects other noise sources as well. The closer you are to what you are recording, the less likely you are to pick up other sources of sound, and those sounds you do pick up are not as loud. Vocals that have a close mic are more prone to popping and other mouth noises.

Given those two variables, a good way to find out what works is to open up a session in Pro Tools, mic the instrument or vocalist up, route your inputs and outputs, arm the track, set levels, and experiment with microphone direction and distance. Try different microphones if you have them. Some are going to sound better than others, and it doesn't really matter why. Use the best-sounding mic in the best-sounding direction at the best-sounding distance!

Stereo Miking Techniques

Several stereo miking techniques take advantage of using directional microphones to capture different signals in two channels. You can record anything in stereo, but some of the most popular sources range from the ubiquitous drum kit, piano, choirs, and ensembles to orchestras, nature, and sound effects.

With the exception of the M-S technique, you should use a pair of the same mics in each application. You can often buy stereo pairs of microphones to ensure they are, within certain tolerances, identical.

Coincident? *Coincident,* or *coincidental,* means the microphone capsules (the part that picks up the sound) are on top of each other as you look straight down on them. They might be facing different directions horizontally, but they are aligned vertically.

Stereo miking techniques are shown in Figure 9.2 and described in the following bulleted list.

- **Spaced Pair:** This technique uses two directional mics spaced roughly 3–10 feet apart. They should be parallel to each other. In other words, don't point them at the same cymbal. Point them both straight at, or down on, the instrument. Spaced pair mics should be three times farther apart from each other than they collectively are from the sound source. This is known as the 3:1 rule.

- **X-Y:** This technique uses two directional, coincident microphones pointing 135 degrees from each other.

- **ORTF/NOS:** This technique uses two directional mics whose "tails" point at each other and whose capsules are angled 110 degrees and 90 degrees from each other, respectively. The capsules are "near coincident" and should be roughly 7 inches and 12 inches apart, respectively.

- **M-S:** This technique, known as Middle-Sides or M-S, uses two coincidental directional mics. One should be cardioid, and the other must be bidirectional (also known as Figure-8). The cardioid mic is pointed at the source of the sound, and the bidirectional mic is used to pick up signals from each side. This technique requires an M-S decoder plug-in to convert the middle and side signals into left and right. The left channel is derived from taking the middle and summing with the side signal ($L = M + S$). The right channel is calculated by subtracting the phase-inverted side from the middle ($R = M–S$, whose phase has been inverted).

Recording Direct

The one instance where you don't need to worry about microphone placement is when recording direct. Technically speaking, this topic should not be in a section on microphone placement, but it seems to fit here.

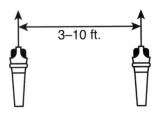

Spaced Pair

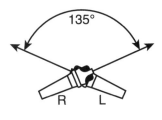

X–Y

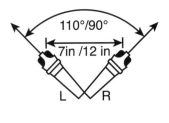

ORTF/NOS

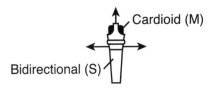

M–S

Figure 9.2 Stereo microphone placement techniques.

Recording direct applies to instruments that generate an electrical signal, either internally (keyboard/synth) or through pickups (guitar/bass). In contrast to instruments going through a speaker, like a bass combo amp or speaker cabinet, you take that electrical signal and route it directly to your interface, bypassing the amplifier and speaker.

Keyboards and synths make this very easy. They often have a line-out signal, often composed of left and right mono channels through 1/4-inch jacks, that you simply take and plug into your Pro Tools interface, making sure to use line-in settings. It's easy.

Guitars and basses are a little more complex, but not much. They should be plugged into some form of Direct Injection (DI) box, which converts their unbalanced, high-impedance, instrument-level signal into a balanced, low-impedance, microphone signal suitable for any preamp that can accept a microphone input.

DI boxes come in many flavors and prices. You can buy active DI boxes, which are powered by batteries or phantom power, or stick with passive DI boxes, which require no additional power. Active DI boosts the signal with an internal preamp so that the instrument's pickups don't have to power two cable runs and the DI box itself. Passive DI simply transforms the signal and passes it on.

Bass guitars are quite often recorded direct. The bass signal lends itself well to this process, and a bass recorded well direct sounds as good as if it were coming from an amplifier. Guitars are a different story. Guitar amps are a pretty big part of an electric guitar's sound, so recording a guitar signal direct, without any other processing, sounds weak and puny. Thankfully, you can find guitar amplifier emulator plug-ins that can take a direct recorded guitar signal and make it sound like it was coming from a $2,000 amp. In fact, recording a clean, unamplified guitar signal direct is the best way to take advantage of these plug-ins.

Recording Tips

Here are some recording tips and techniques:

- **Shockmount:** Mount good vocal mics in a shockmount that screws into the stand. It keeps vibration from the floor from being picked up by the mic. Remember, you're in a recording studio, not a live sound situation.

- **Pop filter:** Always use a pop filter to keep the vocalist's plosives (B's, P's, and other hard sounds) under control. This helps reduce wind/breathing noise as well.

- **Windscreen:** This is not strictly necessary in a studio. Use it if you've got a real heavy breather; otherwise, tell them to breathe "off mic," that is, to look away when taking a deep breath.

■ **Vocals:** The vocal is often the most important part of the entire song. Don't rush it. Make sure to set levels based on the loudest the singers are going to sing/scream. Remind the singers they don't have to eat the mic. That's why you have preamps. They can stand pretty far back and belt it out, and it's just fine. Some singers need a music stand to remember their lyrics and possibly a side-table handy to set a warm drink on for their throat. Point the mic toward the center of the room unless it's a well-isolated booth (even then), so the mic doesn't pick up reverberations coming off a wall.

■ **Acoustic guitar:** As with all acoustic instruments, the sound you get depends on where you place the mic. Many track acoustic guitars in stereo. Unlike electric guitar, you must isolate an acoustic guitar from external noise.

■ **Electric guitar:** You can mic the amp or go direct. Experiment with mic placement on the amp. Center the mic on the speaker cone or offset it, close mic, or back off for different bass levels and ambience. Use mics that can withstand high sound pressure levels if you are cranking the amp.

■ **Electric bass:** This can easily be recorded direct. If miking an amp, make sure to use a mic that has enough low-end range.

■ **Drum kit:** You can go minimal with two or three mics (left and right room, plus kick) or max yourself out by placing a mic on every drum. You have lots of choices and options here. Minimizing bleed is important when miking up all the drums, so use directional mics. Use mics that can withstand high sound pressure levels on most drums.

■ **Other percussion:** This is similar to miking pianos (for things like xylophones and marimbas) or vocalists (for shakers, tambourines, and so on).

■ **Piano:** Most people mic grand pianos in stereo, and many use an X-Y technique. Smaller or upright pianos may require different mic placement. Always try and get close to the sound board on a piano.

■ **Strings:** Unlike acoustic guitars, violins and cellos (to name a couple) do not have large sound holes. Position the mics to point at the strings or bridge. Be careful to give the players room to maneuver their bows.

■ **Horns:** Point at the bell and vary to suit what sound you like. This is similar to miking a guitar amp speaker cone. Use mics that can withstand high sound pressure levels.

- **Groups:** In contrast to cases involving an individual vocalist or instrument, here you are looking to cover an area, or part of an area. Set the mics far enough away to gather the sound but not so far that they introduce too much ambience. If desired, set up a room mic for ambience (and crowd reaction).

Recording in Pro Tools

Now it's time to record some audio in Pro Tools. I'm going to go through the entire process from start to finish and record a few bars of a piece I'm working on. I am using my electric guitar and bass for this. You can, of course, substitute your favorite instruments in your own projects!

Creating the Pro Tools Session

First, create the session. This is something you can do each time on the fly or, if you're dealing with clients, well beforehand. You can also create a Pro Tools session and turn it into a template, which makes creating sessions with the same settings much faster.

Making Templates   Windows and Mac users: first, open Pro Tools and create a session you want to serve as the template. Create tracks, assign busses, inserts, and so forth. Save the file and close Pro Tools. Next, find the session file in Windows Explorer (Windows) or the Finder (Mac). Windows users: right-click the session file and click read-only. Mac users: click the file to select it, choose File >Info from the Finder menu, and check both the Stationery Pad and Locked checkboxes.

Open the template file as you would normally. Windows users should immediately choose File>Save As and create the appropriate folder to store the session in. Mac users are given the option of editing the template or saving a session based on the template's settings.

It makes your job of setting up the Pro Tools session easier if you have some idea beforehand of what you're going to record and how many tracks you might need. Those details are nothing that you can't amend on the fly, but you should give it some thought going in.

1.   Make sure the Pro Tools LE or M-Powered interface is connected and powered up. Make sure any iLoks that might be required are correctly inserted.

2.   Launch Pro Tools.

3.   Select the File>New menu to create the session.

4. Determine where to save the session and choose a name, as shown in Figure 9.3. The new session is stored in a folder with the same name as the session file within the folder you are currently in. Choose your other options if you like. For the Mbox 2, my choices are WAV audio file type, 48 kHz sample rate, and 24-bit bit depth. The last used I/O setting might be good, or not, depending on your last session. You can choose another if you like.

Figure 9.3 Creating a new session.

5. Press Save to save the session and get started.

6. Pro Tools generates the session file and kicks you to the Edit window to get started. This is a clean slate: no tracks, no busses, no Master Faders—nothing.

7. Select the Setup>Playback Engine menu. Set these settings to maximize performance while recording. Now is not the time to experiment. You should

know what settings work and trust their reliability. Lower the buffer to a low, but well-known safe level to reduce monitoring latency. You might be able to reduce Real Time AudioSuite (RTAS) processors because you should not be using many plug-ins while you track.

8. Set a session tempo (see Figure 9.4). Make sure the Tempo ruler is visible and double-click the red triangle to set the initial tempo. If you don't know the tempo, you can come back and set it later.

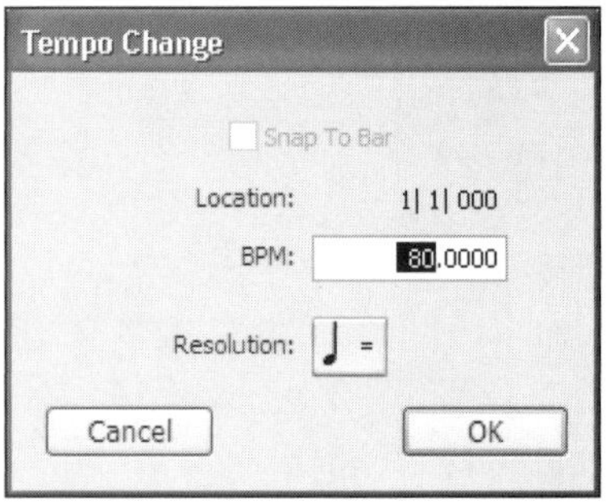

Figure 9.4 Setting the initial tempo.

9. Configure the click from the Setup>Click/Countoff menu. I choose "Only during record" so that when I'm playing back I don't have to mute the click all the time.

10. Create the click track (you can set Pro Tools up to automatically create a click track when you create a new session from the MIDI Preferences) by selecting the Track>Create Click Track menu.

11. Open the Click plug-in (Figure 9.5) to alter how the click sounds (accented versus unaccented beats only).

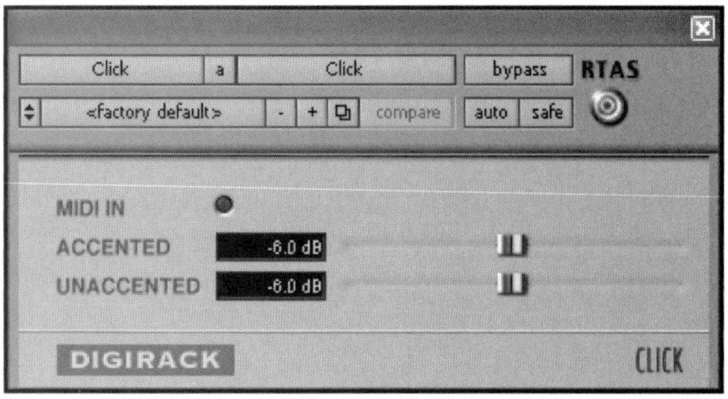

Figure 9.5 Altering click levels.

12.   Now is a good time to save your session.

13.   Next, create the tracks. In this example (see Figure 9.6), I'm going to create four mono audio tracks for recording, two stereo Aux Input tracks, and a stereo Master Fader to control the session's overall level (normally set to 0 dB, which neither amplifies nor cuts level, but is handy to have if you want to mute the entire session or automate a fade-in or fade-out later). Select the Track>New menu to create the tracks.

Figure 9.6   Creating several tracks at once.

14.   Name the tracks by double-clicking the first track name and enter a new name. Click Ctrl (Windows) or Command (Mac) + right arrow to go to the next track. For this example, I named my tracks "EG 1.1," "EG 1.2," "Lead," and "Bass"; my Aux Input tracks I named "Verb" and "Delay." Do this now, before you record, because Pro Tools incorporates the track name into the file name it saves. This makes it easier to keep track of what's what if you need to look at regions or files.

15.   If you like, name your I/O paths from the Setup>I/O menu or load previously saved settings.

16.   Select the correct Input settings (see Figure 9.7). I prefer to do this now rather than wait until I need each track. I input everything on In 1. I also select the input busses for my two Aux Input tracks.

17.   Change any Output paths if you have any mix busses or other circumstances where you want to redirect output.

18.   Save your session.

That about does it for setting up the Pro Tools session. Next, it's time to dive into loading in and making connections.

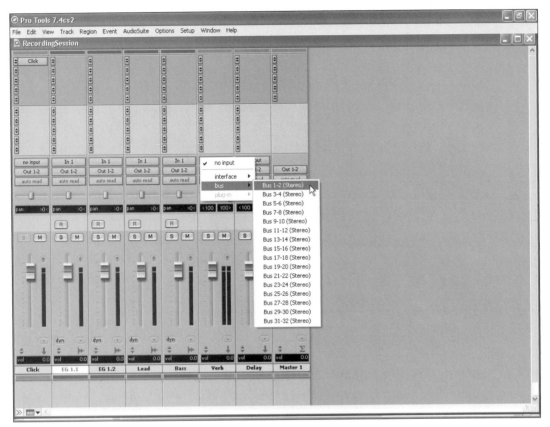

Figure 9.7   Setting input paths.

Loading in and Making Connections

Load-in is the time you schedule a band or musicians to start unpacking and settling in at the studio. It should be well before the time they expect to start recording. It takes time to unpack a drum kit, piece by piece, carry it inside, assemble it, mic it up, test the connections, and get warmed up. Even vocalists who have very little to unpack need time to get "in the groove."

About the only time you don't need to worry about this sort of scheduling is when it's just yourself. For me, that means my amp is already here, plugged in and ready to roll. Most of my connections are set, my guitar is sitting in its stand, my bass is in its case. Everything is close at hand, and the time I need to get ready is much less than with a client. Still, I plan for taking time to get the equipment warmed up, make any changes to my setup that I might need, and get tuned up.

Band Focus   I have a "band focus" as I write this. I realize you might be the only person involved. Like me, you're the musician, engineer, and producer in your home studio. Maybe you've got a rapper coming in or a person who makes beats. The information presented here might or might not directly apply to you. I think it's good to present it from this perspective and let you take from it what you can. I put notes next to the steps that most apply to solo acts, which is how I work at home. Now, back to our regularly scheduled broadcast.

Here's a quick checklist for loading in and making connections:

1. Pro Tools is on and your interface is plugged in and ready to go. The session is loaded and ready.

2. Bring in the equipment and start setting it up. In my case, that's been happening for some months and all the gear is already here. It helps to have your own home studio.

3. Set up mood lighting and music stands. Turn off any distracting lighting.

4. Make sure everyone has pencils and paper for notes.

5. Make sure people know where refreshments and the facilities are.

6. Start miking things up and running cables. Set any user-selectable patterns or other switches such as bass rolloff on the mics now. I operate a little differently here at home. I take the speaker signal from my tube guitar amp and route it through a combination DI box/load attenuator/speaker simulator, then into the interface. As a result, I don't mic anything up. That enables me to record at any time, day or night, and not bother everyone else. Have people tune up now.

Digital I/O   If you're recording over a digital connection such as S/PDIF, make sure to set the clock source (Setup>Hardware).

7. Turn preamp levels down to their lowest level. No need to blow anything up yet. Make the connections to your interface. Be sure to make the correct connections. Line inputs should go to line, microphone to mic, and instrument to instrument inputs. If you are using a system with a mic/line switch, set it correctly.

8.   Now it's time to test signal flow. For the first track you want to record, select the Record Enable (Arm) button. The button should turn red, and you might see the level meter jump around some. If you're running an 003, you should do this for each track you plan on recording, which could be several. Systems like the Mbox 2 might be recording only one or two tracks. Raise the preamp gain and have the musician or vocalist play/sing to establish the fact that everything is working. Now is the time to find bad cables, connectors, instruments, or other problems. I recommend this test be done now rather than later.

That does it for setting up. All the gear is set up, running, connected, and working. Cables are connected to the interface, and you've got signal on each track. Next, it's time to set preamp levels.

Setting Preamp Levels

This is a critical part of the recording process. Don't cheat yourself and rush through this in your sessions. Give yourself the time to do it correctly. However, strive to be able to do this fast enough on each instrument that you don't tire everyone out just setting preamp levels. That's a drag, man. Wear headphones. This dials your ears in and blocks out distracting sound.

Your first goal should be to avoid clipping. You can't easily recover from that.

Your second goal should be to produce a line-level signal coming out of the interface. Yes, that's right, a line-level signal. If you're running 24 bits, that equates to peaking about −12 dB, which is where the green level meter starts to turn yellow. There's a reason for that color change. Many people, myself included, have fallen into the trap of tracking too "hot." I used to shoot for a signal strength of between −3 dB and 0 dB. What I didn't realize is that at that level, the preamp is working way too hard and ends up frying the sound. You don't need that. In fact, the gear isn't designed to do that. It's designed to produce an optimum signal at line-level strength.

Your third goal should be to get a strong enough signal that you can record. If you shoot for −12 dB, you are going to be fine. Make sure to get it up there!

Here are general steps for setting preamp levels. Follow them for each input.

1.   Pro Tools is on, and your interface is plugged in and ready to go. The session is loaded and ready. Mics are set up and connections made.

2.   Arm the track.

3. Conduct some talking or "Can you hear me?" tests. Make sure the artist can hear themselves through their headphones. Tweak mix and headphone levels throughout to make sure they hear what they need to.

4. Have the musicians or vocalist begin in earnest. Have them warm up by working on the song you're going to record. Don't set preamp levels in a vacuum.

5. Raise the gain on the preamp until you see the level meter in Pro Tools peak out somewhere at −12 dB (Figure 9.8). Ctrl (Windows) or Command (Mac) click the track's level readout to see where it peaks.

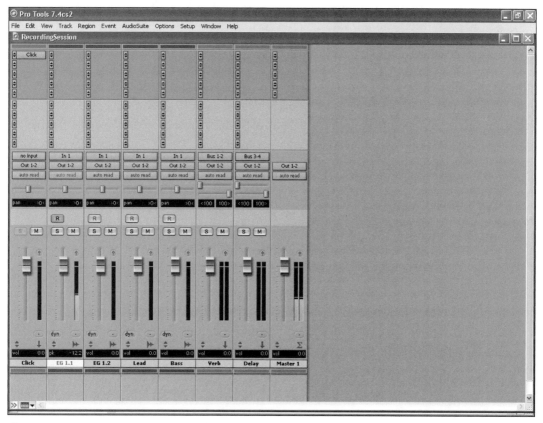

Figure 9.8 Setting correct preamp level.

6. You are going to quickly realize if you need to engage a pad on the interface or on the microphone. Do so if you clip with the gain all the way down.

7. If you're not getting the sound you want, reposition the microphone.

8. When you're done with an input, move on to the next.

Recording

Okay, believe it or not, it's time to record. Recording, in and of itself, is actually pretty easy. You get everyone ready; press Record, then Play (or like I do just hit 3 on the numeric keypad); tell everyone that "tape is rolling"; and Stop (or spacebar) when the take is done or when someone decides to stop in the middle. If someone makes a mistake and stops, don't Undo too fast. You might be able to use most of what you just recorded.

Here are the general recording steps that I follow:

1. Pro Tools is on, and your interface is plugged in and ready to go. The session is loaded and ready. Mics are set up and connections made. Preamp levels are set. Make any final tuning adjustments to instruments.

2. Press Enter (Windows) or Return (Mac) to locate the Play Start marker to the beginning of the session.

3. Give everyone a "Standby" signal.

4. Press Record, then Play. You can also press 3 on the numeric keypad (or hit actual buttons on some systems). You should see Pro Tools recording.

5. Give everyone the "Recording" signal. This tells them they can start.

6. Listen. Listen for good stuff, flubs, intonation problems, and anything else that might trash this take. Note the song structure. I'm recording along in Figure 9.9.

7. Press Stop, or spacebar, to end.

8. Ask everyone what they thought. If the feeling was good, you all might want to listen to the take. In cases where you are an artist involved in the session or producer, you have more leeway in telling someone the good and bad points. If you are strictly the engineer, be careful what you say and how you say it.

9. Depending on the situation, you might want to do one of the following: redo the take, move on to record other tracks, punch-in over small mistakes, re-record scratch tracks, or move on to the next song.

You have many recording options and modes. A few techniques that you should become familiar with are as follows:

■ **Click:** Always try and record with a click track. Musicians who don't regularly practice with one might not be easily convinced, but when it comes time to edit the tracks, you have an established timebase to work with.

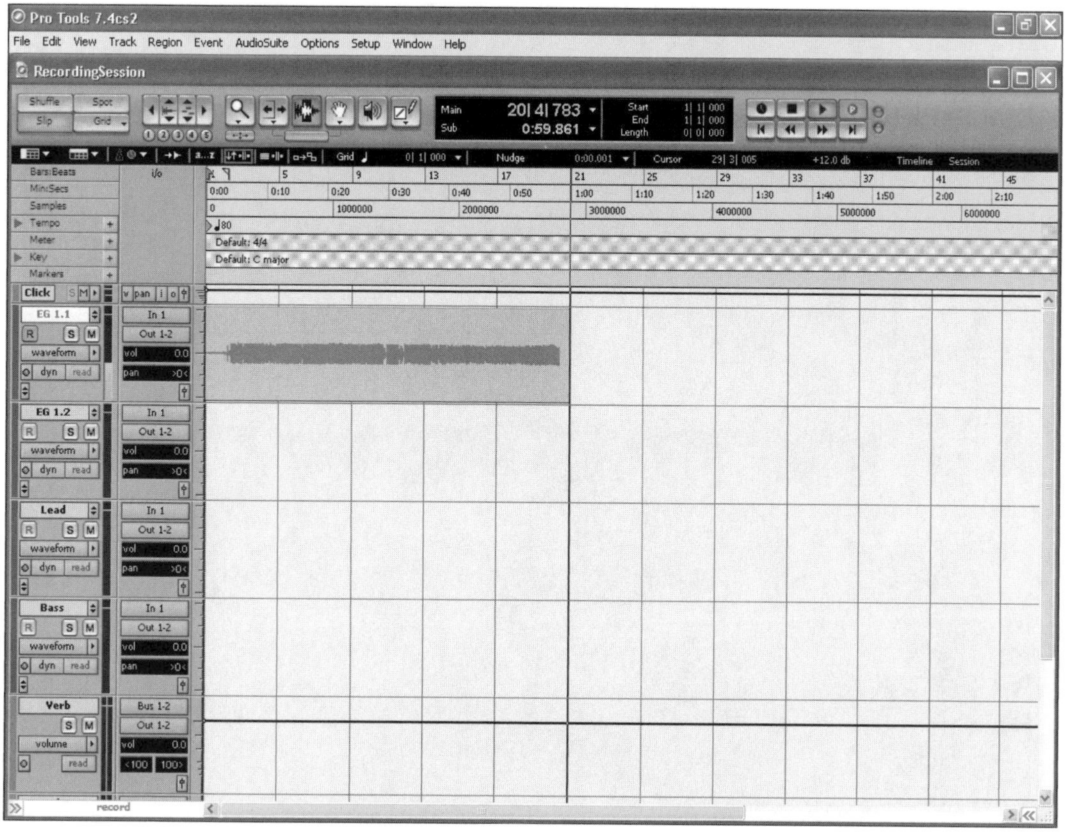

Figure 9.9 Recording.

- **Scratch tracks:** Scratch tracks are tracks you record knowing you intend to record over them at a later time.

- **Overdubs:** This refers to recording additional material to go with the basic tracks, such as extra percussion, lead parts, or other odds and ends. This is about the same as recording material from scratch, only you play along with the previously recorded material. Be careful of recording overdubs on mixes that have a lot of plug-ins. This will drive performance down and latency up. Make tracks and plug-ins you don't absolutely need inactive.

- **Doubling:** This is recording additional takes with the same instrument or vocalist to "beef up" the sound. It can be panned the same or differently. It helps to either mute a prior take or pan it off to the side and lower its level so the artist doesn't confuse the prior take with the current performance. Doubling tracks is vital to get a "wall of sound."

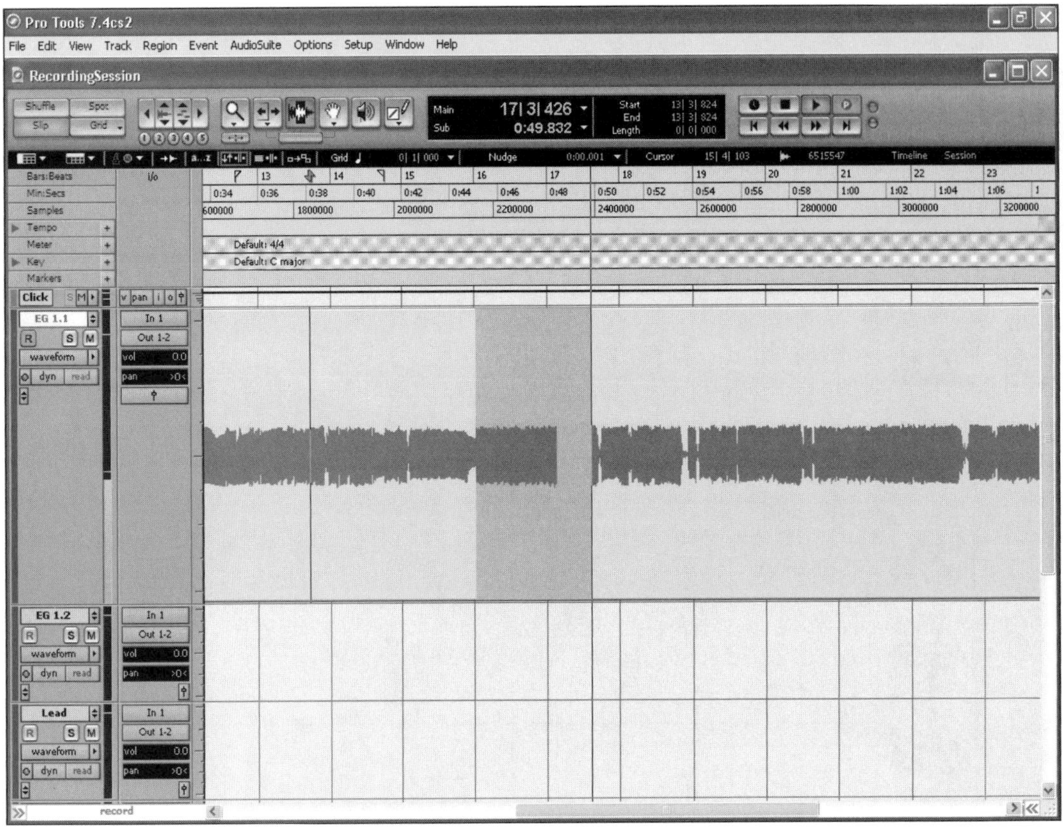

Figure 9.10 Punching in over a mistake.

■ **Punches:** Punching in (see Figure 9.10) and out involves starting playback well before the material you want to record over and having the performer play or swing along. You must be in Quick Punch mode (Options>QuickPunch) and Auto Input mode (Track>Auto Input Monitoring) to do this. Press Play to start playback and then Record close to the section you want to replace. Press Record again to stop the punch but keep playing, or press Stop to stop the take. Punches are a great way of saving a good take from the trash if all that's wrong are a few notes or a measure here and there. You can edit the takes together in editing and never know they were from separate performances.

10 Editing Audio

E diting—yes, we come to editing. People want to hear music on the beat, every time. I don't know about you, but I'm not a perfect musician. I strive to be. I practice, record myself, analyze my performances, and work like a "dawg" at it. For the time being, however, my performance skills fall below how I want to sound. I don't plan on that being the case forever. But in the meantime, I turn to editing to clean my tracks up and sound as professional as I can.

I can let you in on a secret. Do you think anyone is as perfect as what you hear on the radio or through iTunes? Do you think that's how it goes down in the studio? One take, perfectly timed, perfectly in tune, perfectly performed? Most of the time, that's not the case. Of course, some musical geniuses can nail a song to within a few milliseconds. Even their tracks, however, should be scrutinized and examined for possible areas of improvement.

Thankfully, Pro Tools rocks in the editing department. I'm convinced this is because of its clean interface, intuitive tools, and mixing power. I love editing in Pro Tools, and I'm not ashamed to say it. Developing your editing skills helps you make better music, whether you are rescuing a poor performance that you can't re-record or maximizing a great take. This chapter focuses on four of those editing skills: working with audio regions, the Beat Detective, Elastic Audio, and automation.

Working in the Edit Window

The Edit window is, not coincidentally, where you spend most of your editing time. Become familiar and comfortable with all the interface elements, track controls, and possibilities. I'm going to quickly cover some basic Edit window skills before I move on to editing audio proper.

Making Selections

Selecting an area from the timeline is different from selecting audio regions. To select a period of time, switch to the Selection tool and click+drag to the left or right on a track (see Figure 10.1). Notice that the rulers and selected audio become highlighted. You can

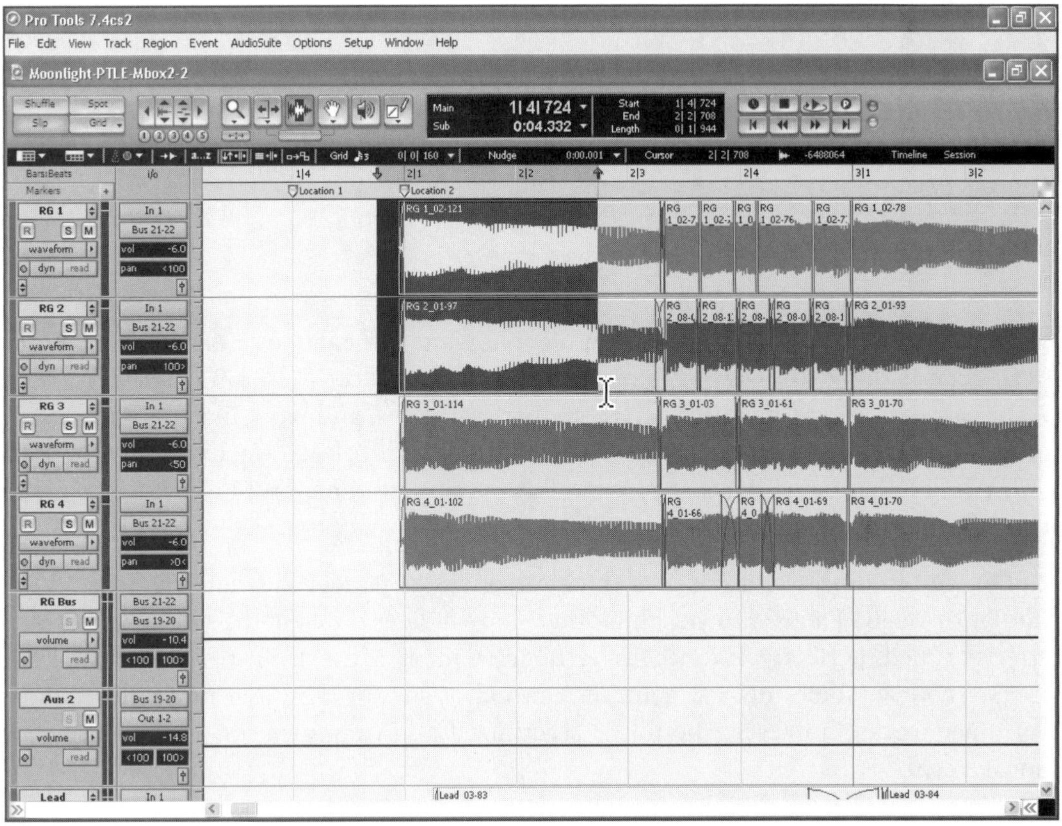

Figure 10.1 Making a basic selection.

drag your mouse up or down to "catch" tracks and audio if you like. If you're in Grid mode, the mouse snaps to the grid markers. If you click+drag on the ruler, all tracks are selected.

If the track you make a selection in is part of a group, all grouped tracks are selected. If you want to select the same area in multiple, nongrouped tracks, make your initial selection and then Shift+click on the other tracks (they do not have to be vertically adjacent to one another). The same area is selected.

Selection Scrolling   I often scroll to the right by using my Selection tool and dragging off one edge or another. The Edit window scrolls in that direction.

Notice the blue arrows that appear on the ruler after you've made your selection. They identify the bounds of the selection and can be moved (click+drag them) to change the timeline selection start and end points. This is one way of refining a playback or looped region.

If you have identified memory locations and double-click on the ruler, the time from the first to last marker is selected.

Now that you've selected an area of time, you can play back, loop playback, record, loop record, delete audio (on tracks where you have made the selection), and more.

Selecting Regions

Selecting regions is easy. First, make sure you're not looking at automation or a Warp view. I normally work in Waveform view for editing. The simplest method to select an entire region is to switch to the Grabber tool and click a region (Figure 10.2). It is selected and becomes highlighted. If you're using the Selection tool and don't want to switch, double-click the region, and it becomes selected.

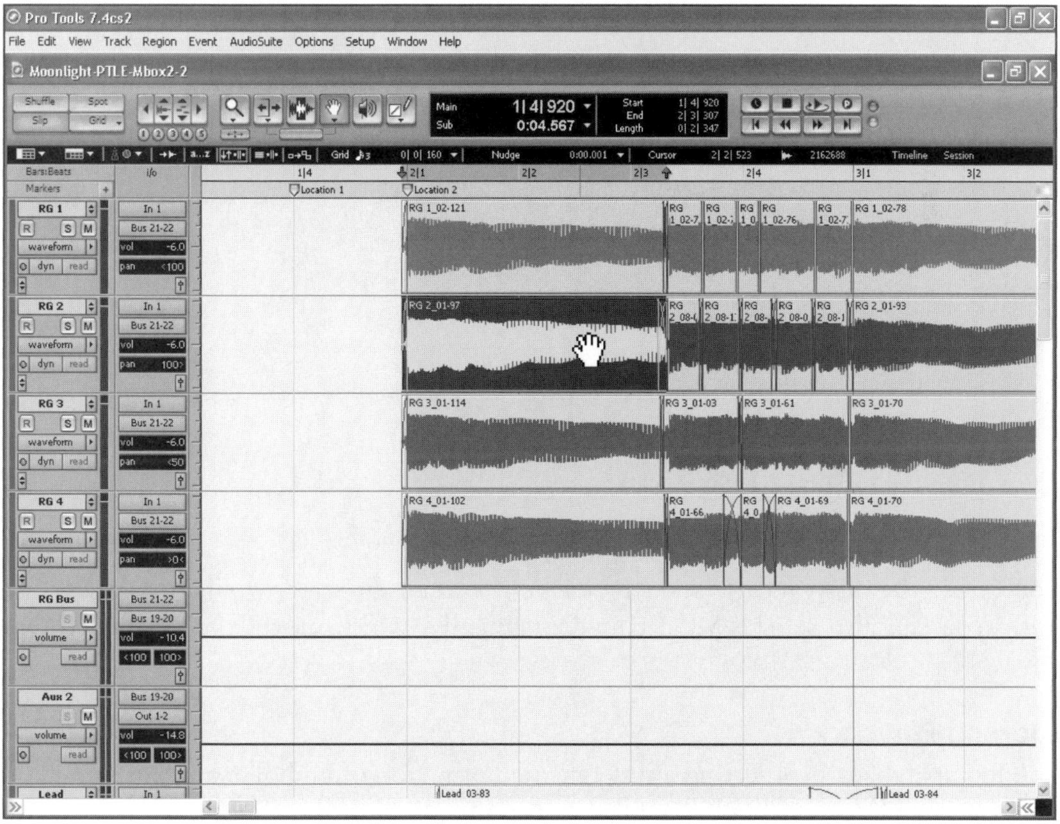

Figure 10.2 Selecting a region with the Grabber.

You can select fades and crossfades with either tool. Click (Grabber) or double-click (Selection) in the bounds of a fade or crossfade to select it. After you've selected a region, you can move it, delete it, nudge it, or apply an AudioSuite plug-in to the region.

Setting the Play Start Marker

The official term for "where you are and where playback starts if you play or record" is called the Play Start Marker. When nothing else is selected, the Play Start Marker appears as a blinking black cursor on one or more tracks (Figure 10.3). It appears on the last track, or track group, you clicked in with the Selection tool. You're given an indication in the ruler where the Play Start Marker is; it is a combination of the blue loop arrows. When you make a selection, those arrows separate and become the start and end loop points. If you make a selection (whether a time-based selection or a region), the Play Start Marker is the start point of the selection.

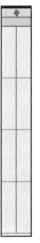

Figure 10.3   The blinking Play Start Marker.

You can set the Play Start Marker by clicking in the Edit window where you want to start. You can also set the Main counter manually, which moves the marker to that point.

Looping Playback

You loop playback by selecting a timeline area or region of audio, enabling Loop Play-back from the Options>Loop Playback menu, and pressing Play. If your selection is too small (under 500 ms), looping does not occur; the selection plays once and stops.

Working with Alternate Playlists

Playlists are great ways of recording multiple takes and conveniently storing them out of the way, but in a place where they are still accessible. Playlists are available on Audio, MIDI, and Instrument tracks. Click the double-arrow beside the track name in the Edit window to access the Playlist menu (Figure 10.4). The pop-up menu enables you to create a new playlist, duplicate a playlist, delete unused playlists, and choose from playlists.

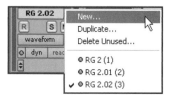

Figure 10.4 Accessing multiple playlists.

Edits you make (with the exception of automation) on one playlist do not affect any others. However, you cannot have a normal audio playlist and an Elastic audio playlist on the same track. As soon as you enable Elastic Audio, it is active on all playlists.

Keyboard Focus

Remember the Keyboard Focus button, introduced in Chapter 8? This is when you see the power of that. When editing, click Commands Keyboard Focus to switch the Commands. This opens a plethora of quick and easy keyboard commands that make editing a breeze. Have a look in the Digidesign Keyboard Shortcuts Guide for the full list (study the section titled "Commands Keyboard Focus Mode"). Here are a few popular ones:

- Center Timeline selection start: Q, centers the timeline windows where you have the Insertion point located.

- Zoom Out horizontally: R, zooms out, centering where you have the Insertion point.

- Zoom In horizontally: T, zooms in, centering where you have the Insertion point.

- Move Edit selection up: P, moves the Insertion point up tracks, or groups of tracks.

- Move Edit selection down: ; (semi-colon), moves the Insertion point down tracks, or groups of tracks.

- Trim Start to Insertion: A, quickly trims from where you have the Insertion point to the beginning of the region it is in.

- Trim End to Insertion: S, quickly trims from where you have the Insertion point to the end of the region it is in.

- Fade to Start (available if no selection): D, fades from the Insertion point to the beginning of a region. Automatically applies the default fade. No selection is required.

- Fade (without showing Fades dialog): F, this fade requires a selection, so it can be a fade in or out, but it does so without showing the Fades dialog box. Automatically applies the default fade.

- Fade to End (available if no selection): G, fades from the Insertion point to the end of a region. Automatically applies the default fade. No selection is required.

- Separate: B, separates the region where the Insertion point is located.

- Timeline Insertion follows Playback (disable/enable): N, toggles the option where the Timeline Insertion marker follows playback.

Basic Editing

Editing happens in the Edit window, where you can see the audio regions residing on their respective tracks. Most standard editing involves separating and working with audio regions.

Remember that you can switch to Commands Keyboard Focus and make editing, especially fades, very quick work with a keyboard.

Separating (Splitting) Regions

To split a region, switch to the Selection tool and click to set the Play Start Marker at the point where you want to make the split. You can use the grid to help you position yourself, or the Main counter. After setting the cursor, select the Edit>Separate Region>At Selection menu or press Ctrl+E (Windows) or Command+E (Mac).

You can also select an area to separate into its own region. It splits on both sides of the selection (Figure 10.5).

Figure 10.5 Separating regions is a fundamental editing skill.

The great thing about Pro Tools (and, to be honest, other digital audio workstations [DAWs]) is that when you separate a region, you haven't lost anything. You can even delete or trim audio out of a region and then expand it with the Trim tool and recover what you just "lost." If you split a region and it's not exactly where you want it to be, use the Trim tool to adjust its boundaries. You can also heal separated regions that haven't been moved.

Moving Regions

Move regions by selecting them and using the Grabber tool to move them left or right within the same track, or up or down to move them to a different track. You can make an exact placement by switching to Spot mode before you make your region selection. You are prompted for the start point when you make the selection. You can also nudge a region left or right (the distance is set from the Nudge values) by selecting it and then pressing + or − on your numeric keypad.

Manual Beat Mapping   Separating regions, moving or nudging them, and creating fades and crossfades are the three skills required to manually edit audio so that performed notes fall on the correct beats. This is editing bread and butter. These skills can help you make just about any performance better.

Creating Fades and Crossfades

Fades and crossfades are important tools in creating click-free audio. Fade-ins and fade-outs are pretty self-explanatory. Crossfades fade between two audio regions. The crossfade creates an area of overlap and blends the two audio regions together. Always listen to your crossfades, because you might have to deal with phase issues (two regions of audio with different phases being blended together is the definition of a phaser) even if you don't hear pops or clicks. Depending on the regions, you might have to experiment with different-sized crossfades. Sometimes you can have good success creating a very small crossfade (ideally where the audio is at a very low level or at 0 dB), but at other times, you might need a longer blending area to minimize phase misalignment.

To create a fade, select the head or tail of a region (on one or more tracks) from where it starts/ends to the point you want the fade to either start or end (or past it into empty space). Then select the Edit>Fades>Create menu or press Ctrl+F (Windows) or Command+F (Mac) to open the Fades dialog box (Figure 10.6).

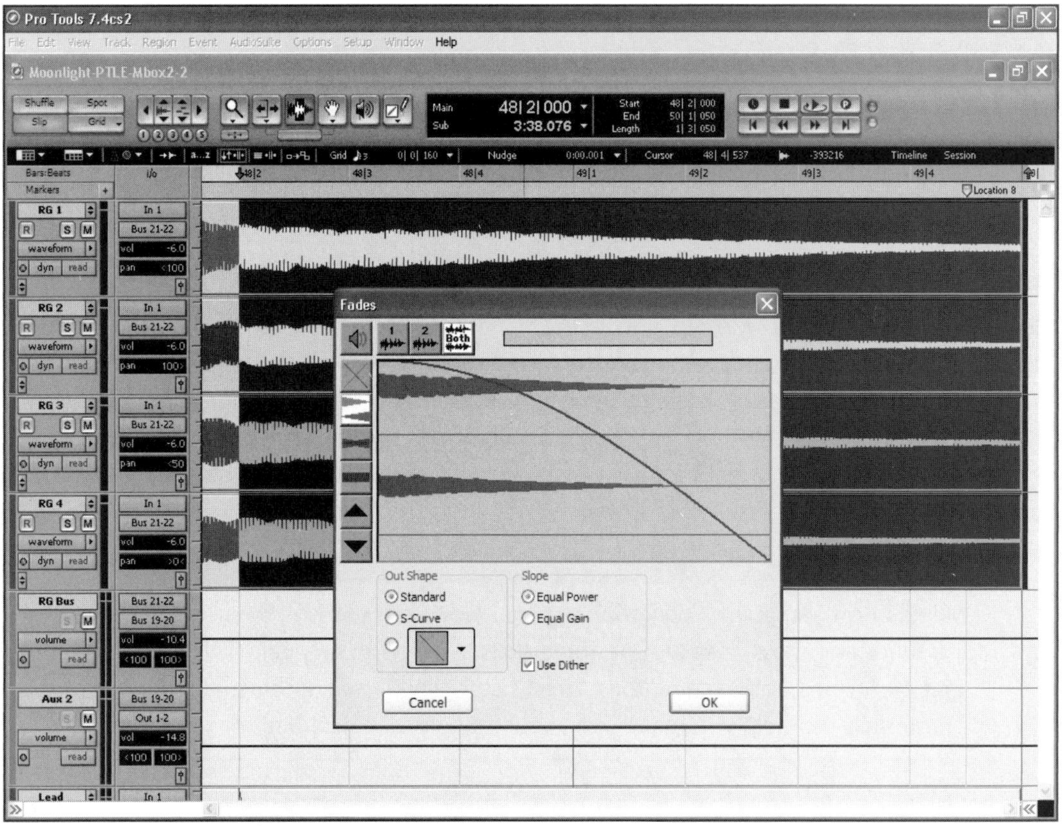

Figure 10.6 Creating a multitrack fadeout.

Select the shape and slope of the fade you want to create from the dialog box. You can then see (and listen to) a preview of the fade. Then press OK.

To create a crossfade, select the area where two audio regions meet, making sure to select from each area, and then create the crossfade the same way as you do a fade. The dialog box gives you the same options as normal fades, only they cross each other (Figure 10.7).

Use the Trim tool to expand the size of the fade or crossfade.

Grouping Regions

Grouping regions is a great way to clean up some clutter in the Edit window and (more importantly) manipulate multiple regions (including applying AudioSuite plug-ins) as if they were one. For example, if you have a lot of regions that you want to copy and paste and want to keep everything together and on beat, group them beforehand. Grouping does not merge them and can be undone.

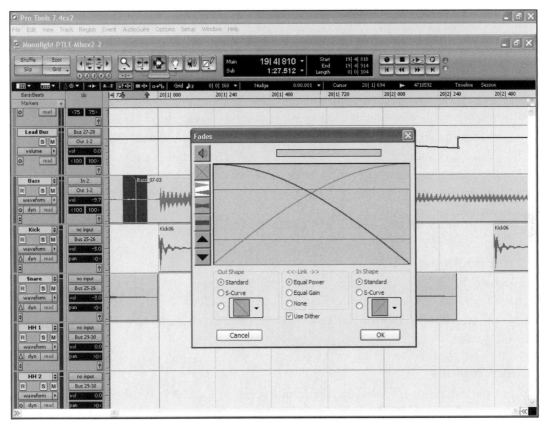

Figure 10.7 Creating a single crossfade.

You can group regions by selecting them and then pressing Ctrl+Alt+G (Windows) or Command+Option+G (Mac).

To ungroup, select the grouped region and press Ctrl+Alt+U (Windows) or Command+Option+U (Mac).

Consolidating (Merging) Regions

All those fades and crossfades are actual files that Pro Tools has to keep in memory and be ready to play at any time. After you get enough regions on a track editing, it can be advantageous to consolidate them into one region that is made up of one complete file.

To consolidate regions, select them and then choose Edit>Consolidate or press Alt+Shift+3 (Windows) or Option+Shift+3 (Mac).

Pro Tools renders this as a separate file.

Fades and Consolidating Fades at the beginning and end of the resulting consolidated region are part of the new file. You don't have to go back and recreate them. By the same token, crossfades are part of the consolidated region as well if you include them in the region selection. I recommend you don't include them or that you remove crossfades between regions you want to consolidate and those you don't. I just completed a test with bass and guitar regions on the same track. I created a crossfade between them and then separated the guitar region into multiple regions for the consolidate test. Finally, I selected the guitar regions, including the crossfade between the bass and guitar, and consolidated the guitar regions. Sure enough, the bass appeared in the consolidated region because it was part of the selected crossfade.

Locking Regions

You can lock regions to prevent further editing. Select the region and choose the Region>Lock/Unlock menu. You then see a little padlock on the region. To unlock, select that region and choose the same menu. Locking is crucial when doing Shuffle edits on a track!

Muting Regions

You can mute regions by selecting them and pressing Ctrl+M (Win) or Command+M (Mac), or by choosing the Region>Mute/Unmute menu. Unmute them the same way. A muted region appears grayed out in the Edit window.

Using Beat Detective

The Beat Detective is another tool for analyzing audio or MIDI regions and determining the beat, bars, or other tempo information from the audio itself. I'm not going to get far into the Beat Detective; just enough to show you the interface and a simple tempo analysis of a portion of a bass track.

1. Launch the Beat Detective from the Event>Beat Detective menu and then select a region of audio (ideally one region on a track with no other regions). I've set up one bar of a bass track to analyze (see Figure 10.8). It's important to begin and end the selection on a beat. I've used the Trim tool to set my start and end points exactly where the beats are in the performance.

2. In the selection portion of the dialog box, enter the appropriate number of bars if you know them. In this case, my region is one bar. That means I start at bar 1, beat 1 and end on bar 2, beat 1. I have 1/8-note triplets in this section as well.

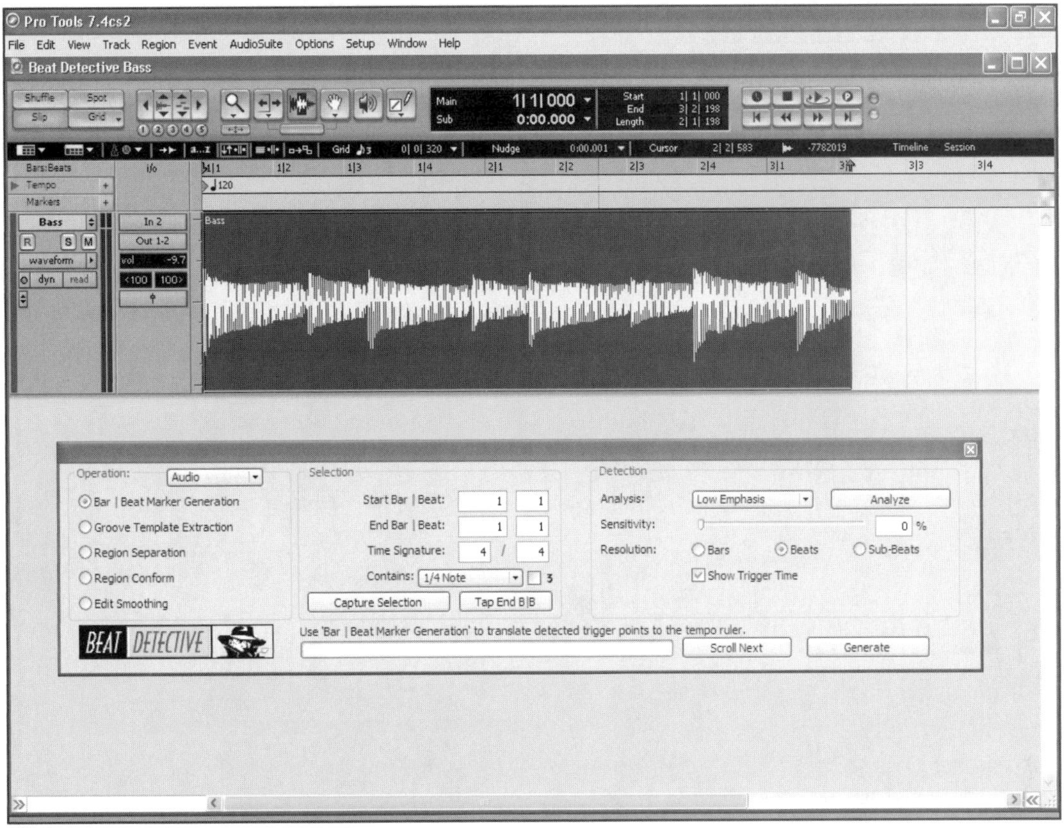

Figure 10.8 Preparing to analyze one bar of bass.

3. Select a method of analysis from the right side of the dialog box, choose a resolution, and press Analyze. In this example, I'm going with beats because the entire region is one bar. Raise the Sensitivity slider until you start seeing beats, as shown in Figure 10.9.

4. Switch to the Grabber tool and move the Beat Triggers manually to set their final position according to the beat. In some cases this isn't much work. In others, it's a lot.

5. Finally, I'm calculating the tempo in this example, so I keep the Operation set on Bar | Beat Marker Generation and click Generate. The result is that the tempo (as derived from my performance) is shown in the Tempo ruler (see Figure 10.10).

This really just scratches the surface with the Beat Detective. I hope your appetite is whetted for more, and you're excited to start experimenting with it!

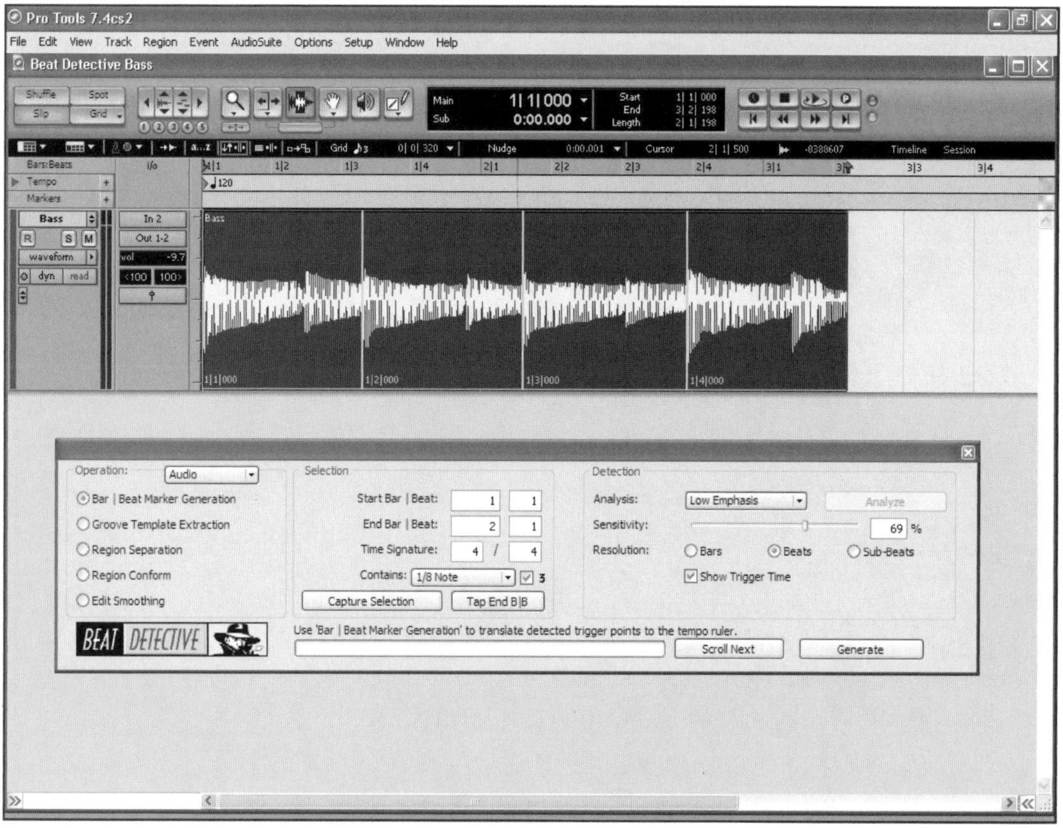

Figure 10.9 Detecting downbeats.

Elastic Audio

Delving into the depths of Elastic Audio is beyond the scope of this book. I do, however, want to introduce you to Elastic Audio so that you are aware of it, have some idea of how to work with it, and see some of its potential.

Simply put, Elastic Audio is a track-based method of time compressing or expanding audio regions to follow a chosen tempo and beat. Time compressing is complex and very resource-intensive. Audio is composed of waves that have a frequency, amplitude, and phase. Frequency and phase are directly tied to time, which means that when you stretch or compress audio, you change its frequency and phase. Elastic Audio works to preserve the original tone while allowing you to match it to new tempos and beats.

Though time compression and expansion have been available in Pro Tools for some time (the Time Compression/Expander [TCE] tool), Elastic Audio represents a major step forward. In contrast to a static, one-time compression/expansion, Elastic Audio

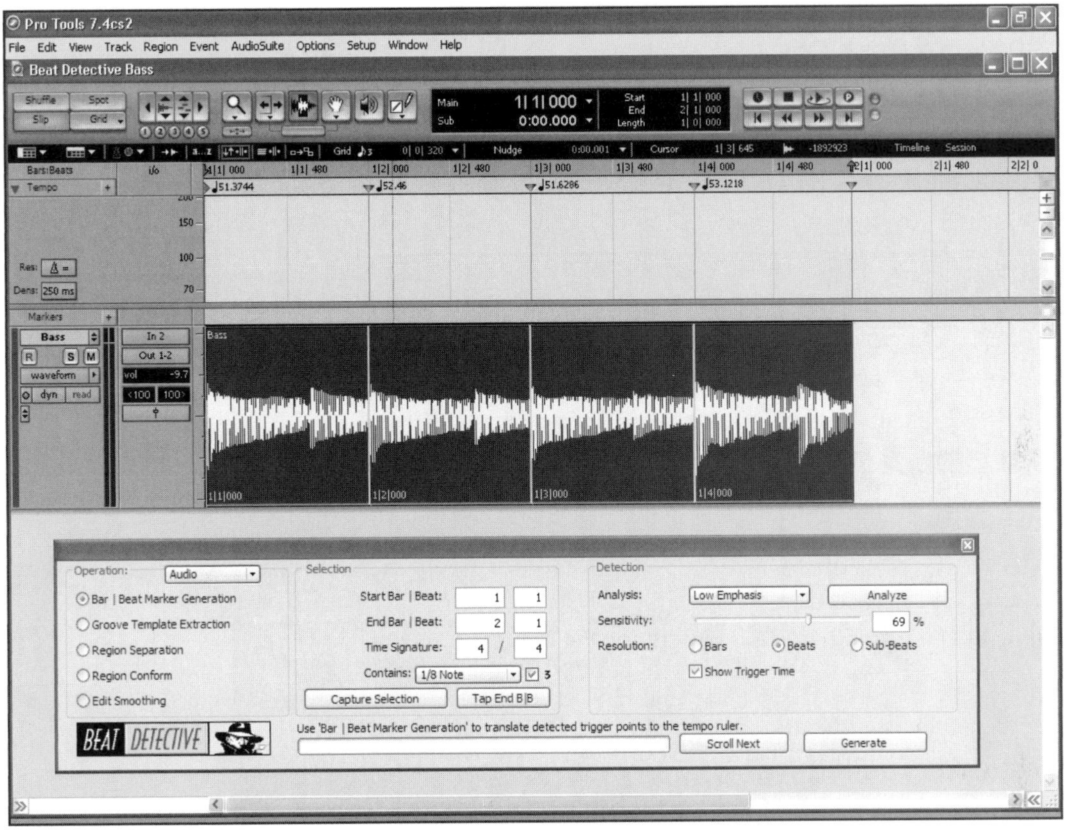

Figure 10.10 I have successfully determined the tempo of the performance.

is a much more flexible and powerful system of event-based (transient beat detection and analysis) warping. In many ways, it's like combining the Beat Detective with the TCE tool and allowing you to do it all in real time.

The main benefits for most people are loop-based audio and the ability to correct slightly off performances. Loops are fun to work with, but Pro Tools has not traditionally been friendly to them. With Elastic Audio, you can match loops to your current session tempo and beat grid. Performance correcting is an alternative option to slicing a recording into regions and manually aligning each beat with the session tempo. That promises to be a major time-saver when you are working with unsteady performers.

Enabling Elastic Audio

Elastic Audio is track-based, which means you enable or disable it on a track-by-track basis. You can automatically enable Elastic Audio in the Preferences (Setup>Preferences,

Processing tab) for all new tracks, or you can turn on Elastic Audio manually from the Elastic Audio Plug-in Selector, which is on the track's channel strip controls. It's the bottom-most button and has top- and bottom-pointing arrows.

To enable Elastic Audio for a track, click the selector and choose an Elastic Audio plug-in, as shown in Figure 10.11.

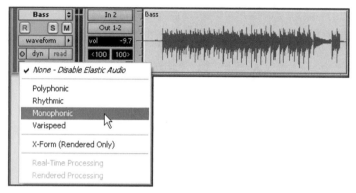

Figure 10.11   Turning on Elastic Audio for the bass track.

Elastic Audio Plug-Ins

You have access to five different Elastic Audio plug-ins. They each handle compression and expansion slightly differently and are optimized for different types of audio. They are as follows:

- **Polyphonic:** This is a good all-purpose algorithm for complex audio.

- **Rhythmic:** This is best for audio that has well-defined transients. This plug-in works very well for drums, but not so well on a soft synth pad.

- **Monophonic:** This plug-in is optimized for vocals and other instruments that most often voice a single note at a time. For example, choose Monophonic for a running bass line, but not for a complex piano track with many notes playing at the same time.

- **Varispeed:** This is more of a special effect plug-in that can sound like a tape machine speeding up or slowing down.

- **X-Form:** This one does not process in real time, so it is more like an AudioSuite plug-in. The tradeoff is that this plug-in delivers the highest quality compression/expansion.

Each plug-in has a plug-in interface, and the Polyphonic and Rhythmic plug-ins each have some simple controls to change their performance.

In addition, with the exception of X-Form, you can choose from the selector menu to have each plug-in operate in real time or rendered.

Event and Warp Markers

Elastic Audio uses two types of markers to show events and warp audio. These are the Event and Warp markers, and they both appear as vertical lines across a track's audio waveform. Event markers do not extend the entire height of a track, but Warp markers do, are a little thicker than Event markers, and end in a small triangle at the bottom.

Event markers (see Figure 10.12) are visible in Warp and Analysis views. They tell you where Pro Tools has evaluated the waveform and thinks there is an event, which is based on its analysis of the attack transient. Normally, this event is a beat of some sort or another. Only you know if it's a downbeat, triplet, or other rhythmic combination. As you warp, you align these markers with your beats, warping the audio to be in time with whatever tempo you choose.

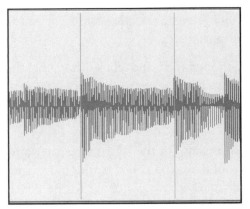

Figure 10.12 Event markers on a track in Warp view.

Event markers are the usual way to warp a given area of audio. You do this by using the Grabber tool and Click+dragging the marker to the left or right while in Warp view. The same action in Analysis view moves the Event marker. That is how you can edit Event markers and reposition them if they're off. Event markers can snap to the grid if you are in Grid mode, but otherwise they are not connected to any point on the timeline.

Warp markers (see Figure 10.13) are visible in Warp view only and are static warp reference points. They hold the audio region in place on the timeline while you warp

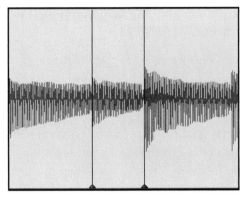

Figure 10.13 Warp markers in Warp view.

around them. You can add, move, and delete Warp markers in Warp view, but they do not appear in Analysis view.

Warp View

Warp view is the main working view for manipulating an Elastic Audio track. This is where you add, remove, and move Warp markers (remember, those are the static markers that hold regions down) and warp Event markers.

You warp Event markers by changing to the Grabber tool and click+dragging the marker left or right. If you're in Grid mode, you snap the marker to the grid. You cannot move, add, or delete Event markers (the ones without the triangle) from the Warp view.

You warp Warp markers (yes, the names do get confusing) in the Warp view the same way you warp an Event marker. Use the Grabber tool to warp. You *can* add, move, and delete Event markers from Warp view. Add Event markers by switching to the Pencil tool and clicking where you would like them to be placed. Move Event markers by clicking them with the Pencil tool and dragging left or right.

Analysis View

Pro Tools does a good job of detecting transients in audio. As a result, you should not need to spend a lot of time (if any) in Analysis view. However, if you find that you need to manually place or reposition Event markers, switch over to the Analysis view.

Add Event markers by using the Pencil tool and clicking where you want them. Move them by using the Grabber or Pencil tool. Delete Event markers by Alt+clicking (Windows) or Option+clicking (Mac) the marker with either the Grabber or Pencil tool.

Correcting a Bass Line

I'm going to load up a bass line I recorded for one of my songs, "Moonlight," and show you how easy it is to use Elastic Audio to correct timing in a performance. The bass has good transient attacks, which makes it a good fit for Elastic Audio.

I've Seen the Light   I sort of pooh-poohed Elastic Audio until I worked with one of my bass lines and realized how incredibly faster it was to correct my timing with Elastic Audio than it was to go through and split region after region, nudging each clip ad nauseam and then messing around with a truckload of fades and crossfades.

It's time to jump into it.

1. I'm going to start this one from scratch and import the bass track from another file. I have the tempo set to 52 bpm. Set the tempo now so you don't forget.

2. Choose File>Import>Session data to import tracks from other sessions. Navigate to the saved file and select it. When you press Open, the Import Session Data dialog box appears.

3. Scroll down to find the track(s) you want to import. In my case, it's "Bass (Mono audio)."

4. Click the list beside the track and select "New Track" (see Figure 10.14). That's going to import the bass track from this session, complete with sends, plug-ins, and automation, into my open session. Click OK to start the import. You might get a warning that the disk allocation has changed. That's okay.

5. Next, I'm going to duplicate everything on the bass track and rename the duplicate "Bass2." I want to be able to compare the unedited original to the warped track when I'm done. To duplicate a track, select it and then choose the Track>Duplicate menu. Decide what you want to duplicate from the many options (see Figure 10.15) and click OK.

6. Enable Elastic Audio on the "Bass2" track. I use the Monophonic plug-in for this example because this is a bass track.

7. Zoom in and switch to Analysis view. Take a look at the Event markers to see if you need to add or move any. It helps to switch to Grid mode and set your grid values to help you identify the beat. My grid is set up to 1/8-note triplets.

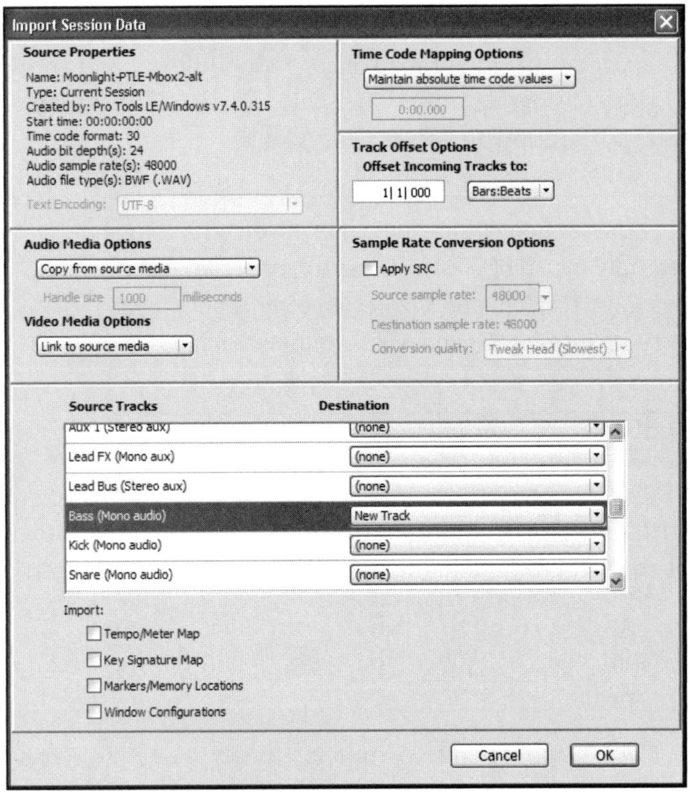

Figure 10.14 Importing a track from another session.

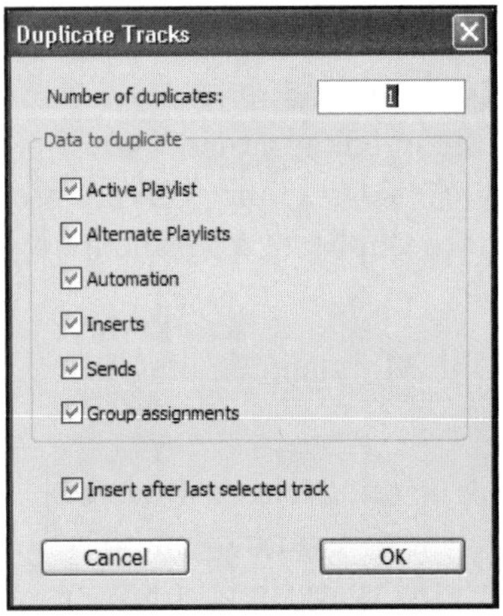

Figure 10.15 Duplicating a track.

Grid Alignment Helper   Here's one of those quirky tips. I find that when I'm looking at audio in Grid mode I can easily lose sight of the grid. To work around this, I create a new Aux Input track for the express purpose of grid alignment. I drag it up or down to where I can see it (see Figure 10.15).

8.   After looking at the Analysis view, if you are satisfied, switch to the Warp view and change to the Grabber tool.

9.   I guarantee you that if you read the Pro Tools 7.4 documentation on this next point you'll be confused. I accidentally found the best way to do this. Shift+click the first Event marker (which turns it into a Warp marker along with the ones beside it) and drag it to the first beat. Keep Shift+clicking your way down the line (see Figure 10.16). This transforms Event markers into Warp markers, which pins the beats to the timeline. That way you can keep working your way along the timeline without continually reshifting beats.

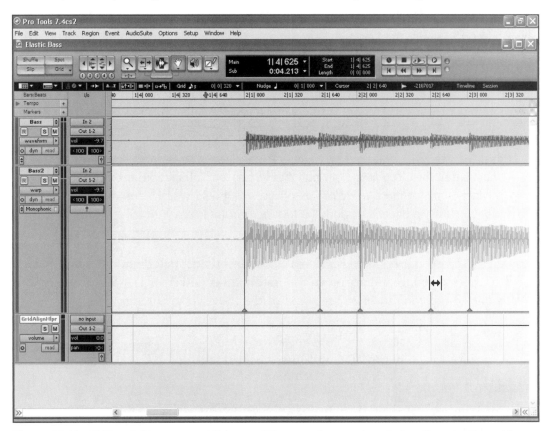

Figure 10.16 Shift+clicking to establish new Warp markers and snapping them to the grid.

10.   If Pro Tools mistakenly puts a Warp marker where you don't want it (in between a beat), delete it by Alt+clicking (Windows) or Option+clicking (Mac) the marker. It reverts to an Event marker, and you should ignore it and go on to the next beat. It's important to delete those extraneous Warp markers; otherwise, you are going to have some weird warping between those beats.

11.   When you're done, the track has been officially warped to match the beat. Listen to it carefully and go back to correct any missed or misplaced beats.

Automation

Wouldn't it be nice if you could program Pro Tools to turn things up or down in certain sections of a song, or perhaps to pan a track around creatively, to automatically control a plug-in, or maybe even to mute a send occasionally? It certainly would be, and you can. The feature is called automation.

Automation goes back further than you might think. You sit at an analog console, and as you bounce your mix, you ride the faders and pots yourself, performing a delicate dance of moving the controls with the music. It's fun, but hair-raising. You can't control many strips by yourself with any degree of comfort, and if you make a mistake, you have to go back to the beginning. Adding more people helps, but the manual process is always prone to human error.

Automate When You Mix   I've put this section on automation in the Editing chapter, but for most workflow purposes you should wait to automate until you're closer to bouncing your mix. Just thought I'd let you know.

Some analog consoles have better automation than others, including motorized faders, but all of these pale in comparison to the automation power of DAWs, of which Pro Tools is one of the coolest. Here are some of the things you can automate:

- **Volume:** All track types.

- **Pan:** Audio, Aux Input, MIDI, and Instrument tracks.

- **Mute:** All but the Master Fader.

- **Send Level, Pan, and Mute:** Audio tracks only.

- **Plug-in controls:** The Pro Tools 7.4 documentation says audio tracks only, but I'm sitting right here automating plug-ins on Aux Input and Instrument tracks as well. Hmm.

- **MIDI:** You can automate MIDI mute, volume, and pan levels.

I want to make one final point before getting into the details—automation applies to all playlists on a track, no matter how many you have.

Automation Modes

Conveniently, you have several different automation modes available to you in Pro Tools LE and M-Powered. Study these modes carefully so they don't trip you up. They aren't complicated. They are as follows:

- **Off:** Okay, so this one's pretty self-explanatory. Set the automation mode to Off if you're not going to use it. I'm not sure if this saves CPU cycles, but you would think so.

- **Read:** This mode reads and plays back any automation information on a track. Think "read-only." This is a safe mode that prevents you from accidentally writing automation unless you draw it. It is also the default mode.

- **Write:** You could probably call this mode "overwrite." It writes automation to the track from where you start playback until you stop, erasing and replacing any existing automation. Write mode writes new automation (whatever the control value is) whether you touch any controls or not.

- **Touch:** Touch is more sophisticated than Write. Pro Tools senses whether or not you're touching (with your hand in some cases and your mouse in others) a control that can be automated and only writes automation if you are. When you release the control, the control value goes from where you are automating back to what was there (in accordance with the AutoMatch Time you have set on the Mixing tab in the Preferences). This is why the 003 has "touch-sensitive motorized faders."

- **Latch:** Latch is a combination of Touch and Write. No automation is written until you touch a control, but when you do, automation continues to be written until you stop playback.

You can change automation modes on the fly.

Safe Mode

Pro Tools has a built-in safeguard to help protect you from accidentally overwriting existing automation or changing output, send, or plug-in values on a track. It's called Safe mode. The "safety" engages if you're writing other automation to that same track. Otherwise, you can change the overall mode to Read and not worry about it. For example, if you want to write plug-in automation but want to protect extensive volume automation you've already done, put the volume control in Safe mode.

Enabling Automation Writing for Specific Controls

Select the Window>Automation window to open the Automation window (see Figure 10.17). This is where you turn on or off the ability to write automation for specific controls like volume, pan, and mute. If you don't turn it off and are in Write mode, you overwrite other automation. This is a major stinger.

Figure 10.17 The Automation window.

For example, if you enter Write mode and make a pass to automate volume on a track and then make another pass in Write mode and automate pan, you have just lost your volume automation. It's gone! You can get around this in some ways by using Automation Safe, but because some controls are tied together (for example, you can't safe volume and write pan), disabling individual controls here is the only way you can "deconflict" them from Write-automating at the same time.

Write Mode Dangers Be careful when you enter Write mode. Whether or not you touch any control, you *will* overwrite all automation that is currently enabled in the Automation window. It's better to turn off automation from the Automation window or to use Touch mode.

This handy little window is a hidden treasure of power and flexibility. Don't forget about it!

Performing Automation

Performing automation is easy. Here's how:

1. Set your Play Start point.

2. Set a suitable automation mode from a track's controls.

3. Open the Window>Automation window and disable controls you don't want to automate.

4. I find it helpful to view the automation you are performing. Select that from the track's display controls.

5. Play.

6. Listen, and where appropriate, move the control you are automating (see Figure 10.18). (Ignore my wild swings please—I wanted you to see it.)

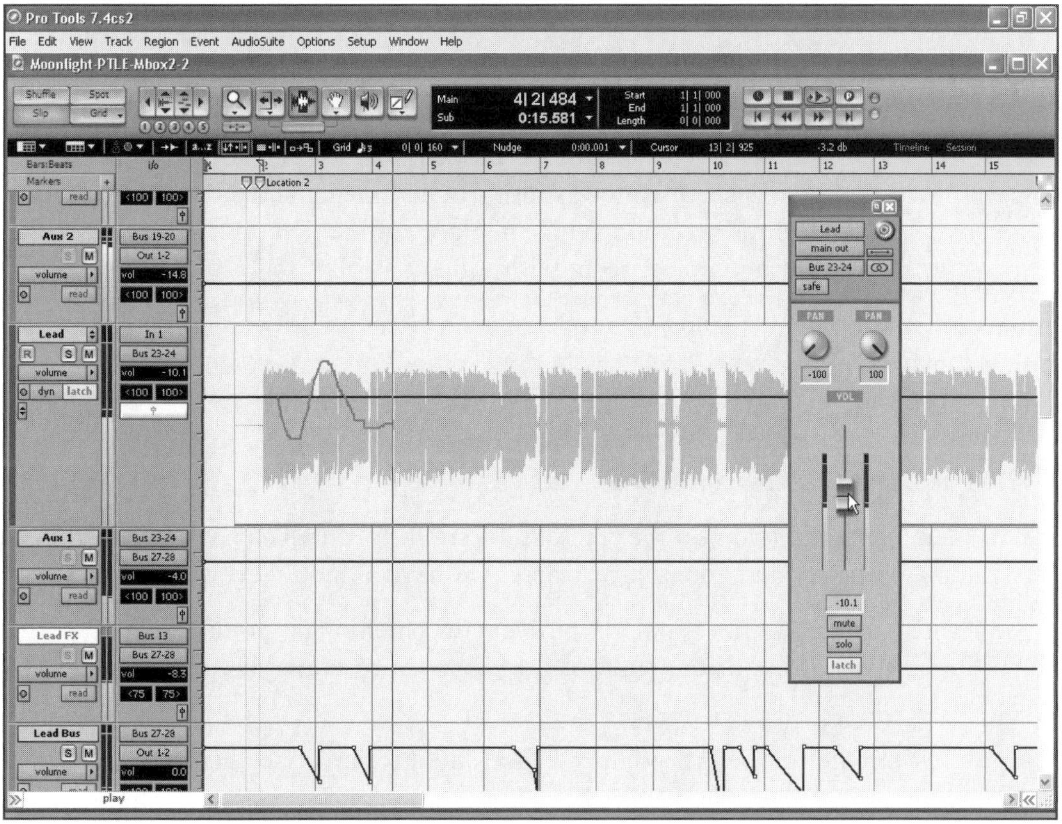

Figure 10.18 Automating volume.

7. Stop playback.

8. Make sure you are not in Automation Write mode and replay to see if the automation you just wrote is what you want.

9. If you don't like what you did, Undo or edit by hand.

It often helps to rehearse more complicated automation passes, but because you can Undo them (and edit them by hand later), you can jump right in. The big thing to remember (creatively speaking) is to know what you want to do.

Write, Then Latch   By default, the automation mode for a track switches to Latch after a Write pass. Don't let that trip you up. You can change that behavior in the Preferences.

Performing automation is one area where it helps to have a control surface. In lieu of that, I tend to draw it by hand.

Drawing Automation

Drawing automation has its pros and cons. It is less exacting from a performance perspective, and you can draw at your leisure because you're not performing in real time. However, it can take longer and is not as intuitive as moving actual control surfaces. The overwhelming benefit is precision. You can place automation points at very precise locations in the timeline and adjust them with total control.

Automation modes, Enable, and Safe mode have no effect on drawing—you are free to draw automation at any time.

Here's how to draw automation:

1. Decide what you want to automate.

2. View the automation on the track in question. It often helps to expand the track vertically and zoom in to where you have a good view of the detail.

3. Switch to the Grabber tool if you want to enter single points. Switch to the Pencil tool (or its various subtools) if you want to draw lines, zig-zags, and whatnot.

4. Click to enter individual points or click+hold to draw (see Figure 10.19).

5. Add new points, or move or delete the points you have. To move a point, switch to the Grabber tool, click the point you want to move, and drag it

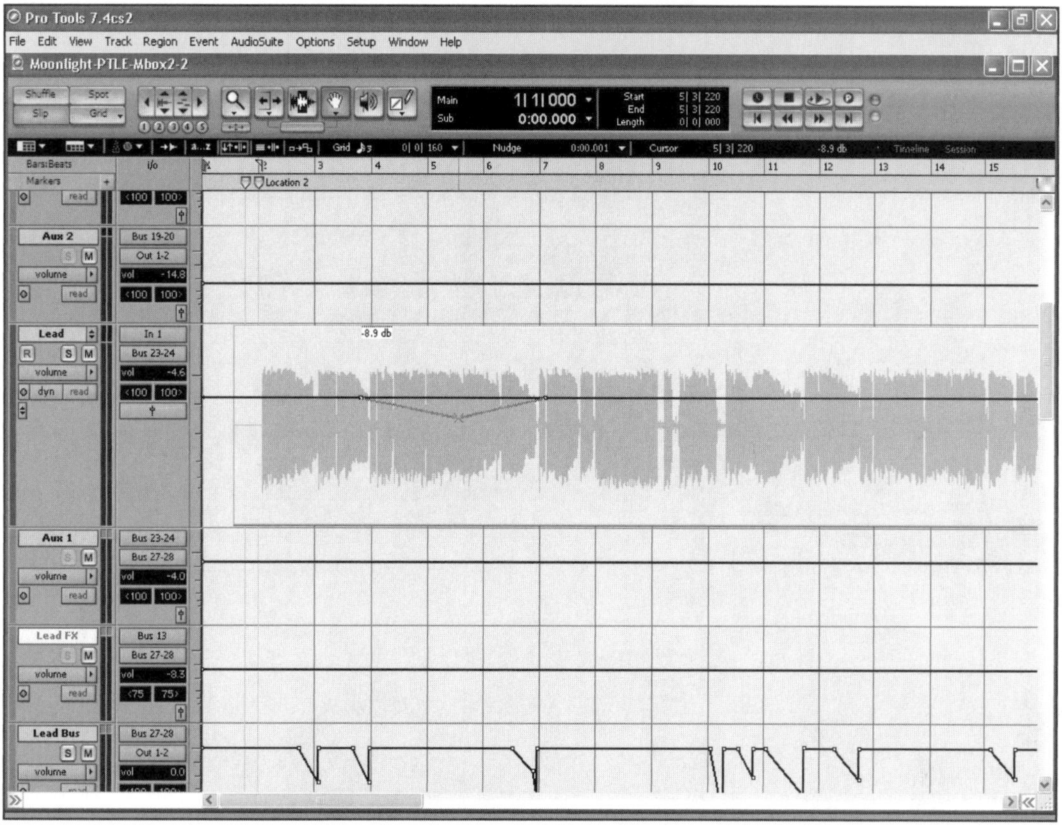

Figure 10.19 Hand-drawing automation points.

horizontally to change its position along the timeline or vertically to alter its value.

Making Fine Adjustments   If you want very precise control, Ctrl+click (Windows) or Command+Click (Mac) points as you move them.

Automating Plug-In Settings

Plug-in automation is probably one of the most overlooked, but useful, automation tools. By default, no plug-in parameters are automated—you have to select them from the plug-in window. Here's how:

1. Select a plug-in you want to automate and open its window.

2. Click the auto button.

3. Select the parameters you want to automate and click Add (see Figure 10.20). You can also remove parameters that have already been added by selecting them and clicking Remove.

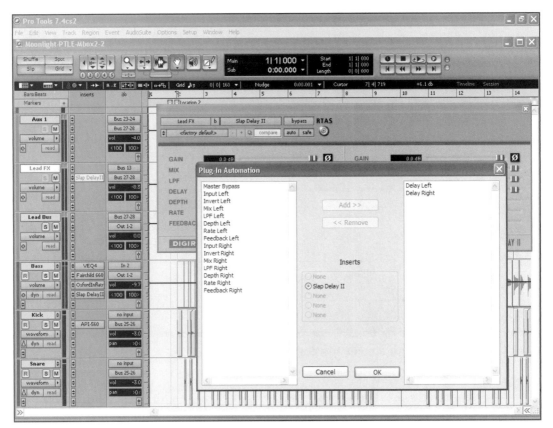

Figure 10.20 Adding plug-in parameters to automate.

4. Click OK to close the Plug-In Automation dialog box. You can also close the plug-in window if you are going to draw the automation by hand. Keep it open if you're going to perform the automation, because you need to access the controls. Notice that automated controls are now highlighted in a different color (see Figure 10.21). In this case, the left and right DELAY sliders are green, indicating they are automated.

5. You can now automate any of those parameters by performing or drawing. You can view them on the track by selecting the parameter you want to see from the track's view menu.

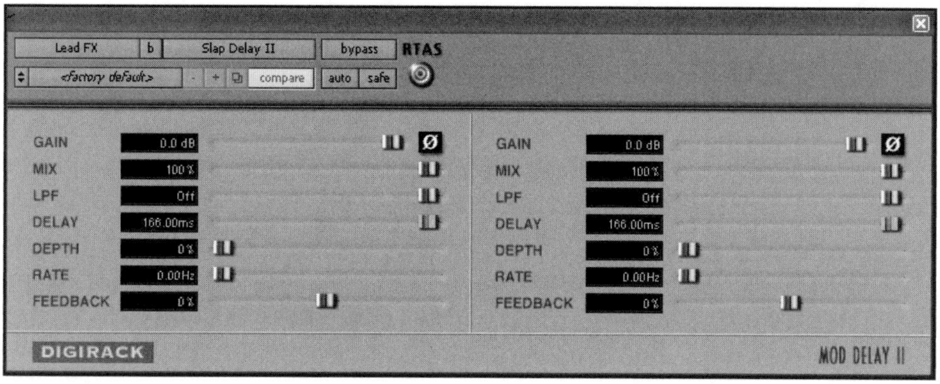

Figure 10.21 Visual indication that plug-in controls are in automation.

Deleting Automation

The safest and least painful way to delete automation is to change the track view to show the automation, switch to the Selection tool, select the area that contains the automation you want to delete, and press Delete. To delete single points, switch to the Grabber or Pencil tool and Alt+click (Windows) or Option+Click (Mac) individual points.

Don't Forget Sends and Plug-Ins!

Don't forget that you can automate sends and plug-ins, not just track volume and pans. This capability can be tremendously useful. For example, if your reverb is muddying up a passage, you have several possibilities to automate it. If the reverb plug-in is on an Aux Input track that is serving as a reverb bus, automate the track's volume or mute it during the passage. You can also automate the individual sends coming from other tracks (best if it's only a few) or automate the setting of the reverb plug-in. Have fun and be creative!

Master Fader Fades

Before you bounce your final mix, automate the volume of the Master Fader track (it's really easy to draw this) to create a smooth fade-in and fade-out. Make your bounce selection (or move your Memory markers) so the song starts and ends when the Master Fader is at negative infinity. This ensures a smooth startup and ending to your songs.

11 Using MIDI

I just got back from the store. I went out to my local Guitar Center and got a 10-foot MIDI cable for a very reasonable price. It's bright red, and because of that, I was able to get twice the length (10 feet versus 5 feet) for the same price as a standard black cable. I wanted to get this MIDI cable because I didn't have one to test for the purposes of this book. Although my MIDI keyboard has both MIDI and USB connectivity, I use USB to connect it to the computer. That's very convenient because the USB bus powers the keyboard (no wall warts to mess with) and some of my interfaces don't have MIDI inputs.

Any time I bring something home that is related to audio and music, my kids are instantly stuck to me like Velcro. So, with my four small children cheering me on, I started getting things hooked up. I tested the cable by connecting one end to the Mbox 2 and the other to my keyboard. I found a power supply and got that connected, turned the keyboard on, and then fired up the standalone version of Analog Factory SE by Arturia (a MIDI virtual instrument that comes as part of the Pro Tools Ignition Pack 2). I set the preferences within the program to receive MIDI input from the Mbox 2 and was very quickly off and running.

I took my turn playing with the keyboard and changing synths in Analog Factory SE, and then each of the kids got their turn. It was a musical MIDI party right here in my home studio, which is why I lead off with this story instead of something "high-falutin'" and esoteric. I'll get to the technical information shortly, but my point here is that MIDI is fun and easy—so easy the entire family can get involved. And it's fun because you can buy one simple MIDI keyboard and, through the use of standalone programs like Analog Factory SE or MIDI Instrument plug-ins within Pro Tools, generate an unbelievably diverse number of incredibly cool sounds. I sound like a MIDI salesman, don't I?

This chapter is meant to help you get started working with MIDI in Pro Tools. I'll cover what MIDI is, and I'll show you how to get your gear up and running; create MIDI tracks; work with Instrument tracks; record, edit, import, and export MIDI. Plus I'll cover all sorts of other MIDI-related tasks within Pro Tools.

What Is MIDI?

MIDI is short for Musical Instrument Digital Interface, and it is a communications protocol. It is not audio. The MIDI standard is a rulebook that defines a series of commands called event messages that two or more MIDI-capable devices can use to "talk," whether that talking is back and forth, back, forth, or through. I'll explain the back and forth stuff shortly.

MIDI and Audio   MIDI is not audio. Remember that and keep the two separate. MIDI is nothing more than digital messages that define the parameters of the music—they do not characterize its sound or generate it. MIDI can be encoded from a keyboard as you play or created by hand in Pro Tools. You can send the same MIDI data to a plug-in and make it sound like an electronic bass and then change the plug-in preset and make it sound like violins. The MIDI remains the same (that's a Zep reference for you "young 'uns").

MIDI Event Messages

At the heart of MIDI, its *raison d'etre* (that's French for "reason for being"), are the MIDI messages. Originally (and in the context I will use in this book), musical events such as "note on" and "note off," which are defined by the MIDI standard, are encoded and transmitted by a MIDI instrument. Upon receipt, another MIDI instrument, sequencer, or sound generator processes the information and takes the appropriate action. Figure 11.1 shows a series of MIDI messages within Pro Tools.

Those messages travel from either the MIDI instrument or MIDI source on a MIDI or Instrument track to an Instrument plug-in (see Figure 11.2), for example. The plug-in determines what the tone sounds like, and the Mbox 2 physically generates the sound that comes out your monitors.

Remember, the MIDI message has nothing to do with what the sound sounds like. It only defines the parameters, such as when the note turns on, turns off, how hard it is struck, the pan position, volume, and so forth. None of these bits of information lock in the actual sound, and they can be sent to completely different plug-ins and sound entirely different as a result.

In fact, you don't need a keyboard at all. You can program these event messages into Pro Tools without any external hardware. This is a boon for those who want to compose in MIDI but can't (or don't want to) play a musical instrument to enter the MIDI data. If you want, MIDI allows you to compose and edit within the confines of the computer and leave the musical instrument alone. On the other hand, if you're a

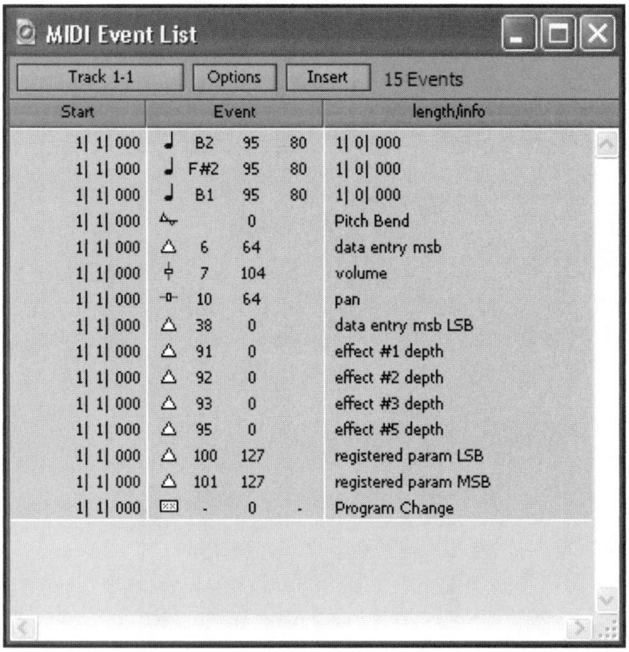

Figure 11.1 This is MIDI.

consummate performer, you can play the music instead of using your mouse to draw each note. Each approach is valid and entirely up to you.

The more you get into MIDI, the more you'll pick up about the specific messages it can send. However, some of the more common messages you'll find in Pro Tools (with possible values) are as follows:

- **Note On:** Turns a note on. You see this in Pro Tools as the beginning of a note.

- **Pitch:** The note to play. In Pro Tools, the pitch is displayed in the Edit window and on the MIDI or Instrument track as the note alongside a piano roll.

- **Note Off:** Turns a note off. In Pro Tools, you see this as the note ending.

- **Attack Velocity (1–127):** Usually determines how hard to "strike" the note. Higher values may sound more pronounced, with an almost percussive attack. Lower values may sound legato. This depends greatly on the instrument being triggered. Some synth patches map attack velocity to different controls like cutoff frequency or even panning. Pro Tools does not allow you to set this to 0.

- **Release Velocity (0–127):** How quickly a note is released. Higher values cause the note to stop playing very quickly. Lower values allow it to "ring" on a bit.

Figure 11.2 Turning MIDI into music.

- **Aftertouch (0–127):** The pressure applied to a key or other note trigger.

- **Volume (0–127):** The MIDI track volume fader.

- **Pan (64 left–63 right):** Pan position from left to right. Be careful on this one. Some applications have this run from 0–127, but in Pro Tools, it ranges from 64 left to 63 right. Sixty-four plus 63 plus 1 (for 0) equals 128, which is the same range as 0–127, 0 inclusive.

- **Mute (0–1):** Mutes a MIDI track.

- **Pitch Bend (-8192–8191):** Bends the pitch of the note by the specified value sharp or flat. This is a useful tool in "humanizing" MIDI or for other special effects.

- **Program or Bank Change:** Changes the operation of the MIDI instrument (hardware or software). Most often, this command switches preset sounds and sound banks. For example, in General MIDI, a Program Change number of 1 is the sound of an Acoustic Grand Piano, whereas Program Change number 19 is Rock Organ. "Program" is often synonymous with "patch," "preset," or "instrument."

- **Sysex:** Short for System Exclusive message. Sysex messages are a type of system message and are most often used to send program information, patches, and other data between devices. The format of the messages is almost always proprietary in that no standard exists for what a sysex should contain other than how it starts.

- **Others:** There are a ton of other messages that are mostly irrelevant to the common user but open lots of options to the MIDI freak (I mean that in a good way). The best way to learn them is by examining the MIDI instrument you use most (hardware or software) and exploring all its capabilities.

MIDI Resolution   Some controllers, like mute, are switches that turn on or off.

Continuous controllers that have ranges from 0–127 are "coarse" controllers. They have a 7-bit resolution. Those that have larger ranges (0–16,384 or from –8192–8191) are "fine" controllers and use 14 bits to store data. Many controllers actually have both a coarse and fine component, such as the Expression Pedal.

You have a greater musical resolution when using fine controllers.

MIDI Connections

MIDI data can be transmitted over three different types of cables: the original 5-pin MIDI cable, and now USB or FireWire. Each has its own pros and cons, and the type of connection you use depends on the hardware you have. If you have a choice between MIDI and USB/FireWire, it's up to your own personal preference. I should note that Ethernet is becoming a popular transport option for MIDI data, but that's beyond the scope of this book as no Pro Tools LE or M-Powered interface can handle that right now.

Originally, MIDI cables (see Figure 11.3) were the only way to connect MIDI devices. These look a lot like standard studio cables from the outside, but they terminate in a 5-pin DIN connector on both ends. (DIN stands for Deutsches Institut für Normung, which is the name of the German national standards organization that standardized this type of connector.)

Figure 11.3   This is my new red MIDI cable.

Standard MIDI cables transmit data in one direction only. This is a key limitation, and it is the reason why traditional MIDI connections are broken out into three types.

- **MIDI IN**: Receives MIDI data.

- **MIDI OUT**: Transmits MIDI data generated by the instrument or device. Even when using MIDI THRU, MIDI OUT transmits only internally generated data, not what is being received from MIDI IN.

- **MIDI THRU**: An out port that transmits all MIDI data received from the MIDI IN connection. MIDI THRU relies on MIDI IN to provide it with the data it transmits.

The Mbox 2 has one MIDI IN and one MIDI OUT port. I can take MIDI data from Pro Tools; route it from MIDI OUT to another device, such as a synth; and use the MIDI IN port on the synth. If the synth has a MIDI THRU, I can use another MIDI cable to connect another device to Pro Tools by using MIDI THRU on the synth and MIDI IN on the third device.

Today, USB and FireWire are becoming increasingly popular MIDI options. My very cheap keyboard has both USB and MIDI capability, which gives me the option of choosing which I want to use. The main differences between USB/FireWire and MIDI are as follows:

- **Directionality**: USB and FireWire are bidirectional and require no confusing IN, OUT, or THRU connections. You just plug them in. Advantage: USB/FireWire.

- **Power**: Devices can often be "bus powered" when connected to a computer over USB or FireWire. In these situations, you don't need an external power supply to power the MIDI device. Advantage: USB/FireWire.

- **Length:** Although USB and FireWire cables come in various lengths, you can buy MIDI cables that are much longer. I just checked online and found MIDI cables up to 30 feet in length. It's theoretically possible (according to the MIDI specification) to have cables 50 feet in length. Advantage: MIDI cable.

- **Interoperability:** USB and FireWire are meant to connect devices to *a computer*, not each other. However, not all interfaces have MIDI ports, whereas all computers have USB and many have FireWire ports. Advantage: Toss-up.

- **Drivers:** Most USB and FireWire connections require you to install additional drivers in your computer. MIDI works at the level of the interface, and Pro Tools interfaces that have MIDI ports work without any additional drivers. Advantage: MIDI cables.

MIDI Channels

MIDI channels are one of the least talked about aspects of MIDI, and therefore, one of the most confusing. Understanding channels is actually very easy, and knowing how to manage your MIDI channels can serve you well if you are working in an environment with several MIDI devices.

MIDI messages are digital and, therefore, much easier to multiplex than standard audio signals. As such, each MIDI cable can carry 16 individual MIDI channels multiplexed into one overall data stream. The channels are numbered from 1 to 16, and each one carries a discrete "directional" signal. In other words, you have no crosstalk between the channels, and they each have both an "In" and an "Out" component (carried over different cables).

This opens doors to a tremendous number of possibilities, but also requires some management overhead. Many MIDI devices can transmit and receive on all 16 channels, effectively making them multitracking wonders. You could send data from a MIDI device that is playing 16 "tracks" of different instruments at once, each assigned to its own channel, and record them onto 16 tracks in Pro Tools.

By the same token, you could daisy-chain several MIDI devices together and assign each device its own separate channel (or range of unique channels). All are transmitting and receiving MIDI over the same communications network (cable) at the same time, but the signals are isolated by virtue of being on different channels.

The upshot of all this is that you're sometimes asked in Pro Tools to identify what channels you want a device or MIDI/Instrument track to send and receive MIDI on. If you're working with one external device, you can safely use "All." However, when you start adding multiple devices, you should manage your channels so you have no confusion regarding what is going to or coming from where.

MIDI Devices

I want to remind you that you can encode MIDI information in Pro Tools without the aid of any other hardware. All it takes is you and your mouse. However, MIDI instruments are popular for a reason. They are very versatile and open up the world of musicality and performance.

MIDI devices can range from the trusty MIDI keyboard to drum pads, guitars, pianos, and more. Here are a few specific examples of MIDI devices and what you would use them for:

- **USB/MIDI Keyboard Controller:** Keyboard controllers, such as the M-Audio Axiom 49 49-Key USB MIDI Controller, offer the perfect combination of keyboard functionality and MIDI control, most often at very reasonable prices. The reason they are relatively inexpensive is that they produce no sound on their own; all they do is send MIDI event messages to your computer or another MIDI instrument. These types of controllers range from the exceedingly simple "keyboard-only" device to those that have more advanced features like sliders, controls, buttons, and pitch bend and modulation wheels. I remember when I got my first MIDI controller. I opened it up, plugged the power supply in, turned it on, and wondered where the sound came out. I kept pressing the keys and nothing seemed to happen. After digging around in the manual I realized I had to install drivers, hook it up to a computer (duh), and assign the controller a software synthesizer that would generate the sound out of my interface. Oh, the good old days.

- **Pad Controller:** The Akai MPD24 USB/MIDI Pad Controller is an example of a pad controller that looks like a series of drum pads. You strike the pads and the unit transmits the appropriate MIDI event to your computer. This is a great way to "play" a drum kit that is actually an Instrument plug-in.

- **Wind Controller:** MIDI can be generated by a diverse set of devices that mimic real-world acoustic instruments. One example is the Yamaha WX5 MIDI Wind Controller, which looks something like a clarinet and whose keys are arranged like a saxophone. You hold it like you would a small wind instrument, blow into its mouthpiece, and "play" it as you change notes with the keys. Your breath is measured by a wind sensor, which translates that information into various MIDI parameters, and is sent out along with the note events generated by your fingers. Cool stuff.

- **Foot Controller:** One foot controller that I've found is the Behringer FCB1010 MIDI Foot Controller. The point here is to control an external MIDI device, such as a multi-effect unit, using MIDI program change commands and MIDI control commands generated by the controller. You can also conceivably use a foot controller to control certain aspects of Pro Tools or control instrument plug-ins with the foot switches.

- **Piano:** Pianos are naturals for MIDI, and I've used acoustic grand pianos that can generate, transmit, and receive MIDI just like "dumb" keyboard controllers. The advantage here is that you're benefiting from the piano's solid feel and construction (as opposed to many controllers), and its own sound, whether it is acoustic or digital. The Yamaha P-140 Contemporary Digital Piano is one such example.

- **Synthesizer:** A good example of a synth that has MIDI capability is the Korg microKORG Synthesizer/Vocoder. By itself, the microKORG generates sound from its internal dual-oscillator DSP synthesis engine. Using MIDI, the microKORG can control other electronic instruments, communicate with computer software, and also generate and transmit its own MIDI performance data. To top it all off, you can record the synth's own internally generated audio by taking the stereo audio outputs from the unit and connecting them to two inputs on your Pro Tools interface. Sounds like a pretty good deal to me.

- **Sampling Workstation:** Sampling workstations are somewhere between synthesizers and pianos, with a good dose of MIDI controller thrown in. The Kurzweil K2600XS 88-Key Sampling Workstation is a great example. Although it has its own oscillators that generate sound, the key feature is that it uses sound samples (saved internally and expandable) to create unique programs such as grand pianos, organs, and others. You guessed it: The Kurzweil also uses MIDI, which, like most other products here, greatly enhances its versatility.

- **Electronic Drum Kit:** Feeling a little cramped by the small pad controller? Then step up and get a full-sized electronic drum kit. The Yamaha DTXplorer Electronic Drum Set is a great example of an electronic kit that generates its own sound and also sends (it does not receive) MIDI.

- **Others:** I'm sure I've left something out (pedalboards, for example). The sky is the limit with MIDI.

Have you noticed something? Most often these MIDI devices mimic their "real-world" counterparts and provide for physical methods of making music rather than using your mouse. MIDI is flexible enough, though, not to be tied to a specific instrument, hardware device, or external hardware at all.

Reasonable Prices? I applaud things like reasonable prices because making music is an expensive business, and if you're like me, you can't afford to go out and buy the most expensive gear on the planet all the time. I have to make choices. I economize where I can to gain a capability and save up for the larger purchases that are important steps in quality. It gets worse if you're a musician *and* an audio engineer. As a musician, I play a guitar (with aftermarket pickups), bass, and keyboard, have cables, stomp boxes, amps, my own DI box, instrument cases, and other whatnot. As an engineer, I invest in things like Pro Tools, extra Pro Tools features (like the MP3 export option) and plug-ins, other DAWs and interfaces, a mixing console, more cables, other preamps and outboard gear, microphones, stands, a computer, headphones, a studio, and more.

If you're a world-class pianist, I'm sure you won't stop at your first inexpensive MIDI controller. You might not even start there. However, it's great having a wide range of options, and the more reasonably priced instruments allow almost everyone to get "in the pool." What you do when you get there, and how long it takes to upgrade to that $2500 synth/keyboard, is where individuals make different choices based on their talents, goals, and budget.

It's important to note that not all keyboards are MIDI-only. A whole range of synthesizers and pianos have their own extensive (and often expandable) internal sound libraries and oscillator/tone generators and can produce their own sound in addition to transmitting MIDI to Pro Tools. In those cases you can treat the instrument as both MIDI and audio-capable by creating a MIDI track and an Audio track in Pro Tools and recording both simultaneously (you can monitor but not record audio on an Instrument track). The MIDI data can be used as a "performance safety" and be held in reserve or tweaked at your leisure. You can create an alternate sound by creating an Instrument track and assigning a suitable plug-in, or "re-amping" the MIDI. Most often done with guitars, re-amping is a technique where you send the recorded signal out to the original instrument (or amp in the case of a guitar track) and record that "canned" performance onto new tracks.

Software Instruments (Plug-Ins)

In the MIDI world you have hardware instruments (discussed previously) and their software counterparts, variously called soft synths, software instruments, MIDI instruments, or Instrument plug-ins. Hardware instruments are physical and real. You press the keys, turn the knobs, and perform just as you would with an acoustic or electric instrument. Sometimes you can select specific sounds from a hardware instrument, as with synthesizers, in addition to generating the MIDI. Others generate MIDI data and no audio.

CPU Load and Instrument Plug-ins Instrument plug-ins notoriously suck up computer power. As a result, although your system might be able to handle many different types of other plug-ins on several tracks, it might choke on more than a few instruments. Test your system out to see where this critical point is and plan accordingly. One technique that saves computer power is to record the Instrument track to an Audio track and disable the Instrument plug-in. I cover that later.

Software instruments reside entirely in the computer. Their job (for the purpose of this chapter) is to read MIDI data and create (indirectly through the interface or with the use of audio samples) the sound you hear. Some make synthesizer sounds. Others specialize in pianos, organs, and orchestral instruments. Several great drum plug-ins use MIDI data to trigger drum samples. Using one plug-in, you often have dozens of choices, with many customizable parameters, to create your own unique sound. You get the idea.

Software instruments are often inserted on Instrument tracks in Pro Tools, just like you would insert any other plug-in on an Audio or Aux Input track (see Chapter 12). Figure 11.4 illustrates an Instrument track with the plug-in assigned and its interface open.

You can become a software instrument guru, just as you can become a MIDI hardware fanatic. The trick is trying out several different plug-ins based on your needs and determining from experience what you like. What does the plug-in sound like? How easy is it to work with? How much does it stress your system? Is it reliable? How much does it cost?

Pro Tools and MIDI

Pro Tools doesn't have the greatest reputation for its MIDI implementation, but it's getting better all the time. Digidesign seems to have realized the importance of having more robust MIDI support within Pro Tools, which gives engineers and artists far greater creative options and opens Pro Tools up to a much wider audience. Lots of people use MIDI, which requires little in the way of traditional studio overhead. You can compose, arrange, and mix MIDI in the car on the way to the grocery store. Shoot, if you're not driving, you can even perform and record MIDI on the way.

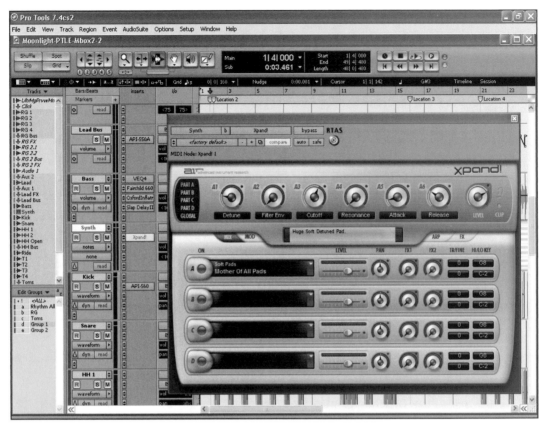

Figure 11.4   An Instrument plug-in inserted on an Instrument track turns MIDI into music.

MIDI-Pro Tools Basics

I'm just scratching the surface in this chapter. I find so much with MIDI in general, and working with Pro Tools and MIDI in particular, that I spend more time trying to decide what to leave out than writing what I've kept in. My choices come down to wanting to provide you with a little MIDI background so you can begin to understand what all the hubbub is about and give you enough specific information to get you started.

I want to review a few fundamental concepts to keep you oriented in the right direction:

- **MIDI:** MIDI is not audio. MIDI is a communications protocol. Pro Tools can use MIDI in either of two ways. Either Pro Tools can receive and record MIDI that is generated when you play an external MIDI instrument, or Pro Tools can use an Instrument plug-in to play MIDI data that you enter manually. Either way, MIDI appears on a MIDI or an Instrument track as notes that you can see and edit.

- **Sound:** MIDI does not describe what something should sound like. It describes only the parameters of the music, such as when notes play and what pitch they are. Instrument plug-ins are what determines whether the note sounds like a violin, a drum, an organ, a guitar, a sound effect, or an other sound. These plug-ins are most often third-party tools that you install separately, such as Arturia's Analog Factory SE, Digidesign's Xpand!, and applications like Propellerhead's Reason.

- **Hardware versus Software:** Your focus can be on creating MIDI from an external MIDI controller, or you might choose to work entirely within Pro Tools and not touch a physical keyboard. Either approach is valid, but they require somewhat different mindsets. When you play and record music from an external device, you have to have it, plug it in, get Pro Tools to recognize it, create an appropriate track, and then record yourself. Manually composing MIDI can be a simpler, but sometimes time-consuming, task.

- **MIDI versus Instrument Tracks:** Pro Tools has two types of tracks that can hold MIDI data: MIDI and Instrument tracks (new in Pro Tools 7). MIDI tracks are pure MIDI, whereas Instrument tracks have some characteristics of Aux Input tracks and are a vast step forward in MIDI-Pro Tools integration. I prefer using Instrument tracks if the plug-ins I assign are compatible. There are times, however, when you may not be able to use Instrument tracks. In those cases, you may have to use MIDI, audio, or Aux Input tracks. One common case is when using a multi-timbral plug-in such as Native Instrument's Kontakt. You will have multiple MIDI channels and multiple audio streams bussed onto their own tracks. Some virtual instruments, especially VSTs that are wrapped using the VST to RTAS converter, will not work on Instrument tracks.

Before I get into details, it's a good time to present you with the bare bones of what to do when you want to record MIDI, and when you just want to create and edit it on your own. I'll cover some more details later in the chapter, but this is what you really need to know.

To record MIDI on an Instrument track, follow these general steps:

1. Connect the external MIDI device.

2. Create a new session or open an existing one.

3. Set up your MIDI hardware if this is the first time you've connected it.

4. Create an Instrument track. You can choose mono or stereo, although most Instrument plug-ins generate a stereo signal.

5. Assign the MIDI Input Selector to your MIDI hardware and the channels you are transmitting (see Figure 11.5).

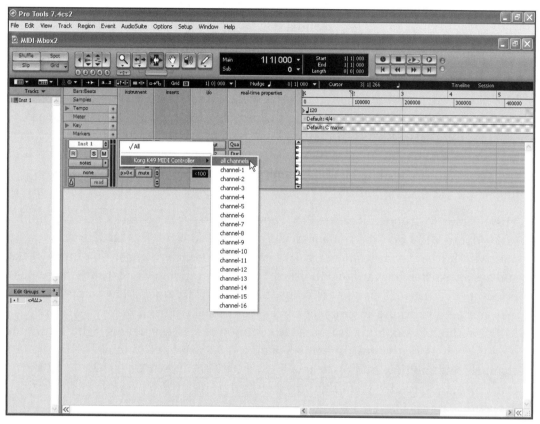

Figure 11.5 Selecting a MIDI input source.

6. Add an Instrument plug-in of your choice as an insert on the Instrument track (see Figure 11.6). This automatically assigns the MIDI Output Selector of the Instrument track to that plug-in.

7. Choose a sound preset from the specific plug-in (see Figure 11.7).

8. If MIDI Thru (Options>MIDI Thru) is enabled, you can test your setup now by pressing some keys on your external MIDI device. You should hear sound being generated by the plug-in and MIDI activity. Make sure the Audio Output path of the Instrument track is set to your main outputs.

9. Arm the Instrument track to prepare for recording.

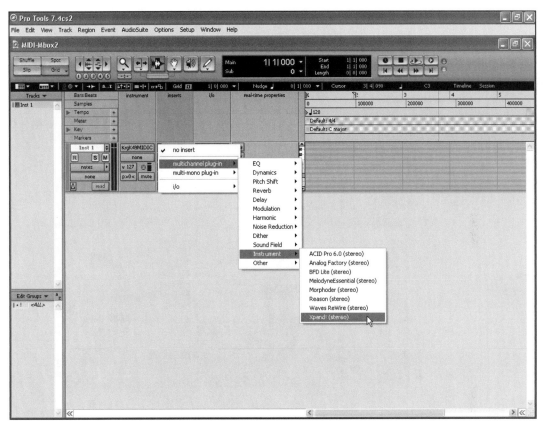

Figure 11.6   Adding the plug-in.

10.   Record your external device (see Figure 11.8).

11.   Stop, and then edit, quantize, or re-record at your leisure. You can also step-record with MIDI, should the piece be hard and you want to be very precise.

What about MIDI Tracks?   I don't use MIDI tracks very often. Your situation, Instrument plug-ins, and goals might necessitate different choices. MIDI tracks are easy to use if you keep in mind that you cannot put an Instrument plug-in on them and must use the MIDI Output Selector to route the signal to whatever track you're using for the plug-in. There are so many different plug-ins and options that your specific plug-in of choice might be the driving force behind what direction you choose.

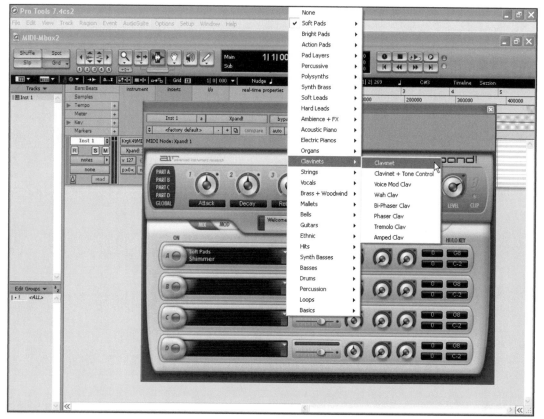

Figure 11.7 Choosing a sound preset.

To create and edit MIDI manually, follow these general steps:

1. Create a new session or open an existing one.

2. Create an Instrument track. You can choose mono or stereo, although most Instrument plug-ins generate a stereo signal. Make sure the Audio Output path of the Instrument track is set to your main outputs.

3. Add an Instrument plug-in of your choice as an insert on the Instrument track. This automatically assigns the MIDI Output Selector of the Instrument track to that plug-in. You don't need to mess with any other inputs or outputs. You're good to go.

4. Choose a sound preset from the specific plug-in.

5. Begin adding notes to the Instrument track and edit away (see Figure 11.9).

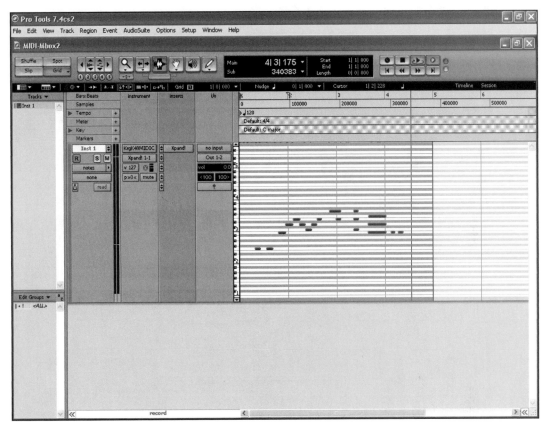

Figure 11.8   Recording MIDI.

MIDI Preferences

MIDI preferences are pretty simple. Select the Setup>Preferences menu and choose the MIDI tab to view them (see Figure 11.10).

MIDI preferences are divided into two areas: Basics and Note Display. The Basics area contains a wide range of preferences that range from *Play MIDI Notes when Editing* (I like hearing what I'm doing) to *Automatically Create Click Track in New Sessions* (another preference I prefer).

I especially like *Use MIDI to Tap Tempo*. With this option enabled, you can tap a tempo on your external MIDI device, and it automatically updates your session's tempo, which is very cool. To enable this preference, open the Tempo Change dialog box (double-click the red tempo arrow or the plus symbol beside Tempo on the ruler area), and tap away. The tempo is updated according to your taps. Stop tapping and close the dialog box to lock the tempo in.

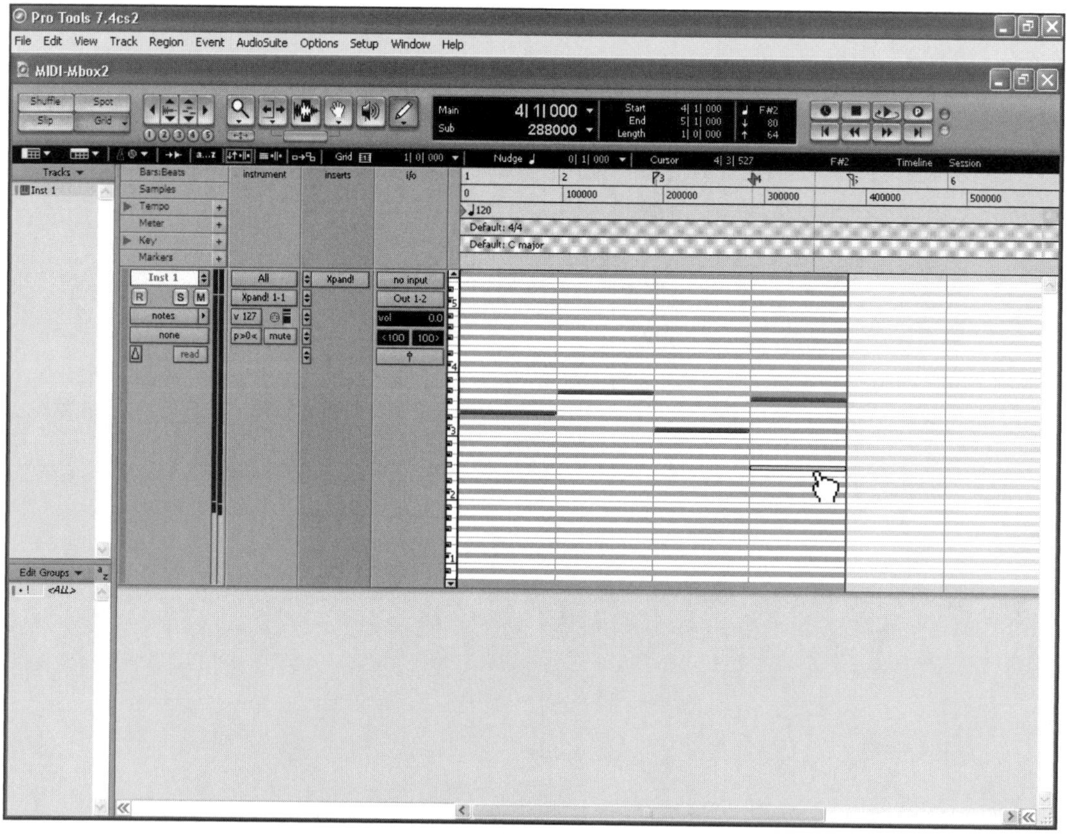

Figure 11.9 Manually entering MIDI data.

The *Default Thru Instrument* option allows you to choose a different MIDI instrument that acts as the default thru instrument. This instrument is what you hear when you are monitoring MIDI tracks. If you have an external MIDI device, you can try this out. Create a few Instrument tracks, and assign a different Instrument plug-in to each track. Enable (or make sure it's on) MIDI Thru by selecting Options>MIDI Thru. You actually don't need to arm the tracks. Select each Instrument track and play a few notes on your controller. With *Default Thru Instrument* set to "first selected MIDI track," you hear the sound from the plug-in on whatever track you have selected, which makes sense. If you change the *Default Thru Instrument* preference to a particular plug-in, you hear that sound, no matter what other Instrument plug-ins are assigned to any particular MIDI or Instrument track.

Global MIDI Playback Offset allows you to enter a number of samples to manually correct for latency.

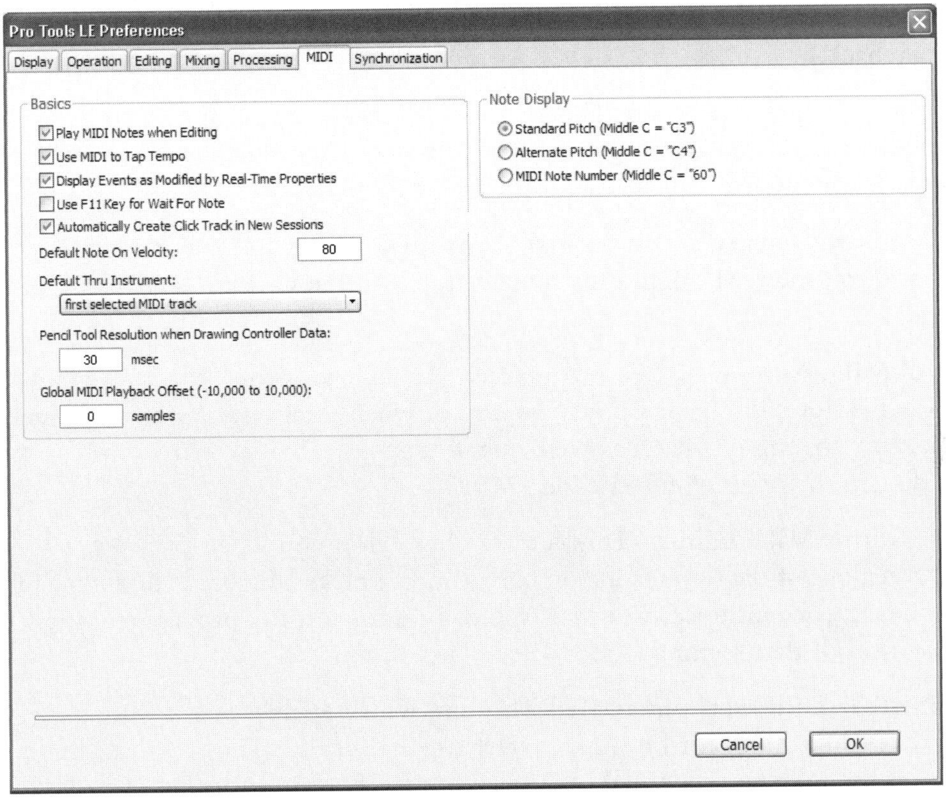

Figure 11.10   MIDI preferences in Pro Tools.

The preferences in the Note Display area determine whether "Middle C" is set to its standard pitch, an alternate, or the given MIDI note number.

Other MIDI Menu Items

I want to quickly review several other MIDI menu items:

- **Event>Event Operations:** This opens the Event Operations dialog box, which allows you to choose from several different types of events and operations. You can quantize a MIDI selection (force the notes to specific start and stop values), change the velocity and duration of notes, transpose a selection, select and split notes, turn Input Quantize on and off, enable Step Input, and Restore or Flatten a performance.

- **Event>MIDI Event List:** This shows the MIDI events within a selected track. You can select and modify individual events from this list.

- **Event>MIDI Track Offsets:** This allows you to enter offsets in samples for specific MIDI tracks.

- **Event>Real-Time Properties:** This allows you to change several MIDI properties during playback.

- **Event>Remove Duplicate Notes:** This removes MIDI notes that appear to be duplicate notes struck quickly together by combining them together or separating them more distinctly.

- **Event>Add Key Change:** This is not strictly a MIDI choice, but you can add key changes and transpose MIDI and Instrument tracks to the new key signature from this menu.

- **Event>All MIDI Notes Off:** This is sort of an "Emergency Stop" command that turns all MIDI notes off. That's pretty important when things get wacky and stuck on. Make sure to stop playback as well if that happens. The keyboard shortcut is hard to discern. It is Ctrl+Shift+Period.

- **Options>Mirror MIDI Editing:** This is a very helpful option when you've got several MIDI regions of the same name on one or more tracks Mirrored editing means that you change one instance, and that change is automatically propagated to all other instances of that region.

- **Options>MIDI Thru:** This turns MIDI Thru on, which enables you to monitor MIDI tracks while you record from an external MIDI device. This is sort of funky. This option has no effect on MIDI or Instrument tracks that are being played through an Instrument plug-in. They play and sound just fine, either way. Say you have an external keyboard connected. MIDI Thru passes the MIDI from the keyboard to a plug-in so you can hear it. Turning MIDI Thru off means you won't hear your external device no matter what. It records properly and you can hear it played back, but you can't hear it on input.

Creating MIDI and Instrument Tracks

Create a MIDI or Instrument track just as you would another type of track. Select the Track>New menu and choose what you want. You can create MIDI tracks (which are not mono or stereo), mono Instrument, or stereo Instrument tracks. You can make either type sample or tick based. Remember, sample-based tracks do not respond to changes in session tempo, whereas tick-based tracks do.

Working with MIDI and Instrument Tracks

After you create them, you work with MIDI and Instrument tracks like other types of tracks. You can move, hide, show, inactivate, activate, color-coordinate, rename, resize, show comments, and group them (to name a few things).

The most obvious difference between MIDI/Instrument tracks and Audio tracks is that MIDI data shows up in these tracks as discrete notes rather than as audio waveforms. MIDI tracks have no inserts or sends, whereas Instrument tracks do. Regarding signal flow, all you can do with a MIDI track is assign MIDI Input and MIDI Output paths. Instrument tracks allow you to assign Instrument (and other) plug-ins and sends and choose MIDI I/O options from one track. You can also select an audio I/O path just like an Aux Input track.

Adding Software Instruments

You can't add software instruments to MIDI tracks, but they are indispensable on Instrument tracks. Simply add them as you would any other plug-in on an Audio (or other type of) track. You can have more than one per Instrument track, but can't have more than one active at any one time, as only one can play.

ReWire

You can use external applications like Reason or ACID Pro as if they were plug-ins through a technology called ReWire. All you have to do is select the application from the plug-ins menu and assign it to an Instrument track like any other Instrument plug-in. You then see a ReWire dialog (see Figure 11.11), which tells you what you are linking to on this insert.

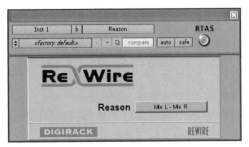

Figure 11.11 ReWire connects Pro Tools to other applications.

The other application launches in ReWire Slave mode. You can open, save, and edit music from within that external application as if you were using it alone. Create whatever you want to, and it's automatically integrated into Pro Tools via ReWire. Awesome.

Composing MIDI

Composing MIDI is a snap. All you need to do is have a MIDI or an Instrument track created and active, switch to the Pencil tool, and click to create the notes, as I did a bit earlier in the chapter. Yes, it's that simple. To delete a note, select it and then press Delete.

If the Instrument track doesn't have an Instrument plug-in it will be darker gray and look inactive, but you can still enter MIDI data on it.

Importing MIDI

Importing MIDI is fairly easy, but one aspect is positively atrocious. You can drag and drop a MIDI file into the Tracks or Regions list to import it or choose the File>Import>MIDI menu to select a file on your system to import. Upon selecting a file with the latter method, you're given a few options as to whether to import the MIDI file as a new track or region. Import the MIDI file as a new track or region according to your preferences.

After the file is imported, the terrible thing is that the MIDI track or region is not named according to your file. It's simply named in numeric sequence, starting at MIDI-01. Awful! I've imported chords from my MIDI chord library and had to rename every single one myself in the Regions list. Pay heed to this and try importing one MIDI file at a time, renaming as you go, if you want to preserve their original names.

Editing MIDI

Editing MIDI is about as easy as entering it. Really, it is. Create a new Pro Tools session, create a new Instrument track, insert your favorite Instrument plug-in, choose a preset, record something, and follow along.

I am going to focus on the graphical method of MIDI editing. You can always open the MIDI Events dialog box, select the notes or message you want to change, and enter new numeric values.

Selecting Notes

Select single notes with the Free Hand tool or the Grabber by carefully clicking them. The cursor changes to a small hand with its finger pointing at the note when you're positioned correctly. That's it. You can select more than one adjacent note by using the Grabber tool and dragging a box around the notes you want to select. Select non-adjacent notes with either tool, but press and hold Shift while you select. The notes change appearance from solid to hollow.

You can also select an area of the timeline with the Selection tool. This selects all MIDI notes in that time frame. You can then move, copy, paste, or delete the notes with the other tools.

Manipulating Note Pitch and Location

You can change the pitch of a note in a few different ways. First, select a note or group of notes with the Pencil tool or Grabber and then drag them up or down to a new position. Drop them on the pitch line you want. You can also select a single note and edit its value from the MIDI indicators, which are up by the counters.

Dragging left or right moves the notes along the timeline.

You can copy and paste notes. Switch to the Grabber or Pencil tool and select the notes you want to copy. Then press Ctrl+C (Windows) or Command+C (Mac) to copy them. Switch to the Selector tool and move the Insertion point to where you want to paste the notes. Then press Ctrl+V (Windows) or Command+V (Mac).

Manipulating Note Duration

Sometimes you want to make a note longer or shorter. You can use the Free Hand Pencil tool or the Trim tool for this. I can illustrate with the Pencil.

Select the tool and then hover it close to one end of the note (see Figure 11.12). The cursor changes to reflect a trim operation (it's a bit larger than normal in Figure 11.12

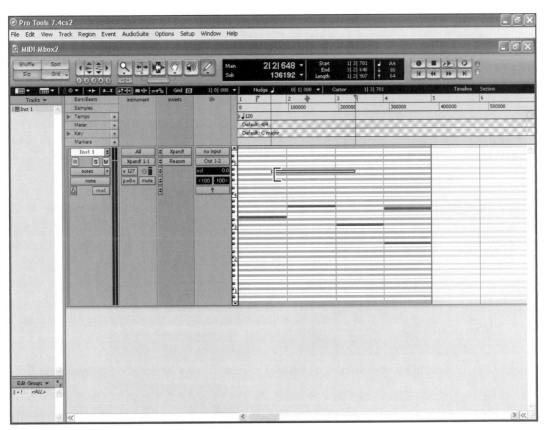

Figure 11.12 Lengthening a MIDI note.

so you can see it). Click+hold and drag the cursor left or right to either lengthen or shorten the note. You can do this from either side of the note.

If things don't act right, you might be in Grid mode. Check to see if you are and what the Grid is set to. If it is set to 1 bar, for example, you won't be able to enter or edit notes shorter than that. Everything snaps to the grid.

Quantizing

Quantizing (Event>Event Operations>Quantize) is a very helpful process that allows you to "magnetically" snap notes to a scheme of your choosing. The Quantize dialog box (Figure 11.13) has a lot of options.

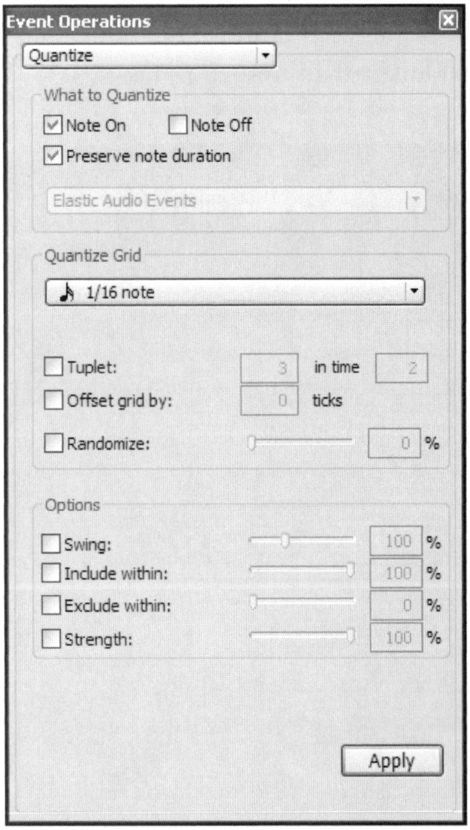

Figure 11.13 Quantizing eases the pain of editing a large number of notes simultaneously.

To quantize a note, it's best to open this dialog box, keep it visible, and then select the notes you want to quantize. After you select them, the different options become active. Make your choices and press Apply to process your decision.

I mainly use quantizing to set note-on messages to the appropriate timing, such as to the closest quarter note. This takes my not-so-professional performance and immediately makes me sound like I can play in time. Play around with the options and see what you like best.

"Printing" MIDI

In the past, MIDI has been somewhat fickle in Pro Tools, and *printing* MIDI tracks was a way to save your work in a form that wouldn't likely disappear. Things have gotten better, but this is still a valid technique to save system resources. It involves creating an Audio track for every Instrument track you have and recording (*printing*, in the parlance of the old days of tape) the Instrument track onto the Audio track. Basically, you convert all the MIDI to audio and then are free to make the Instrument track (and all its plug-ins) inactive to save resources.

When you create your Audio track, set the Output of the Instrument track to match the Input of the Audio track (use the same bus), arm the Audio track, move to the beginning of the material you want to record, and press Record and Play (see Figure 11.14).

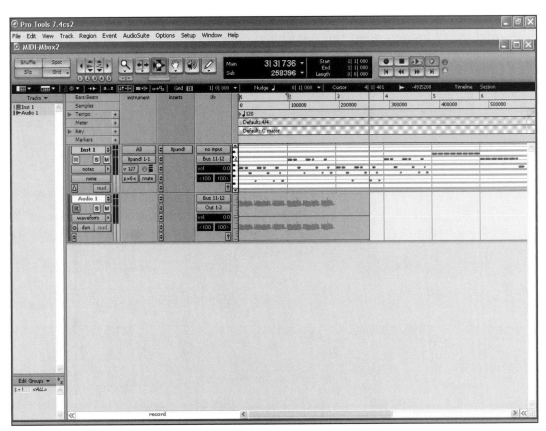

Figure 11.14 Printing MIDI onto an Audio track.

When you're done recording, stop, mute the Instrument track, and listen to make sure everything recorded correctly. Then make the Instrument track inactive.

Working with External Devices

You have several setup options to choose from to make working with external MIDI devices and instruments easier. This is all irrelevant if you're working "in the box" with MIDI and Pro Tools.

It's important to note that MIDI ports do not show up in the Setup>I/O dialog box. All MIDI I/O setup is done from the MIDI Setup menu.

MIDI Setup

Set up external MIDI devices from the MIDI menu, which is located in Setup>MIDI. I cover the four submenus available in the following sections.

MIDI Studio Setup

Windows and Mac users have different mechanisms for setting up MIDI hardware. They both do the same thing—identify MIDI devices connected to your system—only differently. For Windows users, this is optional. As long as they are connected correctly, your MIDI instruments work, but using MIDI Studio Setup makes it easier to recognize and choose your instruments from within Pro Tools.

Windows users, launch the MIDI Studio Setup (MSS) dialog box (see Figure 11.15) from the Options>MIDI>MIDI Studio Setup menu. The MSS allows you to create

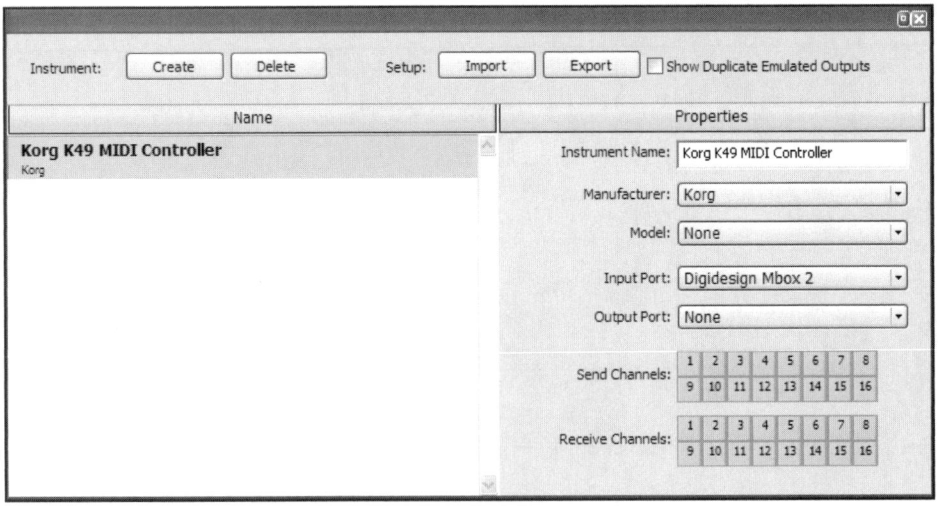

Figure 11.15 The MIDI Studio in Windows.

different MIDI instrument profiles, according to what instruments you have connected to Pro Tools.

Click Create to create a new instrument, and fill out the dialog box with the appropriate details according to your hardware. If you've got something that isn't listed (like I do), do the best you can, choosing None when necessary. The instrument you create shows up by the name you choose within Pro Tools.

Mac users should launch Apple's Audio MIDI Setup (AMS) application from the Options>MIDI>MIDI Studio menu. AMS identifies and allows you to configure your MIDI devices. Click the MIDI tab to scan your system for connected MIDI interfaces (like the Mbox 2). Next, click Add Device to create a new instrument and then connect it to your interface by dragging the virtual cables from the instrument to the interface icons. Double-click your instrument to enter specific data, such as its name, manufacturer, model, and so forth. You can even select a photo to represent your instrument.

MIDI Beat Clock

If your external MIDI device needs to synchronize with MIDI Beat Clock, enable MIDI Beat Clock from the Setup>MIDI>MIDI Beat Clock menu and choose the devices that need to receive it. You must also enable the Conductor from the Pro Tools Transport to transmit MIDI Beat Clock during playback.

Input Filter

The MIDI Input Filter (Setup>MIDI>MIDI Input Filter) allows you to customize what MIDI information is recorded from your external devices. You can chose All, Only (and then select your choices), or All Except (and then choose the exceptions not to record).

Input Devices

You must have MIDI devices enabled from the Setup>MIDI>Input Devices dialog box. If you have not created an instrument profile from the MSS or AMS, you see your standard interface, such as the Digidesign Mbox 2. Otherwise, you see (and are able to check or uncheck) the devices you created earlier.

Making Physical Connections

As mentioned earlier in the chapter, you must physically connect your MIDI device to either your audio interface (via MIDI cables) or your computer (via USB or FireWire).

If you have an interface that doesn't have MIDI IN or OUT ports (like the Mbox 2 Micro), you can still install and use USB- or FireWire-capable MIDI controllers. Pro Tools recognizes and uses them with nary a problem. You might, however, have to install custom device drivers that enable your MIDI device to use the computer. Check the documentation of your hardware to make sure. If your interface has MIDI ports, you can choose whatever connection you like best.

12 Plug-Ins and Mixing

Using plug-ins and mixing are two of the most fun and rewarding aspects of using Pro Tools, and this, the last chapter of this book, covers both. Plug-ins are software inserts that process audio. Some alter the frequency spectrum of audio, whereas others impart delays or add reverberation and other effects. This is where some of the magic of mixing takes place and where Pro Tools sort of steps out of the way and acts as a host rather than the center of attention. Pro Tools ships with many useful plug-ins, but you can find far more third-party plug-ins out there to investigate. After you get the hang of what they do and how to use them, you can use any plug-in on the market with ease.

Mixing goes hand-in-hand with using plug-ins. Mixing is the process where you turn raw recordings (after editing) into a finished audio product that fulfills your creative vision. Professionally produced albums can often be recorded in a few days or weeks, but it can take weeks or months to mix the entire package. That's how important mixing is.

It's time to get to it.

Plug-Ins

I realize I keep bringing up the older world of analog recording and mixing. I'm not doing that because I want to go backwards, and I have limited experience using older technologies. However, you need to understand why things work the way they do in Pro Tools, and most often, you can find the roots of "why" in analog studios. Those studios created the hits we all revere, and they served as the model for most digital audio gear and applications. With an analog console, excepting electronic equalization (EQ) and possibly built-in compression, the only way to apply effects to tracks was to use inserts, sends, and returns.

Inserts are cables inserted into the signal flow of a channel strip that route the signal to a piece of *outboard* gear that sits in a rack to the side of the console. That gear can be a special EQ, compressor, or other effects unit. After the audio is processed, it is patched right back into the signal flow (and hence into the console) from where it departed. Inserts operate on one channel strip.

Sends and returns are wired across all channels. You have *send* level controls on each channel strip with an overall *return* volume control. You can send signal from every channel you like to as many sends as your console has hardwired in. Time-based effects like reverb and multi-effects units are normally handled with sends and returns. Also, headphone or monitor mixes can be easily handled using a console-wide send and return.

TDM Versus RTAS   The world of Pro Tools hosts two different types of real-time plug-ins: time-division multiplexing (TDM) and Real Time AudioSuite (RTAS). TDM is the realm of Pro Tools HD and requires dedicated Digital Signal Processing (DSP) cards to run the plug-ins. RTAS plug-ins, which rely on the host computer to do the work, can be used by Pro Tools HD, LE, and M-Powered software.

The upshot of this is that if you're using Pro Tools LE or M-Powered, TDM plug-ins are useless to you.

You don't have to have a $100,000 console to use the analog tools. I have channel strip inserts, sends, and returns in my Yamaha MG12/4 analog mixing console sitting right here beside me.

The point is that Pro Tools uses this same paradigm. Pro Tools has channel strip inserts where you can assign up to five different plug-ins on each track to process the signal. You can also have up to ten sends from each channel strip. I work them in the same way I would work with them in an analog console. I use my inserts for EQ, compression, instruments, amp emulators, and so forth, whereas I use sends for time-based effects like reverb.

To take advantage of this capability, you've got to have some idea of what sorts of plug-ins are out there and what you can do with them.

EQ

EQ is short for *equalization*, which is the term used for changing the frequency spectrum of a given piece of audio. You can do only two things with EQ: boost or cut, which is implemented and measured in dB. Boosting certain frequencies turns those selected frequencies up by the specified number of dB compared to the rest of the spectrum. Cutting does the opposite.

Figure 12.1 A representative graphic EQ plug-in.

You have two types of EQ: graphic and parametric. Graphic equalizers (see Figure 12.1) have a set number of frequencies that you can boost or cut. These frequencies are built-in and normally controlled by sliders, which present a graphic representation of the frequency spectrum. The specific frequencies and the range you can boost or cut depends on the make and model of the EQ plug-in you're using. Graphic equalizers are great for certain instruments or applications, like room tuning or ringing out feedback in a live sound setting.

Parametric equalizers have several different features that give you more control over the frequencies you boost or cut and how you do that. Some parametric equalizers have a graph (which makes them seem more graphic than a graphic equalizer) that helps you visualize what is happening, and other times (normally old-school, "vintage" equalizer emulations) you have to play it by ear.

Parametric equalizers (see Figure 12.2) have these general features:

- **Bands:** As few as one and as many as ten adjustable frequency bands.

- **Filter Type:** Bell (peaking), low or high shelf, low or high pass.

- **Enable/Bypass:** You can often bypass filters individually.

- **Q:** The bandwidth. A higher Q affects a narrower bandwidth, whereas narrower Q values affect a wider bandwidth. It's backwards to what you would think. Sometimes Q is translated to octaves or simply called bandwidth.

- **Frequency:** The center frequency of the EQ filter on the specified band.

- **Gain:** Sometimes called boost or cut; it's how much you're going to turn those frequencies up or down.

- **Input/Output:** Most equalizers (graphic and parametric) have input and output gain controls that let you boost or cut the overall signal so that it is either strong enough to work with or soft enough not to clip.

- **Display:** Often, parametric equalizers show you the frequency spectrum and the effect of your decisions.

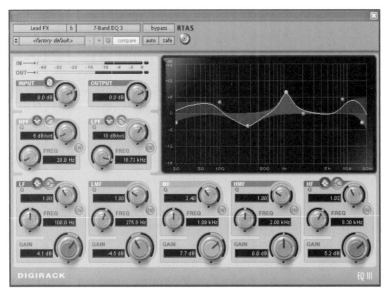

Figure 12.2 The EQ III parametric equalizer.

Some parametric equalizers, most often those modeled on specific real-world hardware, have more limited options than newer "super EQ plug-ins." For example, you might have only three bands to work with: a low shelf, a peaking mid band, and a high shelf. Each band might have a limited number of frequencies that you can select, and that's it. Try these out anyway. Don't let their limited nature fool you. Often the best and most effective tools (historically and today) have fewer bells and whistles.

With judicious EQ, you can make most things sound better. Use EQ to cut rumble from the low end, mud from the middle, and boost an instrument's "key" frequencies to accentuate it.

Pro Tools ships with a basic but very capable EQ plug-in, the EQ III.

Stereo Versus MultiMono Plug-Ins Some plug-ins have both a stereo and multimono version, whereas others have only one or the other. A stereo plug-in links its effect between the two channels. Multimono plug-ins can work on both channels of a stereo signal, but they do not interact in any way. It's like having two mono plug-ins, one on each channel.

Compression and Limiting

Compression and limiting affect the dynamic range of audio. In both cases, you're concerned with "squeezing" peaks down so they are closer to the strength of the rest of the piece. Afterwards, you can turn the overall gain up, resulting in audio with louder lows (be careful of that noise floor—you're turning that up too) and a greater average volume.

Compression allows audio to get louder based on a ratio of input to output, such as 4:1. A 4:1 compression ratio means that for every 4 dB increase in signal strength of the original audio (above a certain threshold), the compressor allows only a 1 dB increase in actual gain.

Limiting is essentially the same, but hard limiting in DAWs enforces a hard ceiling on peaks and says "None shall pass," no matter how much louder they are driven.

You see these controls on most compressors or limiters:

- **Ratio:** The compression ratio. Higher ratios mean more compression. A good starting value is 4:1.

- **Threshold:** The level the incoming signal has to pass in order to trigger compression. A good starting place is to set the threshold so you get 6 dB of gain reduction and then see from there what sounds good.

- **Attack:** How fast the compressor "kicks in." Fast attack values catch fast transients (like drum hits) whereas slow attack values let them through uncompressed.

- **Release:** How quickly the compressor releases. Faster times can result in an audible "pumping" sound, whereas longer times tend to sound smoother. Try to gauge the release time to the music and when notes naturally decay.

- **Gain:** Also called Gain Makeup, this is how much you want to turn the compressed output up. A good rule of thumb is to turn it up by how much gain you're taking out or to listen and make it as loud as the original signal.

- **Knee:** Affects the threshold. "Hard" knee implements compression (which is still dependent on the attack time) immediately after the threshold is crossed. "Soft" knee makes it "spongier" and allows for a softer compression onset.

- **Gain Reduction:** This display tells you how much gain (dynamic range) you are compressing out.

Compression and limiting are hot topics in the audio world, as overcompression and hard limiting have resulted in a "loudness war" that has literally squeezed out the dynamics of modern music. The theory has been that people respond to louder music on the radio or on CDs in jukeboxes, and because louder is always better, all music must be as loud as possible.

Pro Tools comes with a few compressors: the Compressor/Limiter Dyn 3 (see Figure 12.3), the De-Esser Dyn 3 (de-essers work to reduce sibilance in vocals by compressing the frequencies that cause it), and the Bomb Factory BF76.

Expansion and Gating

Expansion and gating are the opposite of compression and limiting. Rather than limiting dynamic range, they increase it. They do this by turning down (or off) audio that falls below the threshold. Gates are simply expanders that turn the signal off below the threshold. Figure 12.4 shows a sample expander. Looks a lot like a compressor!

Expanders and gates have similar controls to compressors and limiters, but remember, they work in the opposite way.

- **Ratio:** The ratio used to turn the signal down as it passes below the threshold. For example, an expansion ratio of 2:1 turns the output signal down 2 dB for every dB the actual signal drops.

- **Threshold:** The point below which expansion or gating takes effect.

Figure 12.3   The Compressor/Limiter Dyn 3.

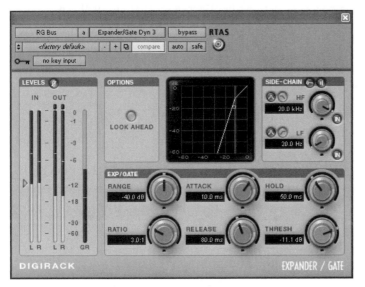

Figure 12.4   The Expander/Gate Dyn 3.

- **Attack:** How fast the expansion "kicks in."

- **Release:** How quickly the expander releases.

- **Hold:** How long the "door" is held open for signal to pass through after the threshold has been crossed (going upwards). This is the minimum time the gate stays open, even if the signal immediately passes below the threshold.

- **Range:** Or floor. How low to turn the signal down when the signal drops below the threshold. Gates turn the signal completely off.

- **Gain Reduction:** This display tells you how much gain is being turned down by the expander or gate when the signal drops below the threshold.

Expanders and gates work wonders to limit guitar noise and isolate drum hits. For example, guitar amps tend to have some buzz to them. You don't want to hear this in your mix, so an expander is a great solution that turns the buzzing down to an almost imperceptible level, but allows the louder signal of the guitar to pass through unhindered.

Drum gates are pretty standard fare in professional audio. Say you mic up a tom-tom but hear the snare bleeding through at a lower level. Gate the tom track so that the snare isn't loud enough to trigger the gate (open it) but the tom is. You've just cleaned up the tom track by removing the snare drum.

Attack and Release   Attack and release times for compressors, limiters, expanders, and gates have the overall effect of smoothing gain changes. If those changes happened instantaneously, that would sound very unnatural and could lead to audio anomalies like pops or clicks. Fast attacks and releases can lead to "pumping," which is sometimes the desired effect.

Pro Tools ships with a capable expander/gate in the Expander/Gate Dyn 3.

Reverb

You hear natural reverberations (reverb) all the time without necessarily thinking about it. Whether you're singing in the shower or playing a guitar in a studio, the direct source is accompanied by a dense pattern of delayed sound that has bounced off one or more surfaces to get to you. That delay occurs very fast—too fast to be perceived as an echo. The nature of the room—its size, shape, the surface texture of the walls, floor, and ceiling—all affects what the reverb sounds like and how long it lasts.

Without reverb, the music you hear would sound very dry and un-lifelike. Studios spend big bucks on ultra-high-end reverb because it is such an important characteristic of sound and music.

Dry Versus Wet   Signal without any effect is called "dry." A completely "wet" signal, on the other hand, is composed entirely of an effect, like reverb. Mixers like Pro Tools allow you to separate the two signals onto different channel strips (say an Audio track and one or more Aux Input tracks) and mix them together very precisely. You can change the mix at any moment because you are not locked in. Many plug-ins also have a mix control so you can use them as inserts and not sends, and still have control over the wet-to-dry signal ratio.

Reverb plug-ins (see Figure 12.5) traditionally are CPU-intensive, because the better the plug-in, the more calculations it does on the dry signal to come up with a realistic effect. Here are a few parameters of standard reverb plug-ins and what they do:

- **Early Returns:** The initial reflections that are better defined than the main body of the reverb. Lots of early returns (also called early reflections) can get in the way of the main reverb; however, early returns give you a good sense of a room's size, shape, and the position of the sound source.

- **Diffusion:** Diffusion refers to how reflections decay. The sound pressure level (loudness) and frequencies level out as the reverb decays, so more diffusion generally sounds "smoother" than less diffusion.

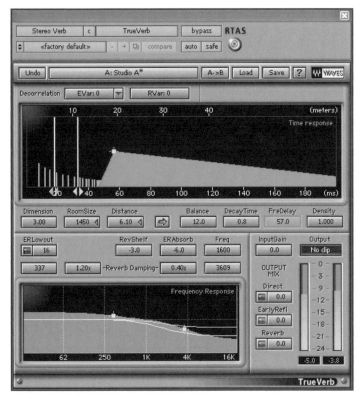

Figure 12.5 Waves' TrueVerb plug-in.

- **Decay Time, or RT60:** The time it takes the reverb to diminish by 60 dB of its original strength.

- **Pre Delay:** Delays the onset of reverb by the chosen amount. Useful for cleaning up reverb so it doesn't step on the original audio. Having some predelay allows you to hear the early reflections better.

- **Direct:** How much of the original signal is heard in the mix. You might have a mix control, which allows you to set the mixture of direct versus reverb. If you're using reverb as a plug-in on an Aux Input track, most often the mix is set to 100 percent wet. You control the mix by the amount of signal you send to the plug-in from each track and the fader level on the reverb channel.

- **Damping:** Allows you to equalize the reverb and damp out either high or low frequencies.

Pro Tools ships with the graphically challenged D-Verb reverb plug-in. D-Verb is getting very long in the tooth and is probably the weakest reverb plug-in that ships with the current crop of DAWs. If you're going to invest in any third-party plug-ins, put buying a new reverb plug-in at the top of your list.

Delay

Delay (see Figure 12.6) is another time-based effect, like reverb, but in this case the time it takes for the reflections to return is long enough for you to perceive it as a distinct echo. Delays most often are synced with the tempo of the song. Very small delays thicken a sound rather than cause an echo.

Pro Tools has several delay plug-ins, based on the length of delay. They are the Extra Long Delay II, Long Delay II, Medium Delay II, Short Delay II, and Slap Delay II. That's a lot of delay!

Modulation

Modulation effects are a hallmark of guitar stomp boxes, but they are also very valuable tools for other tracks. Here are some tried-and-true modulation plug-ins:

- **Chorus:** Caused by (at least) doubling a part and pitch-shifting one or both so they are no longer identical, and then typically panning the parts. Chorus is meant to thicken a sound and cause you to think it was created by an ensemble rather than one person or instrument.

Figure 12.6 The Moogerfooger Analog Delay.

- **Doubling:** Similar to chorus, but the effect is not so much to make you think more than one instrument was used as it is to thicken a sound and enhance the stereo effect.

- **Flanging (also wow and flutter):** The flange effect was the result of slowing a tape machine during playback by putting a finger on the reel's flange and then letting it speed back up to normal and recording the result. Wow and flutter are caused by irregular tape machine playback.

- **Phaser:** Combines the original signal with a slightly out-of-phase signal, resulting in a signal that suffers from comb filtering, which produces the phasing effect.

- **Panners:** Oscillate the pan position.

Pitch Correction

Pitch correction is very easy to understand. You take the original, possibly out-of-tune signal, and change the pitch by the amount you specify. Some pitch correction plug-ins are called auto-tuners, and they specialize in analyzing and correcting vocalists (normally, but this applies to any instrument playing a single note rather than a chord) who can't sing the correct notes or are out of tune. These plug-ins typically place a very heavy load on the CPU. Consider using AudioSuite or "printing" (recording the audio to a new track and making the original track inactive) a track with an RTAS plug-in before you run out of power.

Other Plug-Ins

There are a boatload of other types of plug-ins that do a lot of different things. I'm probably missing some, but this list gives you a good idea of the wide variety of other plug-ins that you can bring to work in your Pro Tools toolbox.

- **Time Adjusters:** Pro Tools comes with three time adjusters, which are handy tools to slip audio by a certain number of samples. This way you don't have to nudge it on the timeline.

- **Amp Simulators:** These puppies take some CPU horsepower, but are very fun to play with. The key is to track a guitar or bass direct and insert an amp sim on the track. Instead of having to buy $10,000 worth of amps to get different tones, you've got pretty good simulations right at your fingertips.

- **Stomp Boxes:** These (see Figure 12.7) typically model a wide range of guitar and bass effects units such as distortion, overdrive, chorus, panning, and so forth. You can use them on anything you like, however.

Figure 12.7   This is serious fun.

- **Multiband Compressors:** These plug-ins are compressors that operate in three to five bands based on frequency. You can compress lows, mids, and highs separately and, hence, shape the EQ of the final mix without having to use an equalizer. These are most often used in mastering.

- **Noise Reduction:** These types of plug-ins reduce hiss, pops, and other noise.

- **Dither/Noise Shaping:** Necessary when bouncing from a higher to a lower bit depth. These features make a lower bit depth sound as good as a slightly higher bit depth, as well as shape noise so that you hear it less.

- **Sound Field:** Most often concerned with phase and stereo width and balance. Some are informational whereas others let you adjust different parameters.

- **Instrument:** These are your software instruments that transform MIDI into music.

- **Informational:** These plug-ins tell you about what you're hearing. You'll find many types that range from VU meters to spectrum analyzers, clip indicators, level meters, stereo analyzers, and more.

- **Psycho-acoustic:** These plug-ins enhance the sound by creating harmonics, aligning phase, or using other techniques to make the music sound better than it actually is.

- **Channel Strips (or Tracks):** All-in-one plug-ins, normally with EQ, gating, compression, expansion, and possibly other features.

Read the Manual!   It's important to read the documentation that comes with the plug-ins you have and buy. Even if you know how to use a compressor, you might learn something new from the manual, and the point of the manual is to tell you detailed information about the specific plug-in you're using. You can't go wrong knowing that!

Using Plug-Ins

Using plug-ins is a snap. The hard part is knowing what you want to do (which plug-in to use) and then making the correct adjustments to the plug-in settings.

Inserting Plug-Ins

To insert a plug-in on a track, click an empty Insert Selector on the track you want to add an insert on and then choose the insert you want from the pop-up menu (see Figure 12.8). You can do this from the Edit or Mix window. If the Insert area of the channel strip is not visible, turn it on from the View>Edit Window (or Mix Window)>Inserts menu.

Remember, inserts affect only the track they are on unless you are sending signal to the track with the insert from one or more other tracks.

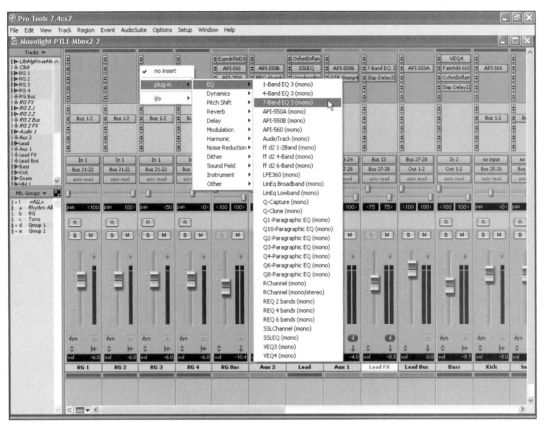

Figure 12.8 Inserting a plug-in.

You can create hardware inserts by choosing an insert from the I/O menu instead of selecting an interface or bus when you add an insert.

Removing Plug-Ins

To remove an insert, select the plug-in Insert Selector and choose *no insert* from the pop-up menu (see Figure 12.9). That deletes the plug-in. One word of warning: You can't undo this step. If you're unsure, bypass the plug-in or make it inactive first. Then, when you're sure you don't need it, remove it.

Opening and Closing Plug-Ins

To open a plug-in, click its name in the Inserts region. It pops up and is ready to use. If you click the name again, it closes. Drag it around the screen to where it's most convenient to use.

Figure 12.9 Removing a plug-in.

Moving and Copying Plug-Ins

To move a plug-in, click the plug-in name in the Inserts region and drag it to a new position within the same channel strip or move it to another channel strip entirely.

To copy a plug-in, hold down Alt (Windows) or Option (Mac) as you move it. You actually move a copy with the same settings as the original. This same technique works for sends.

Bypassing/Unbypassing Plug-Ins

Bypassing a plug-in takes it out of the signal flow but does not free up CPU resources. Use Bypass to quickly toggle a plug-in on and off to hear the audible difference between using it or not. To bypass a plug-in, right-click its name and choose Bypass. You can also bypass plug-ins from their dialog boxes.

Bypassed plug-ins are shown as very dark gray boxes with white text labels (see Figure 12.10).

Figure 12.10 Bypassed plug-ins are much darker.

To remove the bypass, choose Bypass again. The checkmark that appears by the menu disappears.

Making Plug-Ins Inactive/Active

Deactivating plug-ins is a way of turning them off and freeing up CPU power. Follow the same general procedures as you would to bypass a plug-in, only choose Make Inactive from the pop-up menu (see Figure 12.11). You can't deactivate a plug-in from its interface.

Figure 12.11   Making a plug-in inactive.

Inactive plug-ins are shown as slightly darker gray boxes with italicized black text labels. Inactive plug-ins that are also bypassed are shown as inactive. If you activate them, they appear bypassed.

To reactivate a plug-in, choose Make Active, which takes the place of Make Inactive in the pop-up menu.

Using Presets

Some plug-ins have presets that you can load up and use. Be careful with presets. Some might be so good that you don't have to fiddle with them. At other times, you might use a preset as a starting point. Don't hand your authority as engineer over to someone you don't know without listening to what's going on. Just because the preset might say "best EQ ever for guitar" doesn't mean it's right for you, the guitar track you're listening to, or the song you're mixing.

AudioSuite Plug-Ins

AudioSuite plug-ins are the same as RTAS plug-ins, but they do not operate in real time. This takes some getting used to, but can lessen the processing load on your computer. I see this done with pitch correction (a notorious CPU hound) a lot.

One great advantage AudioSuite plug-ins have over inserts is that they can be applied to specific audio regions and not to an entire track. The downside is that you are locked into the change.

To apply an AudioSuite plug-in, follow these steps:

1. From the Edit window, select the region of audio to which you want to apply an effect.

2. Select the AudioSuite menu and choose the plug-in of your choice.

3. Make changes to the settings and hit Preview to hear a preview of the effect.

4. Press Process to apply.

Other Cool Plug-In Tips

Here are a few cool tips on working with plug-ins, inserts, and sends.

- **Keep a plug-in open:** Click the red "bull's-eye" on the plug-in you want to stay open.

- **Bypass all inserts or sends on a given line:** Press and hold Alt (Windows) or Option (Mac), then right-click a plug-in or send, and select Bypass. To reverse the procedure (to turn bypass off), do the same thing.

- **Deactivate all inserts or sends on a given line:** Press and hold Alt (Windows) or Option (Mac), then right-click a plug-in or send, and select Make Inactive. To reverse the procedure, choose Make Active as the last step.

- **Delete all inserts or sends on a given line:** Press and hold Alt (Windows) or Option (Mac), then select No Insert or No Send from the insert or send position you want to globally delete.

- **Create the same insert or send across all channels:** Press and hold Alt (Windows) or Option (Mac), then select the insert or send you want to globally add.

Creating and Using Sends

In this section, I'm going to create an Aux Input track that has a reverb plug-in on it to illustrate using sends and returns. To create a send that is received by an Aux Input track, follow these steps:

1. Switch to the Mix window. Create a stereo Aux Input track from the Track>New menu.

2. Double-click the new track name and rename it Reverb.

3. Click on the Input Path Selector and choose an open stereo bus. For this example, I chose Bus 1-2 (see Figure 12.12).

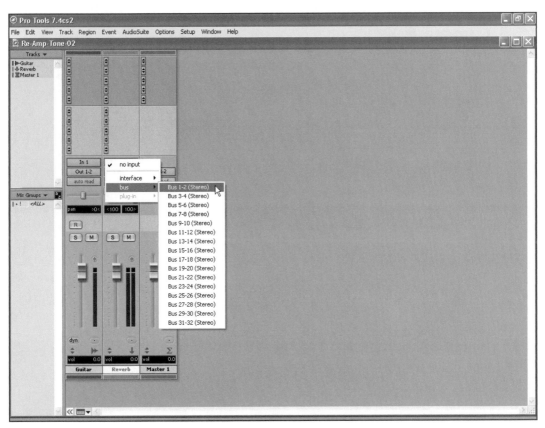

Figure 12.12 Selecting the input path.

4. Add a reverb plug-in to the Reverb track by selecting the Insert Selector on the track and choosing a reverb plug-in from the pop-up list (see Figure 12.13). Select the type of reverb you want from a preset or create your own customized settings.

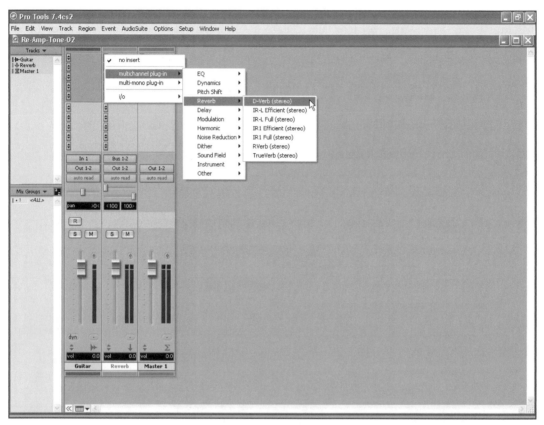

Figure 12.13 Adding the reverb plug-in to the Aux Input track.

5. Select a track with audio on it, click one of the Send Selectors, and create a send to the bus you just selected as the input to the Reverb track—in my case, Bus 1-2 (see Figure 12.14). If the send area is not visible, turn it on from the View menu. The most common mistake here is to select an interface send and to not use the correct bus. Double-check to see that you're sending signal to a bus and that the bus is the correct stereo pair. You should be rewarded by a dialog box with send controls popping up.

6. Drag the send fader up until it is at unity gain (0 dB). You can go lower or higher, but it is common practice to set sends at unity and control the volume of the effect from the Aux Input track (which acts as the return). Set the pan

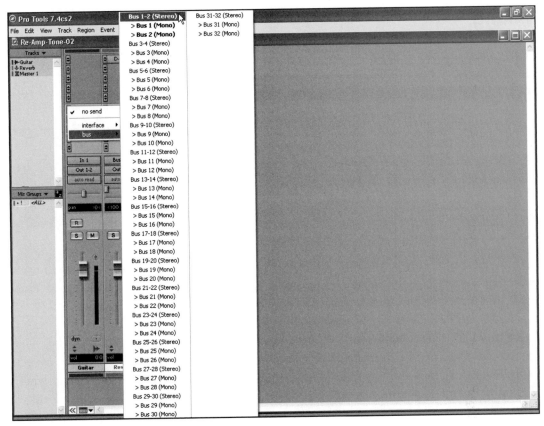

Figure 12.14   Creating the send.

potentiometers to match that of your audio, although for certain effects it is good to change them. You can close the send controls.

7.   I like to solo-isolate Aux Input tracks with effects on them. To do this, Ctrl+Click (Windows) or Command+Click (Mac) the reverb track's solo button on the channel strip. This ensures that you hear reverb even when you have another track soloed. The Solo button becomes grayed out and inactive when you solo-isolate a track.

8.   Select an area in the Edit window timeline and start playback. Open up your plug-in and start setting it to the desired effect. You should also control its return level from the channel strip fader.

9.   The beauty of sends is that you can create one Aux Input track and assign one reverb plug-in to it, and then create sends from as many other tracks as you want to have reverb on.

Mixing

Mixing, which relies entirely on the multitracking paradigm, is the process where you take individually recorded tracks and blend them together using a variety of creative and technical tools. Aside from jamming out with my guitar and making my own music, mixing is my thing.

When I was first introduced to mixing, my jaw dropped and hit the floor. For the first time I realized how much more there is to professional audio production than simply the performance of the artists. Great artists, producers, and engineers form a team. A bad mix can kill an otherwise stellar performance. By the same token, fantastic mixing can make even a high school band sound killer. Artists looking for that "produced" sound are in many ways looking for an engineer that can mix their material and make it sound comparable to successful artists in their genre.

You have more creative freedom mixing your own music, of course. One of the real challenges of professional audio is to stay true to an artist's vision if it differs from your own.

The Heart of Pro Tools

Pro Tools is many things, but at its heart it is a mixer. Leaving its other aspects aside, Pro Tools is designed to play back a number of previously recorded audio tracks (32 simultaneously or up to 48 with the DV or Music Production Toolkit installed); set pan and bus assignments for each track; control levels with faders; host plug-ins that manipulate the audio in many ways; and digitally sum everything together to create a stereo "2-mix" (see Figure 12.15), which is what you hear coming out of the left and right monitors. Let me try to say it a little plainer. Pro Tools takes up to 48 "source" tracks and mixes them together to output a mono, stereo, or surround (Pro Tools HD only) product.

Pro Tools LE and Delay Compensation   I've heard many complaints about Pro Tools LE not offering automatic delay compensation, and many people have offered solutions. However, while researching this book, I ran across posts by Digidesign (Digi Tech Support) on the DUC (duc.digidesign.com) that stated quite definitively that Pro Tools LE (and I assume M-Powered) automatically accounts for delay up to the number of samples you have set in the hardware buffer. This setting is in the Setup>Playback Engine dialog box. So, as long as you're not running any plug-ins that delay beyond what your H/W Buffer Size is, you should be good to go.

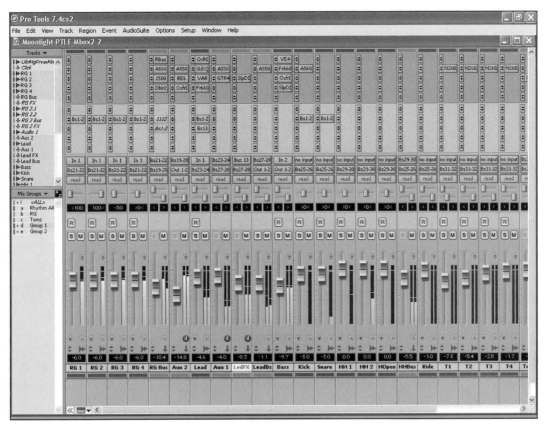

Figure 12.15 A completed mix in Pro Tools in narrow view.

Mixing Theory

Several elements make up a mix. It's your job as engineer to find the right "mix" (pardon the pun). These elements are as follows:

- **Volume:** How loud things are in comparison to each other, and in the end, how loud your mix is and whether it has any dynamic range or not.

- **Width:** Where things fall from left to right in the stereo field.

- **Depth:** The perceived depth of vocals and instruments.

- **Attention:** An elusive quality. What is grabbing your attention? Is it the vocals? Is it an annoying cowbell? You have many, many ways to resolve what elements get the most attention and how to spread that around. That's the challenge of mixing.

- **Quality:** Does it sound good? This is the ultimate criteria. Nothing else matters. No one cares if you used a compression ratio of 4:1 or 2:1 if it sounds bad. And, paradoxically, no one (consumers or fans) really cares what you did to make it sound good. It'll just be good.

Now I want to quickly take a look at some techniques to achieve good mixes in more detail.

Volume

Normally, not everything should be at the same level. Make things louder for emphasis or perceived closeness and softer for distance. Volume can be used creatively to help separate sounds. If you run out of fader room, compress tracks to bring up their average gain. Louder isn't always better. Sometimes a softer track that stands out has more psychological impact. Often, carving out EQ regions for separate instruments (or highlighting a natural emphasis) means you don't have to turn the track up as loud. For example, a bass guitar and hi-hat don't compete in the same frequency spectrum, so neither has to be turned up over the other.

Occasionally, take a step back from the work you're doing and listen to how the volume balance of your mix changes over time. EQ, compression, reverb, and delay change this balance. Do the drums sound too loud now? Is the organ just right? Is the solo guitar irritatingly loud? Tweak. Listen. Repeat often.

Panning

Panning helps spread a mix out from left to right. Create space on the stage. Doubled parts are prime candidates for panning left and right. You can also use plug-ins to change the stereo width. Don't forget that you can often pan sends, returns, and effects. Automate panning carefully.

Time-Based Effects

Time-based effects such as reverb add depth and realism. You can customize the effect by altering a reverb's characteristics, panning, and return level. In addition, you can have more than one type of reverb or time-based effect in a song. For example, I sometimes put spring reverb on guitars with a hint of delay to thicken them up, but use a different reverb for other instruments.

Delays and echoes are great at creating width. Try panning the echoes to the opposite side of the dry signal or wide left and right of a centered track. A little goes a long way here. Too much reverb or too many echoes bouncing around can quickly muddy a mix.

Close Your Eyes   Close your eyes at certain points when you're mixing and listen. This makes you rely on your ears to hear where an instrument is in the mix and not your eyes. No one is going to judge your music by what your mix looked like in Pro Tools.

Modulation Effects

Modulation can have a dramatic effect on the mix. I think it's one of the best tools to use when you have a lot going on and you want to bring attention to something without having to turn it up to 11. Stereo chorus effects, doubling, or quadrupling, for example, turn an instrument into something "real," as opposed to a flat mono-sounding track. Other modulation effects can create movement, using an oscillator to change pan, phase, and other characteristics.

Pitch

Pitch begins with the arrangement and continues through mastering. Arrange and equalize your music like you would conduct an orchestra. Use different instruments, tones, octaves, and timbres to create separation. Carve out different frequency regions for the same or like-sounding instruments with EQ.

Timing

Timing is an often overlooked mixing tool. Use your sense of musical and dramatic timing to place parts along the timeline. Don't always have everything happening at the same time. Create some variety and interest in a song. Make people want to listen to it again.

Automation

Volume automation and side-chain compression are two tools you can use to make sure tracks stay out of each other's way at the right times.

Use Those Busses!

I use the heck out of Pro Tools busses. After all, that's why the program has so many. Here are some of the ways I use them:

Busses and Aux Input Tracks   Busses and Aux Input tracks are not the same thing, but Aux Input tracks receive input from busses so often they sometimes seem to merge together. A bus is a signal path. You can assign track output to a bus and receive audio input from a bus. Aux Input tracks are channel strips. They are one method (albeit a ubiquitous one) of managing and controlling the audio bussed to, you guessed it, a bus.

- **Sends/returns:** Standard fare here. Create sends and returns that point to a bus and use an Aux Input track to control it.

- **Sub-mixes:** I send signal from several tracks to a bus and use an Aux Input track as a group fader. This is also a good way to consolidate group plug-ins, like compressing all four rhythm guitar tracks slightly at the same time on the Aux Input track rather than having four compressors on each separate Audio track. I do not use sends for this. I route the output of the Audio tracks to a bus and then use that bus as the input to the Aux Input track.

- **Mixing multiple effects:** I often use several different effects on my guitars, each assigned to a different Aux Input track that is the control point for its own stereo (or mono to stereo) bus. For example, I might have reverb, delay, chorus, and flanging effects on four different Aux Input tracks, each assigned to a separate bus. I can create individual sends from my main guitar track to each bus and control the overall mix from the Aux Input track faders. Much fun!

- **Automation:** Sometimes, automation is a hassle. At times, I send audio to a bus, create an Aux Input track that receives the input of that bus, and put the automation on the Aux Input track. That way I can still control the volume from the Audio track and not worry about stepping all over the automation.

- **Extra inserts and sends:** Each track can have up to five inserts or ten sends. You aren't likely to run out of sends, but having a shortage of inserts can sometimes be a problem. In this situation, assign the output of that Audio track to a bus, create an Aux Input track, and assign its input to the bus. Presto—five more inserts and ten more sends.

How to Mix

I hesitate to call this section "How to Mix," because that's a profound and in many ways individual subject. You can write entire books on, and spend a lifetime learning, how to mix. I want to give you some concrete steps, however, to start with and learn from. Start here. Use this as a checklist if you like. Switch the order around if something else works better for you.

1. Listen to the song a few times through to get a sense of it. Fiddle with the faders, solo tracks, and mute others so you are aware of everything that's going on.

In other words, don't crank the rhythm guitars and miss the tambourine. Analyze the piece and ask yourself what the most important element(s) is/are. Most often this is the lead vocals, but that can change, depending on the structure of the song at a given time.

2.   Start putting together a rough fader mix. This is where you broadly determine how loud the elements are going to be in relation to each other, such as the drums versus the bass, where the guitar fits in, and how the vocals come through or if they need help.

3.   As you are dialing in the faders, start panning elements out. Often, rhythm guitars and doubled parts are panned hard left and right. Drums, the bass, and lead vocals are generally left in the center. Many people pan the toms, however. Make sure you pan stereo pairs if they are multiple mono tracks.

4.   Start the process of equalizing each track. Many people start with the drums, proceed to the bass, then move on to guitars (and any other instruments), and finish with the vocals. Although some people solo tracks to equalize them, I've found this to be a very bad idea. For example, the only measure of whether a kick drum is equalized properly is how it sits in the mix. You could have the best-sounding kick drum in the world soloed, and when you bring in the other instruments, it can sound terrible. Guitars are particularly susceptible to this.

Equalize with Your Ears   I love Pro Tools, but a potentially disastrous side-effect of having such a pretty program running such cool-looking plug-ins, which have such a sci-fi (or retro, take your pick) vibe to them, is falling in love with moving the doodads and what nots on the screen and therefore equalizing (and doing other engineering tasks) with your eyes and not with your ears. Don't even!

---

5.   Add compression, if desired. This is an incredibly overused tool, so be careful. Make sure to bypass the compressor and listen to the track "before and after." Often, I will put a compressor on and then take it off because it just doesn't make anything sound better. It should!

6.   Add gates, expanders, and other plug-ins.

7.   Add modulation effects.

8.   Add time-based effects like reverb and delay.

9. Keep listening. Listen to how all the changes you've made affect the overall mix. Does it sound better? Is it balanced? Have you lost sight of the objective?

10. One of my last steps is to add automation. After you add automation it can be hard to quickly change a track's level. However, toward the last stages of a mix you should have most things locked down.

11. Take a break. This is probably the most idealistic point I make here. Take a break from working on the song and leave it alone. That might take a day or a week. Get it out of your head so when you come back, you have forgotten the notions that have been cementing themselves in your mind and can listen fresh.

12. Listen again. Review your settings and see how things sound. Tweak as necessary. Throughout the process you might want to bounce intermediate mixes and burn them on a CD or load them into your MP3 player to listen in another environment. Make one last "pre-final" bounce and listen to it elsewhere to see how it comes across. If required, make changes to the mix.

13. Make your final bounce. This is what I call a final mix, but it's not really done until it's been mastered.

Bounce to Disk...

I would like to thank you for purchasing this book and making it to the end with me. The world of professional audio (even if done as a hobby) is rewarding and fun, but it is also demanding. Making music with Pro Tools requires an understanding of a wide range of specialized information and the knowledge of how to apply it. You have to have the time and money to invest in it and the courage to find out where your creativity can take you.

I've just scratched the surface with this book. I intentionally embraced the mindset as I wrote that you weren't on a deserted island in the South Pacific without access to any other Pro Tools information (if you are, give me a holler). I approached my work determined not to simply rewrite a pretty good series of Digidesign manuals. I tried to pick and choose what I thought was the most important information, the most potentially confusing, and the most likely for you to need to get started in your Pro Tools studio. I fully expect you to learn and advance outside of the confines of this book. By all means, don't stop here. I continue to learn and grow every day, and my journey is closer to the beginning than it is to the end.

Come visit me on the web and drop me a line if you need something or want to share your experiences with me. I have a book support page online with any errata, questions, and answers as I get them, and who knows what else. My URL is www.robertcorrell .com, and you can e-mail me at protools@robertcorrell.com. I can't wait to hear from you!

Robert Correll

Index